The Role of International Large-Scale Assessments: Perspectives from Technology, Economy, and Educational Research

Matthias von Davier • Eugenio Gonzalez
Irwin Kirsch • Kentaro Yamamoto
Editors

The Role of International Large-Scale Assessments: Perspectives from Technology, Economy, and Educational Research

 Springer

Editors
Matthias von Davier
Educational Testing Service
Princeton, NJ
USA

Irwin Kirsch
Educational Testing Service
Princeton, NJ
USA

Eugenio Gonzalez
Educational Testing Service
Princeton, NJ
USA

Kentaro Yamamoto
Educational Testing Service
Princeton, NJ
USA

ISBN 978-94-007-4628-2   ISBN 978-94-007-4629-9 (eBook)
DOI 10.1007/978-94-007-4629-9
Springer Dordrecht Heidelberg London New York

Library of Congress Control Number: 2012944183

Printed on acid-free paper

Springer is part of Springer Science+Business Media (www.springer.com)

Preface

This volume consists of the papers presented at the International Large-Scale Assessment conference held at Educational Testing Service (ETS) in March 2011. The conference was designed to present and discuss multidisciplinary issues related to the use and implementation of international large-scale assessments. It was geared towards funders, policymakers, managers, and technical staff of international large-scale assessment programs. The conference covered the following topics: large-scale assessments as change agents; technologies in large-scale assessments; the role of assessing cognitive skills in international growth and development; the utility and need for assessing noncognitive skills in large-scale assessments; the contributions of international large-scale studies in civic engagement and citizenship; and the role of large-scale assessments in research on educational effectiveness and school development.

The different perspectives brought together in this volume reflect the changing landscape of these surveys both in terms of the widening group of researchers and policymakers interested in these data and the issues that should and could be addressed. Among these new directions is a surge in the use of large-scale assessment data in the field of economics as well as an increased interest in how these assessments can inform and the use of technology in education and assessment. In addition, research in civics and citizenship studies as well as investigations focusing on motivation, interest, and self concept indicate great interest in the data collected in international comparisons of education and skills.

Bringing together expert authors to produce such a volume would not have been possible without the generous support of ETS. ETS provided funding for the speakers and sustenance for all conference participants. Also contributing to the success of the conference was the set of invited experts who agreed to provide reflection and discussion of the invited presentations. We would like to thank Esther Care, from Assessment & Teaching of 21st Century Skills Project, Melbourne, Australia; Guido Schwerdt, from the Program on Educational Policy and Governance, Harvard University, United States; Erik Amnå, Professor of Political Science, Örebro University, Sweden; Patrick Kyllonen, from ETS; and David Kaplan, Professor of Quantitative Methods, University of Wisconsin-Madison. These discussants helped to sharpen and shape the questions and answers and, finally, to shape the final version of the chapters presented in this volume.

Finally, we want to acknowledge individuals at ETS who made the conference and this publication possible. The conference would not have been possible without the help of Judy Mendez and Judy Shahbazian, who helped with organization, arrangements, and general support of this endeavor, and Larry Hanover, who provided editorial reviews.

Matthias von Davier
Eugenio Gonzalez
Irwin Kirsch
Kentaro Yamamoto

Table of Contents

Contributors

Jo-Ann Amadeo, Ph.D. Department of Psychology, Marymount University, Arlington, 22207 VA, USA
e-mail: jamadeo@marymount.edu

Michal Beller, Ph.D. RAMA—The National Authority for Measurement and Evaluation in Education, Ministry of Education, 125 Begin Blvd. 12th Floor, Tel Aviv 67012, Israel
e-mail: mbeller.rama@education.gov.il

Henry Braun, Ph.D. Center for the Study of Testing, Evaluation and Education Policy, Lynch School of Education Boston College, 140 Commonwealth Ave, 02467 Chestnut Hill, MA, USA
e-mail: braunh@bc.edu

Dr. Matthias von Davier Educational Testing Service, Rosedale Road, MS 13-E, 08541 Princeton, NJ, USA
e-mail: mvondavier@ets.org

Eugenio J. Gonzalez, Ph.D. Educational Testing Service, Rosedale Road, MS 13-E, 08541 Princeton, NJ, USA
e-mail: egonzalez@ets.org

Eric Hanushek, Ph.D. Hoover Institution, National Bureau of Economic Research and CESifo, Stanford University, Stanford, CA 94305-6010, USA
e-mail: hanushek@stanford.edu

Irwin Kirsch, Ph.D. Educational Testing Service, Rosedale Road, MS 13-E, 08541 Princeton, NJ, USA
e-mail: ikirsch@ets.org

Dr. Eckhard Klieme Center for Research on Educational Quality and Evaluation, German Institute for International Educational Research (DIPF), Goethe University, Schloßstraße 29, 60486 Frankfurt am Main, Germany
e-mail: klieme@dipf.de

Marylou Lennon Educational Testing Service, Rosedale Road, MS 13-E, 08541 Princeton, NJ, USA
e-mail: mlennon@ets.org

Henry M. Levin, Ph.D. Teachers College, Columbia University, 525 West 120 Street, New York, NY 10027, USA
e-mail: HL361@columbia.edu

Dr. Jo Ritzen Empower European Universities, International Economics of Science, Technology and Higher Education, Maastricht School of Governance, UNU-MERIT, Kloosterweg 54 Bunde, Netherlands
e-mail: jo.ritzen@empowereu.org

Judith Torney-Purta, Ph.D. Department of Human Development and Quantitative Methodology, University of Maryland, College Park, MD 20742, USA
e-mail: jtpurta@umd.edu

Dr. Ludger Woessmann Ifo Institute for Economic Research and CESifo, University of Munich, Poschingerstr. 5, 81679 Munich, Germany
e-mail: woessmann@ifo.de

Kentaro Yamamoto, Ph.D. Educational Testing Service, Rosedale Road, MS 13-E, 08541 Princeton, NJ, USA
e-mail: kyamamoto@ets.org

Chapter 1
On the Growing Importance of International Large-Scale Assessments

Irwin Kirsch, Marylou Lennon, Matthias von Davier, Eugenio Gonzalez and Kentaro Yamamoto

Large-scale assessments that compare the skills and knowledge demonstrated by populations across countries are relatively recent endeavors. These assessments have expanded in scope over time in response to increasing concern about the distribution of human capital and the growing recognition that skills contribute to the prosperity of nations and to better lives for individuals in those nations. Broadly defined, large-scale assessments are surveys of knowledge, skills, or behaviors in a given domain. The goal of large-scale assessments is to describe a population, or populations, of interest. As such, these assessments focus on group scores and can be distinguished from large-scale testing programs that focus on assessing individuals. The major themes laid out here—that these large-scale assessments have expanded over the past 50 years to include a greater number of surveys focusing on a broader range of populations and skill domains, that this work has led to new methodologies and modes of assessment, and that these assessments have grown to address the increasingly challenging questions posed by researchers and policymakers around the world—will be addressed in greater detail in each of the remaining chapters. We begin here by providing a general overview of the history of international large-scale assessments and the broadening role that these surveys have played in influencing policymakers around the world.

I. Kirsch (✉) · M. Lennon · E. Gonzalez · K. Yamamoto · M. von Davier
Educational Testing Service, Rosedale Road, MS 13-E, 08541 Princeton, NJ, USA
e-mail: ikirsch@ets.org

M. Lennon
e-mail: mlennon@ets.org

M. von Davier
e-mail: mvondavier@ets.org

E. Gonzalez
e-mail: egonzalez@ets.org

K. Yamamoto
e-mail: kyamamoto@ets.org

M. von Davier et al. (eds.), *The Role of International Large-Scale Assessments: Perspectives from Technology, Economy, and Educational Research,*
DOI 10.1007/978-94-007-4629-9_1, © Springer Science+Business Media Dordrecht 2013

Large-Scale Assessments of Student Populations

Prior to the late 1950s, no systematic or standardized comparative data focusing on skills and knowledge had been collected at national or international levels. The foundational work in this area began with a focus on student skills. In 1958, a group of scholars met at the UNESCO Institute for Education in Hamburg to discuss issues associated with collecting systematic data about schools and education systems in a cross-country context. That meeting led to a study designed to investigate the feasibility of developing and conducting an assessment of 13-year-olds in 12 countries. The pilot 12-country study focused on five domains including mathematics, reading comprehension, geography, science, and non-verbal ability and was conducted between 1959 and 1962. The results of this pioneering study demonstrated the feasibility of conducting a large-scale international survey in which common cognitive instruments worked in a comparable manner across different cultures and languages (Naemi et al. in press).

A parallel effort in the United States began around this same time under the leadership of several prominent American scholars and policymakers. Francis Keppel, the US Commissioner of Education in the mid-1960s, was responsible for reporting to Congress about the condition of education in America. Keppel was concerned about the lack of systematic data on the educational attainment of students in the country. As he pointed out, most of the information that had been collected to date focused on the inputs of education—such as the number of classrooms, dollars spent, and school enrollment figures—rather than on the output of education in terms of skills and knowledge. This concern led Keppel to invite Ralph Tyler, Director of the Center for Advanced Study in the Behavioral Sciences at Stanford University, to develop a plan for the periodic national assessment of student learning. With Tyler as chair, the Carnegie Foundation funded two planning meetings for national student assessments in 1963 and 1964. A technical advisory group was formed in 1965 and chaired by John Tukey, head of the Department of Statistics at Princeton University and Associate Executive Director of Research Information Systems at AT&T Bell Laboratories. This work led to the National Assessment of Educational Progress (NAEP), which conducted its first assessment of in-school 17-year-olds in citizenship, science, and writing in 1969.

Rather than build an assessment around classical test theory models that focused primarily on measuring individual differences, Tyler's vision for NAEP was to focus on what groups of students knew and could do. In this scheme, groups were defined by educationally relevant variables such as gender, immigrant status and ethnic background. Tyler's idea was to convene panels of subject-matter experts, to have them identify key educational objectives within the domains to be assessed, and then to develop test items based on those objectives. Reports from these assessments would then focus on the performance of national populations or subgroups rather than individual students. Additionally, Tyler was adamant that assessment results not be based on any type of norm-referenced perspective such as grade-level norms.

As surveys such as NAEP progressed, one of the criticisms that arose was that interpretations were quite limited because they were fixed to the individual items used in the assessments. In the 1980s, Educational Testing Service (ETS) bid on and won the contract to conduct NAEP based on a monograph written by Samuel Messick, Albert Beaton, and Frederic Lord. In "National Assessment of Educational Progress reconsidered: a new design for a new era," they introduced the idea of using Item Response Theory (IRT), an analytic approach with important advantages compared to the classical methods used previously in that it directly supports the creation of comparable scales across multiple forms of a test. In addition to incorporating IRT-based methodology, the work on NAEP led to developments of new methodologies including marginal estimation procedures that could optimize the reporting of proficiency scales based on very complex designs (von Davier et al. 2006).

NAEP and other surveys began by using a version of matrix sampling, an approach that is based on utilizing multiple, partially overlapping test forms. The introduction of balanced incomplete block (BIB) spiraling to large-scale assessment was another important innovation introduced in the 1980s. The goal of these developments was to broaden the item pool represented in the BIB-spiraled test forms in order to maximize the coverage of the constructs of interest. As an example, NAEP 8th grade mathematics assessments include a large number of test items across five subdomains of mathematics: number properties and operations; measurement; geometry; data analysis, statistics and probability; and algebra. Using BIB spiraling, each student is asked to respond to only a small subset of these items, reducing the burden on the test taker. Striking this balance of construct coverage and the reduction of test taker burden requires utilizing covariance information to create proficiency scales and the ability to generalize to populations of interest.

The use of IRT in combination with BIB-spiraling and covariance information among domains has made it possible to both broaden content coverage to include relevant facets of the cognitive constructs of interest and to extend inferences beyond individual items to the underlying construct. Just as we sample individuals and then make generalizations to populations, these scales, constructed with the help of IRT, represent a construct broadly and therefore make it possible to generalize beyond the specific items in the assessment to the construct domain that those items represent. These methodologies originally developed for NAEP are utilized in all the large-scale assessments covered in this volume, including the studies currently conducted by the International Association for the Evaluation of Educational Achievement (IEA) and the Organisation for Economic Co-operation and Development (OECD) that will be described next. Methodological innovations such as these have contributed to the growth and expansion of international large-scale assessments and allowed us to move beyond the questions raised by Tyler and others in the 1960s and 1970s and focus on increasingly complex questions raised by policymakers today.

Following the initial work that occurred from the 1960s through the 1980s, international large-scale assessments of student skills have expanded tremendously in terms of the number of assessments and participating countries. IEA continued to conduct important periodic large-scale international studies and, starting in 1995, began to conduct continuous assessment cycles for the Trends in Mathematics and Science Study (TIMSS) followed by the Progress in Reading Literacy Study (PIRLS) in 2001. TIMSS is conducted every 4 years and focuses on achievement in mathematics and science at the fourth and eighth grades. PIRLS runs on a 5-year cycle and assesses how well children read after 4 years of primary school. By 2007, some 60 countries participated in TIMSS and over 40 countries participated in PIRLS. At the end of the 1990s, the OECD began the Programme for International Student Assessment (PISA) cycle of studies. PISA assesses the skills of 15-year-olds with the goal of gathering information about how well students have acquired the knowledge and skills essential for full participation in society. The first assessment was conducted in 2000 in over 30 countries and focused on the domains of reading, mathematics, and science. Since then, PISA has expanded in terms of the number of participating countries, with over 65 in the 2009 cycle, as well as the range of domains assessed, with cross-curricular areas such as problem solving and financial literacy being added to the assessment.

Large-Scale Assessments of Adults

In the 1990s, policy interest in the skills of adult workers and citizens led to the first international large-scale assessment focusing on adults ages 16–65. Working with Statistics Canada, ETS conducted the International Adult Literacy Survey (IALS) between 1994 and 1999, with 22 countries participating over three cycles. This assessment focused on prose, document, and quantitative literacy skills[1] and demonstrated the feasibility of conducting a household survey of adult literacy skills in an international context, maintaining comparability across countries and cultures. As such, IALS laid the foundation for subsequent surveys of adult skills and knowledge. The Adult Literacy and Life Skills Survey (ALL), which focused on a somewhat expanded set of adult skills including literacy, numeracy, and analytical problem solving, was conducted between 2003 and 2008 with some 11 countries participating.[2] The most recent adult survey, the OECD's Programme for the International Assessment of Adult Competencies (PIAAC), was conducting its first cycle in 2012 with 25 countries participating in 33 languages. PIAAC is a significant step forward in that it is the first computer-based household survey of adults, with interviewers taking laptops into people's homes and asking respondents to complete a background questionnaire and cognitive items on the computer. A parallel paper instrument is utilized for adults who are unable or unwilling to use the laptop equipment. For those adults taking the assessment on the computer, electronic reading tasks as well as scenario-based tasks assessing problem solving in technology envi-

---

[1] For definitions of these three literacy domains see Organisation for Economic Co-operation and Development and Statistics Canada (2000).

[2] For definitions of the ALL domains and more information about the survey see Statistics Canada and OECD (2005).

ronments complement the more traditional literacy and numeracy tasks that utilize texts, tables and static print-based stimulus material. PIAAC expands large-scale assessments by utilizing technology to administer the survey and, at the same time, embracing the fact that today's literacy-related tasks often take place in technology-based contexts such as web-based environments, spreadsheets and databases, or electronic mail.

The countries participating in today's student and adult large-scale surveys represent the overwhelming majority of GDP in the world and interest in the data these surveys yield continues to grow. For example, within the context of large-scale assessments, many countries now include special studies focusing on populations of particular interest such as the elderly, immigrants, and incarcerated adults. There is also interest in longitudinal studies as is the case in Canada, which is planning to use PIAAC to measure skills over time. Given that countries are looking more and more toward these assessments for data to drive and inform policy, it is likely that we will see international large-scale surveys continue to expand over time.

The Expanded Range of Large-Scale Assessments

As the aforementioned studies demonstrate, not only have we seen an expansion of who is assessed in terms of the range of participating countries and populations within those countries, but international large-scale assessments are also broadening the horizons in terms of what is being assessed. Earlier studies focused on in-school populations and measured typical academic domains such as mathematics, reading, and science. While these continue to be areas of interest, student assessments have expanded to measure a wider range of competencies and interests, reflecting a growing recognition of the need for lifelong learning as a tool to succeed in rapidly changing economies. Large-scale comparative surveys of adult populations began with a focus on literacy and quantitative skills and have expanded to include numeracy and problem solving in everyday adult contexts. With the growing importance of information technologies, measures of Information and Communication Technology (ICT) literacy skills, digital reading, and problem solving in technology environments have also been included in a number of studies.

The growing interest in assessing technology-related skills and knowledge has led to a growing interest in delivering assessments via computer. As has been mentioned, PIAAC is a household survey delivered on laptops. The call for tenders for PISA 2015 also focuses on moving that assessment more fully towards a computer-based platform. Computer-based assessments are making it possible to include new and innovative item types such as interactive scenario-based items and to collect a broader range of information including timing data and information about the processes test takers engage in when completing assessment tasks. This capability is, in turn, leading to a broadening of the cognitive constructs being measured. Additionally, computer-based assessments make it possible to take advantage of psychometric advances such as the use of adaptive testing, which allows for more targeted and time efficient measures.

Another significant development in the history of international large-scale assessments has been the growing interest in broadening the information gained from cognitive measures through the use of extensive background questionnaires. Recent student and adult surveys typically include quite extensive background questionnaires. Student questionnaires address a range of topics including general attitudes and interests, day-to-day learning and leisure activities, and educational resources at home.

For adult assessments, questions about job requirements, literacy related activities at home and at work, and social outcomes such as engagement in civic activities have been included. Applying IRT scaling methodologies to these questionnaires has made it possible to create derived scales based on attitude and interest questions as well as on self-reported literacy-related activities and uses of technology. The use of IRT allows us to study differences across participating countries in terms of background characteristics along the same scales and in the same detail as is possible for the cognitive scales. Data from these questionnaires, in conjunction with the cognitive measures, are being used to inform increasingly complex policy questions about the relationships among learning, skills and outcomes.

Both the broadening of the cognitive constructs being addressed in large-scale comparative surveys and the interest in expanded coverage of policy relevant information collected in background questionnaires have driven the need to develop new methodologies for survey design and data analysis. What began as a basic desire to collect descriptive data in the 1960s and 1970s has now expanded to a much broader range of questions of policy interest. There is clearly growing interest on the part of stakeholders from different disciplines to address policy and research questions that are of interest both at the national and the international level.

Evidence-Based Policy Information

It is important to remember that the foundation of international large-scale assessments has always been some call for comparable information about the skills possessed by populations of interest and an understanding of how those skills are related to educational, economic and social outcomes. As such, the development of international large-scale assessments represents a cycle, as shown in Fig. 1.1. The initial work is motivated by policy questions which then drive the development of assessment frameworks and the design of instruments to address those questions. The desire to assess new aspects of existing constructs as well as to include new domains leads to advances in design and methodology that, finally, facilitate the analysis and interpretation of the survey data. This assessment data and the possibility of assessing new constructs as an outcome of more advanced methodologies leads, in turn, to new questions that then form the basis of the next cycle of assessment.

Fig. 1.1 The development cycle of evidence-based educational policy utilizing data from large-scale international assessments of skills

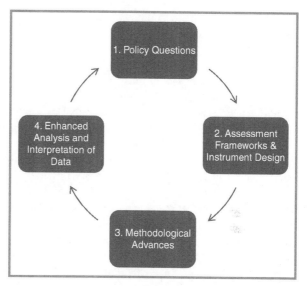

Current and future assessments will continue this cycle, enriching the databases available to researchers around the world to address questions arising in educational research and policy. And the most recent step towards computer-based assessments leads us to the next era of international large-scale assessments. While opening up new sources of information about how students and adults solve technology-based tasks, this move towards computer-based assessments also poses challenges. First and foremost, the ongoing development of new cycles of assessments and the move to new modes of technology-based delivery have to be reconciled with the desire of policymakers to measure trends—particularly for student populations—by comparing skills over cycles of these assessments. In addition, as technology develops, the platforms used for delivery of large-scale assessments will surely evolve and change more quickly than their paper-based predecessors. Finally, we can expect that new domains and new constructs may be added to the ones currently assessed, and additional information will be collected in the background instruments. These innovations will continue the development cycle, likely leading to new assessment methodologies, new interpretation models, and new areas of focus for large-scale assessments.

Perspectives on International Large-Scale Assessments

The contributions in the remaining chapters of this volume are based on invited presentations given during the International Large-Scale Assessment (ILSA) conference, held at Educational Testing Service in March of 2011. The range of perspectives reflected by the presenters and participants reflects the ever broadening range of stakeholder groups with an interest in international large-scale assessments and the role that these assessments play in educational policy. The present volume includes the views of thought leaders from a variety of disciplines, all of whom have profound interest in international large-scale assessments.

In Chap. 2 "International Large-Scale Assessments as Change Agents," Jo Ritzen, Chair of the NGO Empower European Universities, focuses on ILSAs from the policy perspective. He discusses the impact that international large-scale assessments have had on educational policies, using PISA as a focus. He presents a series of national examples, illustrating how data from PISA 2006 resulted in a range of policy outcomes across participating countries. In addition, the role of transmission mechanisms, with a focus on the media in particular, in translating the results of assessments into institutional change is discussed. Ritzen concludes that international large-scale assessments provide transparency by allowing countries and institutions to evaluate the quality of their educational programs and compare where they stand compared to others. It is this transparency, he argues, that spurs change in policy and practice.

Michal Beller, Director-General of the Israeli National Authority for Educational Measurement and Evaluation (RAMA), focuses on the connection between technology-based assessments and learning. In Chap. 3, "Technologies in Large-Scale Assessments: New Directions, Challenges, and Opportunities," Beller contends that the goals for schools today are much broader than helping students master a set of core subjects. Educational systems in the twenty-first century must assist students in becoming critical thinkers, problem solvers, good communicators and good collaborators. In addition, schools strive to help students become information- and technology-literate, innovative and creative and globally competent. Beller argues ICTs have the potential to enhance the assessment of this broad range of skills. Her chapter addresses the computerized revolution of large-scale assessment and considers whether these new developments will be merely a technological leap forward, or serve as a catalyst for a more profound pedagogical change, influencing the way instruction and assessment will be conducted in the next era. Beller also discusses the role of computer-based large-scale assessments in the integration of twenty-first century skills into all content areas, as well as in creating new methodologies for a better use of technology in the service of learning.

Eric Hanushek of Stanford University brings his focus on economic analyses of educational issues, including efficiency, resource usage, and economic outcomes of schools, to the discussion of international large-scale assessments in his chapter. In Chap. 4, "The Role of Assessing Cognitive Skills in International Growth and Development," Hanushek notes that while most analyses of growth and development emphasize the central role of human capital, measurement issues have plagued both research and policy development. Specifically, attention to school attainment and enrollment rates appears misdirected. In contrast, Hanushek explains, recent work has shown that measures of cognitive skills derived from international assessments greatly improve the ability to explain differences in economic growth rates across countries. Moreover, higher levels of cognitive skills appear to have dramatic impacts on the future economic well-being of a country, suggesting that policy actions should focus directly on school quality and other means of improving cognitive skills.

Henry Levin of Teachers College, Columbia University also looks at large-scale assessments in the context of the economics of education. However, Levin extends that focus beyond measures of traditional cognitive skills in Chap. 5, "The Utility and Need for Assessing Noncognitive Skills in Large-Scale Assessments." Levin notes that most attention in large-scale assessments of educational progress and outcomes is focused on cognitive measures of student proficiency. In part, this focus is due to the assumption that "skills" are cognitive in nature and have a high predictive value in terms of productivity. However, the predictive value of cognitive scores on worker productivity and earnings is more modest than commonly assumed. In fact, attempts to relate cognitive test scores from surveys to economic output, although meritorious, require substantial liberties in the interpretation of data. At the same time, there is considerable evidence that noncognitive skills are as important as—or even more important than—cognitive attributes in predicting both school outcomes and economic productivity. Noncognitive outcome measurement is more challenging to assess than cognitive because of its highly diverse dimensions and difficulties in sampling performance on these dimensions. This chapter addresses the developing knowledge base on the potential importance of noncognitive aspects of students and schools, issues of measurement and assessment, and their predictive value on adult outcomes.

In Chap. 6, "The Contributions of International Large-Scale Assessments in Civic Engagement and Citizenship," Judith Torney-Purta of the University of Maryland shares the perspective of researchers and policymakers interested in social policy. She focuses on three studies conducted since the 1970s that have addressed the topic of measuring civic engagement and citizenship and examined patterns of student achievement in attitudes and skills as well as knowledge. Because of the complexity of preparing for citizenship and workplace readiness in different democratic systems, these civic education projects have had an innovative edge in both assessment development and the analysis undertaken. Results from these studies have led to insights into political events, such as the difficulty of establishing civic education after a dictatorship, the rise of anti-immigrant parties, and changes in the political participation of young adults in Europe and the United States. These studies provide information about how students are able to get along with others in society, acquire norms, and participate via democratic means to implement change. In addition to considering civic studies in an international perspective, this chapter presents results of secondary analyses of CIVED data to illustrate the utility of these studies, and discusses analyses relevant for policy and for researchers in political science and psychology.

Eckhard Klieme, Director of the Center for Research on Educational Quality and Evaluation at the German Institute for International Educational Research, brings the perspective of researchers interested in school quality and school development to the discussion of international large-scale assessments. In Chap. 7, "The Role of Large-Scale Assessments in Research on Educational Effectiveness and School Development," Klieme contends that policymakers are primarily interested in large-scale educational assessments as indicators that monitor the functioning, productivity and equity of educational systems, while researchers tend to perceive large-scale assessments as a kind of multi-group (i.e., multi-country) educational effectiveness study. Aside from describing strengths and challenges with regard to student performance and the conditions of teaching and schooling in participating countries, researchers also want to understand why students achieve certain levels of performance. Klieme argues that, because large-scale assessments provide only observational data, it is exceedingly difficult to draw causal inferences, such as concluding that a particular educational policy or practice has a direct or indirect impact on student performance. He proposes that a productive interplay between large-scale assessments and effectiveness research may be established in several ways by implementing enhancements to the assessment design. Two examples of such enhancements are presented and discussed: (1) a national large-scale assessment on language competencies in Germany reassessed students 1 year after the first large-scale assessment, allowing researchers to study the impact of school-level factors on classroom instruction and student growth and (2) a reassessment of Germany's schools performed 9 years after initial participation in PISA.

In Chap. 8 of this volume, "Prospects for the Future: A Framework and Discussion of Directions for the Next Generation of International Large-Scale Assessments," Henry Braun of Boston College describes a set of essential conditions that international large-scale assessments must satisfy in order to contribute to constructive change. These include that reported outcomes of these assessments must be credible, relevant, and correspond to national goals, that stakeholders must be spurred by the results to propose new policies and allocate (or reallocate) resources, and that policymakers must maintain a sustained but flexible focus on these policies. Braun situates the topics covered in this volume within this framework and concludes by examining how the positive impact of international large-scale assessments can be increased. In his view, forward-looking strategies require that these assessments provide more useful information, enhance the value of that information, and extend their reach through approaches such as developing strategies to allow a wider range of jurisdictions to participate and to share resources and expertise to build capacity.

As these brief summaries show, the authors in this volume cover a range of topics and perspectives related to the role and impact of international large-scale assessments. As such, they very much reflect the range of questions that international large-scale assessments will be asked to address as we strive to better understand where we are in terms of educational effectiveness and human capital development and how we might best move into an increasingly interconnected and challenging future.

References

Messick, S., A. Beaton, and F. Lord. 1983. *National assessment of educational progress reconsidered: A new design for a new era* (Report 83–10). Princeton: Educational Testing Service.

Naemi, B., E. Gonzalez, J. Bertling, A. Betancourt, J. Burrus, P. Kyllonen, J. Minsky, P. Lietz, E. Klieme, S. Vieluf, J. Lee, and R.D. Roberts, (in press). Large-scale group score assessments: Past, present, and future. In *Oxford handbook of psychological assessment of children and adolescents,* eds. Saklofske D., and Schwean V. (Cambridge, MA: Oxford University Press).

Organisation for Economic Co-operation and Development and Statistics Canada. 2000. *Literacy in the information age: Final report of the international adult literacy survey.* Paris: OECD Publishing.

Statistics Canada and Organisation for Economic Co-operation and Development (OECD) 2005. *Learning a living: First results of the adult literacy and life skills survey.* Paris: OECD Publishing.

von Davier, M. Sinharay, S., Oranje, A. and Beaton, A. 2006. Statistical Procedures used in the National Assessment of Educational Progress (NAEP): Recent developments and future directions. In *Handbook of statistics,* eds. Rao C. R., and Sinharay S., (Vol. 26): Psychometrics. Amsterdam: Elsevier.

Chapter 2
International Large-Scale Assessments as Change Agents

Jo Ritzen

Introduction

Transparency to keep you honest: This notion, in a general sense, had been widely embraced in the national legislatures of many countries as an important change agent towards better societal outcomes. But in education, transparency in the form of educational outcomes—to be measured by (large-scale) assessments, among other methods—is a relatively new phenomenon as an intended agent of change.

This chapter is a survey of my personal experience in the recent past with international large-scale assessments (ILSAs) as change agents, with a focus on PISA, the Programme for International Student Assessment, which started in 1994[1] and has had a progressively larger impact on the educational policies of countries. Many countries felt PISA gave them an honest view of where they were in their aspirations to have the best possible talent development. It was not always a happy view. Sometimes it confirmed earlier fears that the country had fallen off track. Sometimes the PISA results were in sharp contrast to previously held beliefs in the quality of the country's education system. This PISA-shock has spurred a rapid change in country policies, with a likely unprecedented upward spiral in the quality of education.

My survey starts with a theoretical framework of transparency as a change agent. This model is based on assessments that allow for comparisons between institutions. It has to be slightly modified for an application to PISA, which provides a

---

The following is an adaptation of the keynote address for the International Large-Scale Assessment Conference at Educational Testing Service in Princeton, NJ, on March 16–18, 2011.

---

[1] While planning and preparation for this endeavor started in 1994, it took until 2000 for the first PISA assessment to be administered in OECD countries.

J. Ritzen (✉)
Empower European Universities, International Economics of Science, Technology and Higher Education, Maastricht School of Governance, UNU-MERIT, Kloosterweg 54 Bunde, Netherlands
e-mail: jo.ritzen@empowereu.org

M. von Davier et al. (eds.), *The Role of International Large-Scale Assessments: Perspectives from Technology, Economy, and Educational Research,*
DOI 10.1007/978-94-007-4629-9_2, © Springer Science+Business Media Dordrecht 2013

comparison among countries. Then I present the main findings of the PISA evaluation in terms of its policy impact within the framework of the theoretical model. Subsequently, I consider transmission mechanics (in particular, the role of the media) in translating the results of assessments into institutional change before providing a concluding section.

The main point is that assessments make comparisons in the accomplishments of different institutions or regions possible. They can take the role of signaling the quality of the educational institutions or the educational establishment of a region or a country. This signal can drive a healthy competition in which all participating partners profit.

Transparency as a Change Agent: A Think Model

Throughout my career both in government as a Minister for Education, Culture and Science in the Netherlands in the 1990s, as well in different capacities (among others as vice president for education, health and social protection) at the World Bank, I have emphasized the role of transparency as an important change agent towards better educational outcomes within countries and between countries. The theoretical model implicit in this emphasis is depicted in Fig. 2.1.

I consider the educational institution as the unit of performance for which educational outcomes are measured in a way that allows for comparisons with the educational outcomes of other institutions. Of course, one can also focus on the educational outcomes of a set of institutions, e.g., in a region, a state or a country.

The transmission of these measurements to "change" in institutions can take place in three different ways, as shown in Fig. 2.1.

1. The first is the direct line of "naming and shaming," which might lead schools to rethink their policies and become more performance-conscious.
2. The second refers to the reaction of consumers (students and their parents) and stakeholders (the community in which the school is located).
3. The third refers to the reaction of local, regional, or state governments to large-scale assessments.

Any sign that their school performs less well than others may have repercussions. I have found evidence for this in the external evaluation of policy impact of PISA (OECD 2008) in Basque country, where PISA results were known by school. Their parents and local stakeholders of some top-performing schools will make every attempt to have their school perform even better the next time around.

Needless to say, "iteration" (repeating the cycle of measurement) is a necessary condition for assessment to have an improvement function. "Consumer choice," whether direct (in an education system that allows choice even within the public system, or for a switch from public to private, or vice versa) or indirect (through migration to school districts with better schools), does have an impact on institutions.

"Choice" is an important transmission mechanism of quality measures towards the energy and dedication to change. The size of the effects of "choice" on

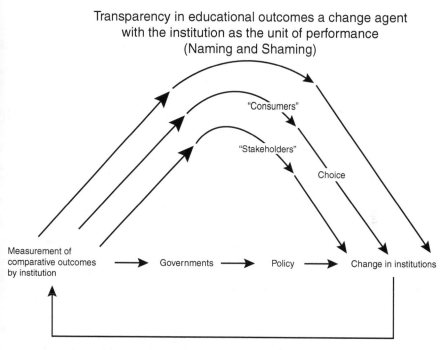

Transparency in educational outcomes a change agent
with the institution as the unit of performance
(Naming and Shaming)

"Consumers"

"Stakeholders"

Choice

Measurement of
comparative outcomes ⟶ Governments ⟶ Policy ⟶ Change in institutions
by institution

Fig. 2.1 Transparency in educational outcomes as a change agent with the institution as the unit of performance (Naming and Shaming)

institutional behavior depends on a great number of factors. First, the measures will—in education—only partially reveal the main features that consumers (students and/or their parents) have sought in the school. As a result, consumers will only partially let their choice depend on such measures. Second, the institutions may not want to react to changes in choice (decreased student number) on the basis of published performance measures, because they believe that those measures do not represent their strategic aims in full. Some schools may prefer to have a smaller student body along with a different educational mission than what is captured in the performance measures.

Some examples of the Netherlands in the 1990s are the higher education "Choice Guide" and the inspectorate assessment of schools.

In the 1990s, the Ministry of Education organized and financed the Choice Guide. In this guide, all degree courses of all higher education institutions were compared annually in groups of similar courses (e.g., medicine, economics, law, etc.), using student evaluations on a large number of items (approximately 30). The evaluations were summarized by grade. The effect on choice was and still is limited. However, the impact on institutions has been impressive. Some institutions have made it their mission (advertised in public) to be among the best evaluated and work hard to correct low evaluation scores. Most institutions do their best to avoid low scores. Those with consistently low scores for degree courses over a number of years are bashed in the press. Although they still may not have lost too many students (presumably because of the geographic limitations of choice), they are under considerable pressure to improve.

Although no detailed analysis exists, it is hard to believe that the annual publication has *not* led to a substantial improvement of higher education (in order of decreasing importance: Ph.D., master's degree, university bachelor's degree, professional education bachelor's degree, community college bachelor's degree), albeit only through choice, when serious alternatives were an issue.

The assessments of secondary schools of the Dutch inspectorate were published in one of the national morning newspapers (*Trouw*) for the first time on a Saturday in 1996. The demand was so overwhelming that the paper was sold out at 8 a.m. The publications did and do affect choice, and schools will do almost everything to ensure they are well evaluated on their performance by the inspectorate.

In Fig. 2.1, I put "stakeholders" next to "choice." In those countries where choice is not used as an allocation mechanism, school boards and other local stakeholders can be the parties that put pressure on institutions to improve in terms of their performance measures.

The third line of change is the one of government. Government may choose to alter policies or even close down schools that are performing badly. The "No Child Left Behind" policy in the United States allows for such an approach in combination with the possibility of revamping the school as a charter school.

Both the United Kingdom and the Netherlands (as examples) have legislation that allows for the termination of public finance for low-performing schools. Needless to say, this refers only to a limited number of cases each year. Policies are not so likely to be altered if the results of assessments are not known by institution.

The direct impact ("naming and shaming"), the impact of stakeholders, and the impact of government agencies are strongly related to the way the public interest is taken up by the media. In the subsequent section, "The Policy Impact of PISA," I will discuss their role more in detail.

To this point, I have taken a "technical" position on assessments and change without asking the more normative question whether such change is socially desirable. This question uncovers the "value-added" debate. Educational accomplishments indeed should be considered in a value-added fashion. Unfortunately, few countries have followed the lead of Poland in showing a willingness to pursue this necessary direction.

When assessments are taken to the country level—as with PISA—and used for cross-country comparisons, the value-added question is less intrusive, assuming that the base distribution of learning achievements of, say, 5-year-olds is not so different among countries, at least those with similar per capita incomes.

The resistance to participation in ILSAs—although substantially different among countries—often comes from the education community. Many education leaders express the fear that assessments drive them "to teach to the test" or that the assessments "label" students. Yet, high quality performance tests that are not used to promote or select students are unlikely to have this effect. The "labeling" of students indeed can take place, because the education environment can be adapted based on the test to serve the student better, as an intended effect.

In the case of the Dutch Choice Guide for higher education, there was originally a strong resentment from the side of the higher education institutions that was expressed as unease with the types of measures used. But one cannot escape the impression that the resentment was based more on unwillingness to be transparent than on concerns about the types of measures used.

The Policy Impact of PISA

PISA is an internationally standardized assessment that monitors the quality of education systems in terms of student outcomes. PISA assesses the ability of 15-year-olds to apply their knowledge in reading, mathematics, and science to real-life problems, rather than the acquisition of specific curriculum content. Assessments take place every three years and use a framework that is jointly developed by Organisation for Economic Co-operation and Development (OECD) countries. Contextual data are collected through background questionnaires for students and schools, with between 5,000 and 10,000 students typically tested in each country.

The first survey was conducted in 2000. It focused on reading literacy and measured students' "capacity to understand, use and reflect on written texts, in order to achieve one's goals, to develop one's knowledge and potential, and to participate in society." The survey was completed by students in 43 countries (29 OECD member and 14 nonmember countries and economies; for 11 of the 43 countries and economies, data was collected in a follow-up study, PISA-PLUS, in 2002).

The second survey was conducted in 2003. It assessed students in mathematical literacy and examined young adults' "capacity to identify and understand the role that mathematics plays in the world, to make well-founded judgments and to use and engage with mathematics in ways that meet the needs of that individual's life as a constructive, concerned, and reflective citizen" (see page 12 in OECD 2006). A total of 41 countries (30 OECD member and 11 nonmember countries and economies) participated in the 2003 assessment cycle.

The third survey was conducted in 2006. It had science literacy as its focus and assessed the capacity of students' "scientific knowledge and use of that knowledge to identify questions, to acquire new knowledge, to explain scientific phenomena, and to draw evidence-based conclusions about science-related issues, understanding of the characteristic features of science as a form of human knowledge and enquiry, awareness of how science and technology shape our material, intellectual, and cultural environments, and willingness to engage in science-related issues, and with the ideas of science, as a reflective citizen." A total of 57 countries (30 OECD member and 27 nonmember countries and economies) participated in this survey.

The fourth survey was conducted in 2009 (see OECD 2010).

In 2007 the OECD commissioned a group of three individuals, of which I was one, to do an evaluation of the impact of PISA on policy. This group produced a report one year later.

The research design consisted of the following two parts:

- A *quantitative* strand: A total of 905 questionnaires were distributed to policymakers, local government officials, school principals, parents, academics and researchers, and media representatives in 43 countries and economies (of which 24 were OECD member countries) via email. Of these, 548 questionnaires were returned. This corresponds to an overall response rate of 61 %. Furthermore, responses were obtained from 42 representatives at the PISA Governing Board, 33 members of the business community, and 36 representatives of teacher organizations.

- A *qualitative* strand: Five case-study countries and economies were selected, taking into account variations in terms of the levels of impact PISA has achieved, performance in PISA, and equity and government structure (centralized/decentralized/federal/regional). Geographical balance was also taken into consideration. The case-study countries and economies were Canada, Hong Kong-China, Norway, Poland, and Spain.

I personally visited Spain and Poland as part of this intensive, in-depth qualitative review.

Let me first focus on the question of whether PISA acted as a change agent, and if so, how. Our model of Fig. 2.1 needs some adaptation because, in this scenario, consumer choice is irrelevant (generally, students will not choose to follow their education in other countries).

The overall level of policy impact of PISA in each country was estimated by combining the respondents' assessment of the extent to which PISA influenced policymaking at the national/federal and local levels in all three PISA assessments. The categories were constructed based on the distribution of answers to the questions of countries that returned more than four questionnaires. Early on, countries asked for and received the assurance that individual country data would not be published by us. Rather, deciles were generated from the distribution of respondents, who judged that PISA was extremely or very influential in informing policy. PISA was considered to have a comparatively low impact in countries falling into the range from the lowest to the third decile. The policy impact of PISA was considered to be medium in countries from the fourth to the seventh decile, and high in countries in the deciles above. This resulted in the following classification:

- Group A
    - *Countries where PISA achieved relatively low levels of impact on policy formation*: Czech Republic, Ireland, Italy, the Netherlands, the Slovak Republic, Turkey, the United Kingdom, Bulgaria, Croatia, Hong Kong-China, Latvia, Lithuania, Romania, the Republic of Serbia, and Uruguay.

- Group B
    - *Countries where PISA achieved relatively medium levels of impact on policy formation*: Australia, Austria, Belgium, Canada, Finland, Greece, Hungary, Iceland, Switzerland, Chile, Chinese Taipei, Colombia, and Qatar.

- Group C
    - *Countries where PISA achieved relatively high levels of impact on policy formation*: Denmark, Germany, Japan, Mexico, Norway, Spain, Sweden, Israel, the Kyrgyz Republic, Macao-China, Slovenia, and Thailand.

Note that this survey took place in 2007. If we had done this after the 2009 PISA results were published in 2010, the picture would have been quite different: The United States and the United Kingdom reacted quite strongly to the PISA observation that their countries continued to belong to the low achievers among the richer countries. All in all, it seems that it takes a while for the PISA message to sink in into the policy domain in those countries that are not top PISA performers.

What then is the framework in which these reactions can be placed? Surely the reactions are rooted in the discrepancy between expectation and realized results. But how do countries come up with expectations regarding PISA results? Several scenarios seem likely:

- Expectations are based on "comparison" (neighboring?) countries (applicable to 2000 PISA).
- Expectations are based on expected changes over time due to national improvement efforts (applicable to 2003 and 2006).
- Expectations are based on a combination of both.
- Expectations are based on the wish to belong to the "world top."

The relation, on the one hand, among the above indicators derived from the PISA scores for 2003 and 2006 and, on the other, the measure of the reaction on PISA, was statistically analyzed without any significant result. Neither "neighboring" country score, average score, nor world top fits the bill as "comparison/benchmarking" for all countries. For Spain and Poland (the countries that I could study in depth), their reaction can only be explained by the ambition to belong to the world top: The benchmark in terms of expectation are to be the very best PISA countries in the world, even if neighboring countries seem to take a more "relaxed" attitude. Digging one spade deeper, I tried to ascertain the level of ambition with respect to the educational accomplishments of 15-year-olds in the country by looking at general government documents (such as annual budgets).

It appears indeed that countries expressing great general ambitions ("belonging to the top 10 in competitiveness"—a goal that at least some 50 countries in the world endorsed in the survey!)—also are more ambitious with respect to education and seem to react more strongly to the PISA results than others.

PISA, of course, showed that educational outcomes differ remarkably among countries, including countries with similar levels of income. Figure 2.2 shows the performance distribution for five different countries and the OECD average.

Finland might be considered to have reached "the production possibility frontier" (as economists would call it), while other countries still have substantial room for improvement.

Figure 2.3 shows that a great majority of questionnaire respondents (85 %) regarded policymakers as the main *stakeholders* responsible for implementing policies in light of PISA, followed by school principals and local government officials. Professional teacher associates and academics and researchers were considered third and fourth. "Consumers" (parents) or stakeholders reflecting the "consumers" side (the business community) are not regarded as important in engendering change based on assessment. If you think that these results are brought about by the framing

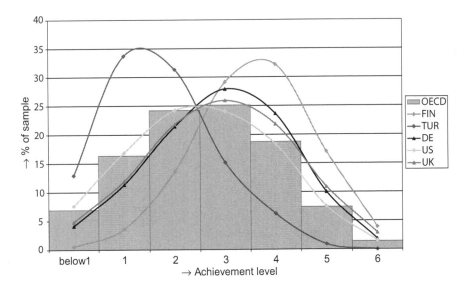

Fig. 2.2 The Academic Achievement Curve (selected countries), *OECD* Organisation for Economic Co-operation and Development countries, *FIN* Finland, *TUR* Turkey, *DE* Denmark, *US* United States, *UK* United Kingdom. (Source: Ritzen 2010, p. 177)

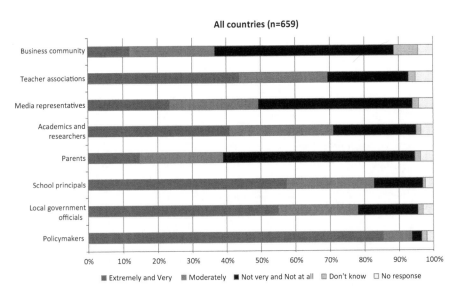

Fig. 2.3 Stakeholders responsible for implementing policies in light of the PISA results, Question: Who would you identify as being responsible for implementing policies in light of the PISA results in your country? Please indicate the degree of responsibility for each stakeholder and specify to which PISA assessment you refer

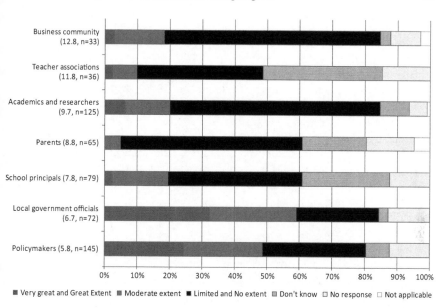

Fig. 2.4 Extent of key stakeholder's own responsibility for results, Question: To what extent do [members of own stakeholder group] feel responsible for your country's results in PISA?

of the questions, then it is good to know that all questions (including, "Who would you identify as the most significant stakeholders in PISA and its results in your country") led to the same result.

One would imagine that the responsibility for the PISA results would be claimed (in case of good results) by all parties (and definitely by the schools). Of course, one would expect all parties to dodge responsibility in the case of not-so-good results. However, the latter seems to be more generic as Fig. 2.4 shows.

All parties dodge responsibility. Thirty-two percent of local government officials and 24 % of policymakers claim responsibility, but *only 2 % of school principals and representatives of teacher organizations respond that they feel responsible.* Unfortunately no analysis was made along the lines of positive or negative responsibility answers in relation to higher or lower scores. For me, this response is beyond comprehension. How can a whole sector ignore its responsibility for the results, as these results would seem to imply? Note that we are not looking at an isolated reply from one country, but at a reasonably well spread group of respondents from a sizable number of different countries.

One might have expected that the link between PISA and "change" would be less if the stakeholders felt that PISA did not adequately address the core mission of education as viewed by education institutions, the government, or the "consumers," as we suggested in our model in the section on transparency as a change agent. This is, however, *not* the case. Overwhelmingly the stakeholders regarded student

performance in reading (78 %), mathematics (75 %) and science (71 %) as well
as international comparisons and rankings (70 %) as extremely important or very
important.

This was also the case when reporting on PISA regarding the relationship between home background and student performance (58 %), the relationship between
school context and student performance (53 %), and student interests, motivation
and attitudes (48 %).

In the qualitative part of the research, for which I was able to visit schools for
whom institutional PISA scores were available, I did find a confirmation of the
hypothesis that schools that do well on PISA also feel more comfortable with the
PISA outcome measurements as reflecting their mission, while schools that under-
perform in PISA indicate that they feel that civic education, socialization, and a
broad development of talents of students are more important than the three domains
as measured in PISA.

This was also found in a question in the quantitative part—to what extent PISA
addresses the policy needs of participant countries and economies. The answers
were less positive than those on the relevance of the measures used, maybe because
of different objectives on the part of stakeholders than those captured in the actual
measurement.

Of course, stakeholders might also be apprehensive of the accuracy of the measurement, but that did not turn out to be the case (OECD 2008, p. 24).

Transmission

Large-scale assessments can only play a role as a change agent if the information derived from these assessments reaches the stakeholder, and even more so if
stakeholders are challenged because of the results of the assessments. The media
play a tremendously important role in this process. However, this turns out to be
an autonomous and rather unpredictable role. One would surmise that the PISA
results would compare to the benchmark of other countries in the same league as a
predictor, according to the same expectation model as was suggested earlier for the
overall impact of PISA on policy (expectations based on the average, the neighboring countries, or the world top).

Again, although not considered statistically, the evidence suggests (as with the
policy reaction) that there is no clear cut case for suggesting any general "expectation" model on the part of the media.

Media are part of the dissemination of PISA results. In general, the dissemination
of results by the media played a substantial role in determining the policy impact.
Some country governments were aware of this and organized dissemination through
press conferences held for representatives of the media, as well as through conferences with stakeholders and schools (as Poland and Spain did). But other countries
simply let PISA run its course and paid little to no attention to dissemination.

Here we recognize the dissemination effort as it relates to the government's interest in policy change. Dissemination (including media coverage) does not seem to be an exogenous, but rather an endogenous variable in the model, with the exception of that part of the media that plays more an "NGO (nongovernmental organization) role."

I found a compelling similarity between the reaction of Lang (2010) to the No Child Left Behind assessments and reactions to PISA at the school level: If you want large-scale assessment to have an impact on schools, then you should disseminate results and discuss them with teachers, parents, school boards, and so forth on the local level.

Also in the PISA evaluation, the local level—where the changes should take place—felt uninformed and uneasy as well.

Even if all were well informed, the question is, What do you do with the PISA results? How should a restructuring of schools take place so that better results can be achieved?

Conclusion

1. ILSAs can be important change agents, provided that the assessment addresses the primary concerns of stakeholders in education. The diversity in the objectives of education and differences in the priorities that different stakeholders place on distinguishable objectives (like mathematics versus citizenship) will generally reduce the impact of large-scale assessment as a change agent to some extent. It is important to include a variety of measures in the assessment that reflect principal components of the diversity in the missions schools have adopted.
2. Most large-scale assessments dodge the value-added question. This undermines their potential for change. The present shortcut to measure only outcomes and not to include value-added is unavoidable, but value-added measures should be conceived and implemented in future assessments.
3. The drawback of "teaching to the test" inherent in the impact of large-scale assessments on policy may be exaggerated, unless the survey results are used as high stakes tests.

For ILSAs such as PISA, policy change seems to depend mostly on the level of ambition of the country as expressed in the comparison/benchmarking. Some countries seem to be happy to follow the mean, or the mean of the scores of neighboring countries. Others aspire to become part of the world top performers.

Overall, we conclude that the competition between educational institutions or educational establishments of regions or countries can have a healthy, quality-improving effect on education, once a proper quality signal in the form of an assessment that allows for comparisons is developed.

References

Lang, Kevin. 2010. Measurement Matters. *Journal of Economic Perspectives,* 24(3, Summer): 167–182.

OECD. 2006. *Assessing Scientific, Reading and Mathematical Literacy: A Framework for PISA 2006.* Paris: OECD.

OECD. 2008. External evaluation of policy impact of PISA. Paris: OECD.

OECD. 2010. PISA 2009 results. Paris: OECD.

Ritzen, Jo. 2010. *A Chance for European Universities.* Amsterdam: Amsterdam University Press.

Chapter 3
Technologies in Large-Scale Assessments: New Directions, Challenges, and Opportunities

Michal Beller

Introduction

Assessment serves a critical role in education. It holds education systems accountable and, at the same time, serves as a gateway to systemic change in education. Assessment signals priorities for curriculum and instruction, and in some jurisdictions, teachers tend to model their pedagogical approach on standardized large-scale assessments. Curriculum developers and designers of educational materials respond to high-stakes tests by modifying existing textbooks and other instructional materials and by developing and marketing new ones suited to test expectations. Ultimately, assessment drives change at all levels, from classroom to legislature, though its effects range from the positive to the negative (e.g., Koretz and Hamilton 2006; Nichols and Berliner 2007).

Therefore, the contents and the mode of assessment should be designed carefully and thoughtfully to ensure the impact on education is positive. For this to happen, assessments should be more aligned with the intended curriculum, embedded in authentic contexts, and fully integrated into the learning and teaching process. Effective integration of assessment in learning and teaching is a challenge, particularly due to the need to balance between formative and summative assessments. Technology can assist in achieving such a challenging goal (e.g., Bennett 2001, 2002).

It is clear that existing innovative technologies, such as smart phones and tablets, as well as future technologies, hold the potential to dramatically change the way assessment will be implemented in the future. However, this chapter deals neither with the pure technological opportunities ahead of us, nor with the technological barriers existing today (e.g., access to computers in schools and bidirectional adaptation of the test platform to various languages such as Arabic and Hebrew).

This paper describes the recent developments of technology-based national large-scale assessments (NLSAs) and international large-scale assessments (ILSAs)

M. Beller (✉)
RAMA—The National Authority for Measurement and Evaluation in Education,
Ministry of Education, 125 Begin Blvd. 12th Floor, Tel Aviv 67012, Israel
e-mail: mbeller.rama@education.gov.il

M. von Davier et al. (eds.), *The Role of International Large-Scale Assessments:*
Perspectives from Technology, Economy, and Educational Research,
DOI 10.1007/978-94-007-4629-9_3, © Springer Science+Business Media Dordrecht 2013

and addresses whether the digital revolution of ILSAs will be merely a technological step forward or serve as a catalyst for a more profound pedagogical change in the way instruction, learning and assessments will be conducted in the future. We look at whether it will foster the integration of twenty-first century competencies and expertise into teaching and instruction of all content areas, and whether it will facilitate the creation of new methodologies for a better use of technology and assessment in the service of learning.

The Role of Technology in Assessment

Information and communication technologies (ICT) assist in automating various phases of testing processes such as designing, presenting, recording, and distributing test materials. However, one main goal of integrating ICT is to enable assessment of those aspects of cognition and performance that are complex and dynamic and have been impossible to assess directly via paper and pencil (P&P). New capabilities afforded by technology include directly assessing problem-solving skills, exposing the sequences of actions taken by learners in solving problems, and modeling complex reasoning tasks. Technology also makes possible the collection of data regarding students' concept organization and other aspects of students' knowledge structures, as well as representations of their participation in socially interactive discussions and projects (Chudowsky and Pellegrino 2003).

By enriching assessment situations through the use of multimedia, interactivity and control over the stimulus display, it is possible to assess a much wider array of constructs than was previously possible. For example, SimScientists uses science simulations to support powerful formative assessments of complex science learning (Quellmalz et al. 2009). The simulation-based assessment tasks are dynamic, engaging, and interactive. They are capable of assessing complex science knowledge and inquiry skills, which go well beyond the capabilities of printed tests.

Advances in measurement, technology and in the understanding of cognition hold promise for creating assessments that are more useful and valid indicators of what students know and can do. Such work involves reconceptualizing assessment design and use and tying assessment more directly to the processes and contexts of learning and instruction (Chudowsky and Pellegrino 2003; Quellmalz and Pellegrino 2009; Bejar and Graf 2010). Success in tying assessment more closely to contexts and specific learning processes is what will make these new developments more effective.

Universal Design of Assessment

There is a push in several countries (the United States in particular) to expand national and state testing and to require that assessment systems encompass all students—including those with disabilities, learning disorders and those with limited proficiency in the language of instruction—many of whom have not been included in these systems in the past.

Technology allows for the development of assessments using universal design principles that make assessments more accessible, effective, and valid for students with greater diversity in terms of disabilities and limited language proficiency (mainly non-native), thus allowing for wider student inclusion (e.g., Johnstone et al. 2009; Thompson et al. 2002). Technology allows for presentation and assessment using different representations of the same concept or skill and can accommodate various student disabilities and strengths. Therefore, presenting information through multiple modalities enlarges the proportion of the population that can be assessed fairly. Similarly, assistive technology can make it possible for students with disabilities and those who require special interfaces to interact with digital resources, allowing them to demonstrate what they know and can do in ways that would be impossible with standard print-based assessments.

Almond et al. (2010) proposed stimulating research into technology-enabled assessments that incorporate conditions designed to make tests appropriate for the full range of the student population by enhancing accessibility. The prospect is that rather than having to retrofit existing assessments to include these students (through the use of large numbers of accommodations or a variety of alternative assessments), new assessments can be designed and developed from the outset to allow participation of the widest possible range of students, in a way that results in valid inferences about performance for all students who participate in the assessment.

The Role of Technology in National Large-Scale Assessments

Efforts are being made for system wide implementation of technology-based assessments in order to extend, improve or replace existing assessment systems, or to create entirely new assessment systems. Kozma (2009) provided a comprehensive list of the potential advantages and challenges of incorporating ICT into large-scale assessments (See exact quote in Appendix 1).

Delivery of national assessments via computer is becoming more prevalent as changes are made in assessment methodologies that reflect practical changes in pedagogical methods. Introducing computer-based testing (CBT) is often viewed as a necessary and positive change in large-scale educational assessment—not only because it reflects changes in classroom instruction, which is becoming more and more computer-mediated, but also because it can provide a number of assessment and administrative advantages (Bennett 2010).

A systemic integration of digital components in NLSA began in the United States with the National Assessment of Educational Progress (NAEP) (e.g., Sandene et al. 2005; Bennett et al. 2007), and is being implemented today in a number of NLSA systems around the globe as part of a process of integrating technology into learning and instruction (e.g., Iceland, Denmark, Hungary, Israel, and Australia). However, results from the NAEP Problem Solving in Technology-Rich Environment study

(Bennett et al. 2007, 2010) made it clear that going beyond traditional testing is still extremely challenging. Recent progress on SimScientist is encouraging—findings from an evaluation study based on six states (Herman et al. 2011) provide recommendations for incorporating these simulation-based assessments into state science assessment systems in addition to the formative classroom use (Quellmalz et al. 2011).

An elaboration on the main relevant developments in Israel and the United States follows below.

Israel

Instruction, Learning, and Assessment via Computers

The Israeli education system went through several phases of integrating technologies into instruction, learning, and assessment (not yet with complete school coverage):

I. 1975–1990: The Infrastructure Phase I—Setting up computer labs in schools, mainly for drill and practice.

II. 1990–1999: The Infrastructure Phase II—Personal computer labs featuring multimedia programs.

III. 1999–2005: The Internet Phase—Proliferation of school websites. Sporadic web-based activities aimed at information literacy and project-based learning.

IV. 2006–present: A shift to web-based content and tools (e.g., CET, Time-to-Know, Galim) aligned with the national curricula (links below).

CET develops both digital content and advanced technology for instruction, learning, and assessment (ILA) by various means. The ILA system provides (in both Hebrew and Arabic):

• Optimal integration of the latest technologies available
• Integrated learning units with assessment tasks
• Classroom–home continuum
• Use of a learning management system for managing learning and assessment
• Customization for students with learning disabilities.

The ILA system takes full advantage of computer capabilities for instruction, learning and assessment, such as simulations and animations; virtual labs; video clips; maps; narration; information literacy tasks on the web, and interactive feedback for the student. For example, the online elementary school system—Ofek (horizon, in Hebrew), a bilingual (Hebrew and Arabic) teaching, learning, and assessment environment, contains a learning management system and a large collection of curriculum-based learning activities and assessment assignments in most subjects (Hebrew, math, science, social studies, Bible, current events, etc.). Ofek also offers innovative generators, such as an online comic strip generator, math exercises generator, writing generator and more, all allowing teachers to create their own teaching material in line with the specific needs of their students (For more on CET, see: http://cet.org.il/pages/Home.aspx and http://ofek.cet.ac.il; on Time-To-Know, see: http://www.timetoknow.com/; on Galim, see: http://www.galim.org.il/fields/english.html).

United States of America

The US education system went through phases similar to the Israeli ones with regard to integrating technologies. However, the US system was one of the first in the world, if not the first, to conduct a large-scale online standardized assessment via its National Assessment of Educational Progress (NAEP).

The National Assessment of Educational Progress (NAEP)

NAEP conducted three field investigations as part of the Technology-Based Assessment Project, which explored the use of new technology in administering NAEP.

The first field investigation was the Math Online (MOL) study. It addressed issues related to measurement, equity, efficiency, and operations in online mathematics assessment. In the MOL study, data were collected from more than 100 schools at each of two grade levels in spring 2001 (Sandene et al. 2005).

The 2002 Writing Online (WOL) study was the second of three field investigations in the Technology-Based Assessment project, and it explored the use of new technology in administering NAEP.

The 2003 Problem Solving in Technology-Rich Environments study (TRE) was the third study and it investigated how computers might be used to measure skills that cannot be measured on a paper and pencil test (Bennett et al. 2007, 2010).

In continuation of the previous studies, NAEP recently completed a multistate field test of online writing assessment for 8th and 12th grades to be operational in 2011. The design of the 2011 NAEP writing assessment reflects the way today's students compose written texts—and are expected to compose texts—particularly as they move into postsecondary settings. The assessment is designed to measure the ability of students in grades 8th and 12th to write using word processing software with commonly available tools (For more, see: http://nces.ed.gov/nationsreportcard/writing/cba.asp).

US State Assessments

West Virginia and Oregon are among the leading states in moving forward on the integration of technology into their state assessments.

West Virginia

West Virginia's techSteps program is a literacy framework based on the National Education Technology Standards for Students (NETS*S) and is aligned with state and Common Core State Standards.

TechSteps is a personalized, project-based technology literacy curriculum that infuses technology skills into core instruction, promoting core subject area outcomes while also teaching skills for the twenty-first century. A Technology Literacy Assessment Profile is built for the student and updated as each new activity is performed and recorded. This approach allows educators to teach and assess technology literacy in an integrated and systematic manner, using authentic performance-based assessment to provide meaningful feedback to students and generate data for reporting purposes. This system provides West Virginia with statewide student data on technology proficiencies at each grade level (For more, see: http://www.techsteps.com/public/home/).

Oregon

The Oregon Assessment of Knowledge and Skills (OAKS), is the name for the larger Oregon statewide assessment system. This new online testing system assesses students' mastery of Oregon content standards. The OAKS Online operational test is now available for reading, mathematics, science, and social sciences (For more, see: http://www.oaks.k12.or.us/).

Recent Developments in the United States

Cognitively Based Assessments of, for and as Learning (CBAL)—
A Research Project

The improvements in large-scale assessments, important as they may be, will not resolve the growing tension between internal and external school assessment. An innovative research project proposed by Educational Testing Service (ETS) is CBAL (Bennett and Gitomer 2009; Bennett 2010), which attempts to resolve this tension.

Technology plays a key role in the CBAL project. The central goal of CBAL is to create a comprehensive system of assessment that documents what students have achieved ("of learning"), helps identify how to plan and adjust instruction ("for learning"), and is considered by students and teachers to be a worthwhile educational experience in and of itself ("as learning"). The computerized system, when completed, will attempt to unify and create synergy among accountability testing, formative assessment and professional support.

Accountability tests, formative assessment and professional support will be derived from the same conceptual base. This base will rest upon rigorous cognitive research, common core or state standards, and curricular considerations. CBAL assessments will consist largely of engaging, extended, constructed-response tasks that are delivered primarily by computer and, as much as possible, automatically scored. CBAL assessments are designed to help students take an active role in the assessment of their own learning.

It should be noted, however, that for such an integrated accountability system to be relevant and effective, the participating educational bodies should be in full agreement as to curricula and standards (For more, see: http://www.ets.org/research/topics/cbal/initiative).

US Department of Education (DOE)

> I'm calling on our nation's governors and state education chiefs to develop standards and assessments that don't simply measure whether students can fill in a bubble on a test, but whether they possess twenty-first century skills like problem solving and critical thinking and entrepreneurship and creativity. (President Barack Obama, address to the Hispanic Chamber of Commerce, March 10, 2009)

In an effort to provide ongoing feedback to teachers during the course of the school year, measure annual student growth, and move beyond narrowly focused bubble tests, the US Department of Education has awarded grants (in September 2010) to two groups of states to develop a new generation of tests. The consortia—the Partnership for Assessment of Readiness for Colleges and Careers (PARCC), and the Smarter Balanced Assessment Consortium (SBAC)—were awarded US$170 million and US$160 million, respectively, to design assessments that evaluate students based on common-core standards by the 2014–2015 school year. The tests will assess students' knowledge of mathematics and English language arts from third grade through high school.

> As I travel around the country the number one complaint I hear from teachers is that state bubble tests pressure teachers to teach to a test that doesn't measure what really matters. Both of these winning applicants are planning to develop assessments that will move us far beyond this and measure real student knowledge and skills. (US Education Secretary Arne Duncan)

(http://www.ed.gov/news/press-releases/us-secretary-education-duncan-announces-winners-competition-improve-student-asse)

The smarter coalition will test students using computer adaptive technology that will tailor questions to students based on their answers to previous questions. Smarter will continue to use one test at the end of the year for accountability purposes but will create a series of interim tests used to inform students, parents, and teachers about whether students are on track.

PARCC's next-generation assessment system will provide students, educators, policymakers and the public with the tools needed to identify whether students— from third grade through high school—are on track for postsecondary success and critically, where gaps may exist and how they can be addressed well before students enter college or the workforce.

With such new technology-based assessments, schools may no longer have to interrupt their routine instructional processes at various times during the year to administer external tests to students, not to mention the time saved on preparing them for the tests. Such a scenario would be made possible when schools implement assessments for both formative and summative purposes in a manner developed now in CBAL.

The cognitively-based assessment of, for, and as learning (CBAL) system has many of the features that are envisioned in the PARCC and SBAC consortia. The CBAL summative assessments are not one-time events, but rather are spread over several occasions throughout the school year. This is a feature that has attracted a good deal of attention in discussions of the consortia plans. CBAL also emphasizes the use of formative assessments by teachers and in teacher professional development. This emphasis on formative assessment and teacher professional development can also be found in the broad outlines of the consortia plans (Linn 2010).

The Role of Technology in International Large-Scale Assessments (ILSAs)

Among the more familiar LSA systems are the international large-scale assessments (ILSAs), which are designed to enrich the knowledge and understanding of decision-makers in education systems in different countries through international comparisons and comparative studies in central areas of education. The major players in this arena are the International Association for the Evaluation of Educational Achievement, or IEA, with Trends in International Mathematics and Science Study (TIMSS), Progress in International Reading Literacy Study (PIRLS), International Computer and Information Literacy Study (ICILS), and others), and the Organisation for Economic Co-operation and Development (OECD) with the Programme for International Student Assessment (PISA), Programme for the International Assessment of Adult Competencies (PIAAC,) and the Teaching and Learning International Survey (TALIS). These international assessments usually involve nationally representative samples composed of thousands of students.

The growing popularity of ILSAs has been accompanied by several phenomena. In many countries today ILSAs constitute de facto standards for learning goals in the subjects assessed, and as a result the curricula in different countries have been aligned with the theoretical framework of these international assessments. In a number of countries the results and rankings of ILSAs have become politically high stakes: ministers of education and governments perceive them as being an indicator of the success of their local policy (e.g., Poland, Germany, and Israel). As such, international assessments intensify the negative consequences that often accompany high-stakes tests in different countries ("teaching to the test," diverting resources, etc.).

In international assessment research programs, as in national and local assessment programs, three different themes are evident in the application of ICT. One is the use of ICT to better assess the domains that have traditionally been the focus of assessment in schools: reading, mathematics, and science. Note that the use of ICT to create richer and more interactive assessment materials increases validity and enables the assessment of aspects within the domains that, up to now, have been difficult to assess. A second theme is the use of technology to assess more generic competencies, such as ICT skills and a broad set of generalizable and transferable knowledge, skills and understandings that are relevant to managing and communicating information. A third theme is the use of technology to assess more complex constructs, which are less well understood and characterize much of the thinking about twenty-first century skills. Such constructs include creativity and collaborative problem solving (as typified by the Assessment and Teaching of Twenty-First Century Skills (ATC21S) Project.

In 2006, for the first time and on an experimental basis, PISA included an optional computer-based component in the assessment of student achievements in science (CBAS). In PISA 2009, in addition to the P&P assessments, countries were offered the opportunity to participate in a computerized assessment of electronic reading of texts (ERA). In 2011, 15-year-old students around the world took part in a pilot study of three computerized assessments (problem solving, mathematical literacy, and reading of electronic texts) as a pilot study for PISA 2012. Also, adults (16–64 years old) around the world were assessed digitally on PIAAC. In 2012, eighth graders around the world will participate in a pilot study in preparation for ICILS 2013. For 2015, PISA plans are to proceed on the assumption that computer delivery will be a significant aspect of the overall assessment. The full extent of computer delivery has yet to be established. A brief elaboration on all these new assessments follows below.

Organisation for Economic Co-operation and Development (OECD)

Since 2006, the OECD has gradually begun introducing technology into its assessments (PISA and PIAAC):

The Programme for International Student Assessment—PISA

PISA is an internationally standardized assessment that was jointly developed by participating economies and administered to 15-year-olds in schools. PISA focuses on young people's capacity to demonstrate their preparedness in the fundamental domains of reading literacy, mathematical literacy, and scientific literacy. Four PISA cycles have been carried out so far (in 2000, 2003, 2006, and 2009). Close to 70 countries and large economies participated in the 2009 cycle.

PISA is different from other international surveys, such as TIMSS, which is curriculum-based, in that it attempts to assess the skills and competencies each learner needs for further study and success in the future. Although the basic skills assessed

Table 3.1 PISA cycles and the digital components

	Reading Literacy	Mathematics Literacy	Science Literacy	Other Domains
PISA 2000	+	+	+	
PISA 2003	+	+	+	Problem Solving
PISA 2006	+	+	+ CBAS	
PISA 2009	+ ERA	+	+	
PISA 2012	+ ERA	+ EM	+	Problem Solving Financial Literacy
PISA 2015	ERA	EM	CBAS	Collaborative Problem Solving

Shaded cells denote the extended domain assessed in a given year, + paper and pencil assessments, *CBAS* computer-based assessment of science, *ERA* electronic reading assessment, *EM* electronic math

in PISA (reading, math, science) are similar to other assessment programs, their definition is different and broader and the tasks are put into the context of everyday situations with which most people will have to deal.

Therefore, it is not surprising that the PISA governing board decided to make use of computer-based assessments, not only to measure ICT literacy skills, but also to allow for the provision of a wider range of dynamic and interactive tasks and to explore more efficient ways of carrying out the main tests of student knowledge and skills in reading, mathematics and science.

The initial goal was to begin the digital implementation in 2003. However, it only materialized in 2006. A list of past, present, and future cycles of PISA is presented in Table 3.1, with the green cells indicating the extended domain assessed in each cycle, and the blue letters indicating digital assessment components (added to or replacing paper and pencil).

Overall, there is a challenge in how to move forward to CBT while keeping the paper and pencil trends of the scores across the years. In a way, the two goals of preserving trends and moving to CBT are incompatible. Changing the nature of tests generally breaks the trends, while keeping assessments unchanged undermines its validity, as the definition of the skills and competencies to be measured are continually changing and evolving. This paradoxical situation should be resolved and, in order to do so, both new technologies and new conceptualizations of what is being measured must be further explored. The 2006 CBAS study and, even more so, the 2009 ERA study, offer an opportunity to closely scrutinize the results of CBT in comparison to paper and pencil.

PISA 2006—Computer-Based Assessment of Science—CBAS (optional component)

The initial goal of extending the PISA 2006 assessment of science to include a computer-delivered element was to administer questions that would be difficult to deliver in a P&P test. In particular, the goals were reducing the load of reading and written expression; motivating students for the assessment task; linking dynamic contexts with data interpretation; enabling student interaction with the media; and allowing assessment of aspects of science not available in paper-based forms. The relevant questions included video footage, simulations, and animations.

The computer-based assessment of science was field tested in 13 PISA countries in 2005, and the main study was conducted in only three of them in 2006: Denmark, Iceland, and Korea. Overall achievement within countries did not change from one test modality to the next, yet there was a tendency for Denmark's performance to decrease on the computer-based test. Korean students outperformed Danish and Icelandic students in the computer-based test just as they did in the P&P test.

In the computer-based test, male performance increased in Iceland and Korea while female performance decreased. Males outperformed females on the computer-based test in all three countries. Females outperformed males on the P&P test of science literacy in Iceland, whereas there was a gender difference in favor of males in the P&P results for Denmark. The association between reading literacy and achievement on the science literacy was weaker for the computer-based items than for the P&P items (Turmo and Svein 2006; OECD 2010).

An international workshop was held in Reykjavik, Iceland in the autumn of 2008 during which the following matters were discussed:

- Comparison between paper-and-pencil tests and computer-based assessment
- Electronic tests and gender differences
- Adaptive vs. linear computer-based assessment (For more, see: http://crell.jrc. ec.europa.eu/WP/workshoptransition.htm).

PISA 2009 and 2012—Electronic Reading Assessment—ERA (optional component)

The PISA 2009 ERA optional component was implemented in recognition of the increasing prevalence of digital texts in many parts of our lives: personal, social, and economic. Even though the core principles of writing texts and the core processes of reading and understanding texts are similar across media, there are reasons to believe that the specific features of digital texts call for specific text-processing skills.

The new demands on reading proficiency created by the digital world have led, in PISA 2009, to the inclusion of electronic reading in the reading framework, an inclusion that has, in turn, resulted in some redefinition both of texts and of the mental processes that readers use to comprehend the texts. ERA 2009 was designed to investigate students' proficiency at tasks that require the access, comprehension, evaluation, and integration of digital texts across a wide range of reading contexts and tasks among today's 15-year-olds.

Nineteen countries participated in ERA. The ERA used a test administration system (TAO) developed through the University of Luxembourg. TAO can deliver tests over the Internet, across a network or (as was the case with ERA) on a standalone computer with student responses collected on an external memory device (USB).

ERA will be offered again as an optional component in PISA 2012 (a pilot study was conducted in 2011 in around 30 countries).

PISA 2012/2015—Computer-Based Problem Solving Assessment (compulsory component)

The development of competency in problem solving (PS) is a central objective within the educational programs of many countries. The acquisition of increased levels of competency in problem solving provides a basis for future learning, for effective participation in society, and for conducting personal activities. Students need to be able to apply what they have learned to new situations.

What distinguishes the 2012 assessment of PS from the 2003 PS assessment is not so much the definition of the competency of problem solving, or the focus on problems that only require low levels of discipline-based knowledge for their solution, but the mode of delivery (computer-based) of the 2012 assessment and the inclusion of problems that cannot be solved without the respondent interacting with the problem online. A pilot study was conducted in 2011 in around 40 countries.

In PISA 2015 a new Collaborative Problem Solving assessment will be added, which will incorporate online assessment of the skills required to solve problems as a member of a group.

PISA 2012—Electronic Mathematical Assessment (optional component)

The definition of mathematical literacy in PISA 2012 explicitly calls for the use of mathematical tools, including technological tools, for judgments and decision making. Computer-based tools are in common use in workplaces of the twenty-first century and will be increasingly more prevalent as the century progresses. The nature of work-related problems and logical reasoning has expanded with these new opportunities, creating new expectations for individuals.

Because PISA items reflect problems that arise in personal, occupational, social, and scientific contexts, a calculator is part of many PISA items. Computers and calculators relieve the burden of computation so that individual respondents' attention can be focused on strategies, concepts, and structures rather than on mechanical procedures. A computer-based assessment will provide the opportunity to extend the integration of technologies—such as statistical tools, geometric construction and visualization utilities, and virtual measuring instruments—into the test items. A pilot study was conducted in 2011 in around 30 countries.

PISA 2015—Recent Call for Tender

The plans for PISA 2015 are proceeding on the assumption that computer delivery will be a significant aspect of PISA 2015. The full extent of computer delivery has yet to be established.

The PISA 2015 call for tenders requires the contractor to develop an electronic platform that is suitable for the assessment of all PISA domains and is capable of all functions from item development to delivery of the assessment, i.e., item development, item review, test compilation, test delivery, and administration. It should be capable of being operationalized through an extensive range of operating systems, including delivery over the Internet, in order to maximize country participation, and should exploit the possibilities that arise from the use of new technologies to assess students' knowledge and skills in everyday tasks and challenges, in keeping with PISA's definition of literacy. It should also be adaptable to allow for evolution over the PISA cycles, e.g., to assess new domains and to cope with new test designs.

Overall, there is a challenge yet to be resolved in how to move to digital assessments while keeping the trends from previous P&P PISA assessments.

Programme for the International Assessment of Adult Competencies (PIAAC)

Over the past two decades, national governments and other stakeholders have shown a growing interest in an international assessment of adult skills that allows them to monitor how well prepared populations are for the challenges of a knowledge-based society. The OECD's PIAAC will be the largest and most innovative international assessment of adult skills ever conducted (Schleicher 2008).

The primary objectives of PIAAC are to: (1) identify and measure cognitive competencies believed to underlie both personal and societal success; (2) assess the impact of these competencies on social and economic outcomes at individual and aggregate levels; (3) gauge the performance of education and training systems in generating required competencies; and (4) help to clarify the policy levers that could contribute to enhancing competencies.

At the core of PIAAC is an assessment of the literacy skills among adult populations, these being understood as the interest, attitude, and ability of individuals to appropriately use sociocultural tools, including digital technology and communication tools, to access, manage, integrate, and evaluate information, construct new knowledge, and communicate with others. In addition, PIAAC collects information from respondents concerning their use of key work skills in their jobs—a first for an international study.

The skills assessed by PIAAC (literacy, numeracy, and problem solving in technology-rich environments) represent cognitive skills that provide a foundation for effective and successful participation in modern societies and economies. Levi (2010) argues that a technology-rich workplace requires foundational skills including numeracy and literacy (both to be tested in PIAAC), advanced problem-solving skills or Expert Thinking (similar to the construct of Problem Solving in Technology-Rich Environments to be tested in PIAAC) and advanced communication skills or Complex Communication (not being tested in PIAAC).

PIAAC will offer a far more complete and nuanced picture of the "human capital" on which countries can count as they compete in today's global economy. It will help policymakers assess the effectiveness of education and training systems, both for recent entrants into the labor market and for older people who may need to continue learning new skills throughout their lifetimes.

Twenty-six countries are currently implementing PIAAC. A field test was successfully conducted in 2010, with the main assessment being conducted in 2011–2012. A second round of PIAAC is planned to allow additional countries to participate in, and benefit from, the assessment. The assessments will be available in paper- and computer-based formats.

The International Association for the Evaluation of Educational Achievement (IEA)

The IEA has conducted various international surveys regarding the implementation of ICT in education around the globe. Twenty-two countries participated in the first stage of the Computers in Education Study and, in 1989, conducted school surveys in elementary, lower secondary, and upper secondary schools. In 1992 the second stage of the study repeated the surveys of the first stage and added an assessment of students. The rapid diffusion of the Internet and multimedia technology during the mid-1990s generated an interest in a new study that, among other things, could investigate the changes in the curricula and classrooms since IEA's earlier study.

The Second International Technology in Education Study (SITES) was initiated in 1996 by the IEA and school surveys were conducted in 1998. The SITES study consists of three modules. The survey data of module 1 were collected in 1998. The module 2 case studies that involved visits to school sites were conducted during 2000 and 2001, and the reports were released in 2002 and 2003. Module 3 was launched in 2001, but the data for the surveys and student assessments was collected during 2004, with the results released in 2005 and 2006.

A new IEA computerized international large-scale assessment for students— ICILS—will be administered in 2013.

International Computer and Information Literacy Study (ICILS)—2013

ICILS will examine the outcomes of student computer and information literacy (CIL) across countries.

Computer and information literacy refers to an individual's ability to use computers to investigate, create, and communicate in order to participate effectively at home, at school, in the workplace, and in the community. Twenty countries have registered so far to participate in this study.

The assessment of CIL will be authentic and computer-based. It will incorporate multiple-choice and constructed-response items based on realistic stimulus material; software simulations of generic applications so that students are required to complete an action in response to an instruction; and authentic tasks that require students to modify and create information products using "live" computer software applications.

ICILS 2013 will be the first international comparative study of student preparedness to use computers to investigate, create, and communicate at home, at school, and in the broader community. ICILS will assess students' capacity to:

- Use technology to search for, retrieve and make effective judgments about the quality and usefulness of information from a range of sources (such as the Internet)
- Use technology to transform and create information
- Use technology to communicate information to others
- Recognize the ethical and legal obligations, responsibilities, and potential dangers associated with digital communication.

ICILS 2013 will provide policymakers with results that will enhance understanding of factors responsible for achievement in computer-based tasks. It will also inform policy on the possible contribution of educational systems to the use of computers for digital communication and information literacy as an essential skill in the twenty-first century.

A pilot study will be conducted in 2012 (For more, see: http://www.acer.edu.au/icils/).

Mega Technology Companies Collaborate to Integrate Technology in ILSAs

Three leading technology companies—Cisco, Intel, and Microsoft—collaborated in 2009 with the University of Melbourne with the goal of transforming global educational assessment and improving learning outcomes—Assessment and Teaching of Twenty-First Century Skills (ATC21S).

The goals of the project are to mobilize international educational, political, and business communities to make the transformation of educational assessment and, hence, instructional practice a global priority; to specify in measurable terms high-priority understanding and skills needed by productive and creative workers and citizens of the twenty-first century; to identify methodological and technological barriers to ICT-based assessment; to develop and pilot new assessment methodologies; to examine and recommend innovative ICT-enabled, classroom-based learning environments and formative assessments that support the development of twenty-first century skills.

The collaboration initiated and produced five important white papers (Griffin et al. 2011) in the first phase of this development project:

- Defining twenty-first century skills
- Perspectives on methodological issues
- Technological issues for computer-based assessment
- New assessments and environments for knowledge building
- Policy frameworks for new assessments.

Through 2010–2012 the focus of the project is on development of the assessment methodologies and dynamic tasks. ATC21S has received the support of major international assessment organizations, as well as participating governments' departments of education, through representation on the ATC21S Advisory Panel (For more, see: http://atc21s.org/).

Conclusion

Neither assessments nor technologies are goals in and of themselves. The merit in both is only if they make a significant impact on education by improving instruction and increasing (directly or indirectly) the opportunity for each pupil to learn and progress. However, the more technology becomes integrated in instruction, the more the need is to adjust assessment to become digital and align with the new instructional environment.

Do all the above new and innovative digital assessments indicate that the educational world is approaching a turning point regarding the incorporation of technology into large-scale assessments? Are schools pedagogically, technologically, logistically, and socially prepared for this development? What are the implications for educators, and for policymakers? What will make this mega-investment worthwhile?

Thoughtful integration of technology into assessment may meet several complementary goals:

- Supporting and enhancing the integration of technology into learning.
- Allowing for an assessment of complex cognitive skills (e.g., Diagnoser, Sim-Scientists).
- Designing a new accountability paradigm, that fully integrates sequential formative assessments and periodic summative assessments via computers (i.e., CBAL).

The present structure and development of electronic ILSAs certainly support the first two goals—enhancing the integration of technology into learning, and providing an appropriate response for the measurement of complex cognitive abilities, thus increasing test validity. Also, beyond measuring twenty-first century skills and broadening the measured construct, computerized international assessments can provide a more useful profile of countries whose students are clustered in particularly high or low levels of performance.

However, new accountability paradigm approaches, proposed by CBAL and the Race to the Top consortia, according to which formative and summative assessment are fully aligned and integrated via technology, may not be easily applicable to ILSAs. That is, the ability to integrate continual formative assessments with periodic summative assessments entails complete alignment of the curricula, the content and standards with the external and internal assessment tasks. It is not clear whether such an alignment is possible, or even desired, with regard to the ILSAs.

Additionally, ILSAs take place on a cycle that is well suited for international comparisons (3, 4 or 5 years). However, as ILSAs have become high-stakes and excelling on them has become a national goal, this cycle causes certain local irregularities in the organization of learning and NLSAs in years that coincide with ILSA cycles. Thus, there is a need to better align the national and international assessments in countries where both systems exist.

In summary, several issues have yet to be resolved before moving NLSAs and ILSAs to full blown digital and online systems: adaptive versus linear administration of the assessments; ensuring gender equality; narrowing the digital divide; school system readiness (personnel, hardware, connectivity); infrastructure adaptation to various languages (including right-to-left languages) and more.

Also, there is a challenge in how to link P&P and digital assessments with the goal of maintaining long-term trends, as the two goals are somewhat incompatible. Changing the nature of tests generally breaks trends, while keeping tests unchanged is unsatisfactory as the definition of the skills and competencies to be measured are continually changing. This paradoxical situation has to be resolved and in order to do so both new technologies and new conceptualizations of what is being measured have to be explored.

Nevertheless, it is clear that technology will continue to advance and improve both NLSAs and ILSAs in an evolutionary manner. Technology even has the potential to revolutionize NLSAs and its alignment with learning and teaching as proposed by the CBAL model. However, the extent to which ILSAs, based on a common international framework that is often not fully aligned with the national curricula, can join this revolution remains a pedagogical and strategic challenge.

Appendix 1

Kozma (2009) provided an extensive list of the potential advantages and challenges of incorporating ICT into large-scale assessments (exact quote):

Advantages

- Reduced costs of data entry, collection, aggregation, verification, and analysis.
- The ability to adapt tests to individual students, so that the level of difficulty can be adjusted as the student progresses through the assessment and a more refined profile of skill can be obtained for each student.

- The ability to efficiently collect and score responses, including the collection and automated or semi-automated scoring of more sophisticated responses, such as extended, open-ended text responses.
- The ability to collect data on students' intermediate products, strategies, and indicators of thought processes during an assessment task, in addition to the student's final answer.
- The ability to take advantage of ICT tools that are now integral to the practice and understanding of subject domains, such as the use of idea organizers for writing, data analysis tools in social science, and visualization and modeling tools in natural science.
- The ability to provide curriculum developers, researchers, teachers, and even students with detailed information that can be used to improve future learning.

Technological challenges

Among the technological challenges that might inhibit the use of ICT-based assessments are:

- Significant startup costs for assessment systems that have previously implemented only paper-and-pencil assessments. These costs would include hardware, software, and network purchases; software development related to localization; and technical support and maintenance.
- The need to choose between the use of "native" applications that would not allow for standardization but would allow students use the applications with which they are most familiar, the use of standardized off-the-shelf applications that would provide standardization but may disadvantage some students that regularly use a different application, or the use of specially developed "generic" applications that provide standardization but disadvantage everyone equally.
- The need to integrate applications and systems so that standardized information can be collected and aggregated.
- The need to choose between standalone implementation versus Internet-based implementation. If standalone, the costs of assuring standardization and reliable operation, as well as the costs of aggregating data. If Internet-based, the need to choose between running applications locally or having everything browser-based.
- If the assessment is Internet-based, issues of scale need to be addressed, such as the potentially disabling congestion for both local networks and back-end servers as large numbers of students take the assessment simultaneously.
- Issues of security are also significant with Internet-based assessments.
- The need to handle a wide variety of languages, orthographies, and symbol systems for both the delivery of the task material and for collection and scoring of open-ended responses.

- The need to keep up with rapidly changing technologies and maintaining comparability of results, over time.
- The need for tools to make the design of assessment tasks easy and efficient.
- The lack of knowledge of technological innovators about assessment, and the corresponding paucity of examples of educational software that incorporates with high-quality assessments.

Significant methodological challenges include

- The need to determine the extent to which ICT-based items that measure subject knowledge should be equivalent to legacy paper-and-pencil-based results.
- The need to detail the wider range of skills that can only be assessed with ICT.
- The need to determine the age-level appropriateness of various twenty-first century skills.
- The need to design complex, compound tasks in a way such that failure on one task component does not cascade through the remaining components of the task or result in student termination.
- The need to integrate foundational ideas of subject knowledge along with twenty-first century skills in the assessments. At the same time, there is a need to determine the extent to which subject knowledge should be distinguished from twenty-first century skills in assessment results.
- The need to incorporate qualities of high-level professional judgments about student performances into ICT assessments, as well as support the efficiency and reliability of these judgments.
- The need to develop new theories and models of scoring the students' processes and strategies during assessments, as well as outcomes.
- The need to establish the predictive ability of these judgments on the quality of subsequent performance in advanced study and work.
- The need to distinguish individual contributions and skills on tasks that are done collaboratively (For more, see: http://www.worldclassarena.net/doc/file17.pdf).

References

Almond, P., P. Winter, R. Cameto, M. Russell, E. Sato, J. Clarke-Midura, C. Torres, G. Haertel, R. Dolan, P. Beddow, and S. Lazarus. 2010. Technology-enabled and universally designed assessment: Considering access in measuring the achievement of students with disabilities—a foundation for research. *Journal of Technology, Learning, and Assessment,* 10 (5). Retrieved from May 2011: http://www.jtla.org.
Bejar, I., and E.A. Graf. 2010. Updating the duplex design for test-based accountability in the twenty-first century measurement. *Interdisciplinary Research and Perspective*, 8 (2/3): 110–129.

Bennett, R.E. 2001. How the Internet will help large-scale assessment reinvent itself. *Education Policy Analysis Archives* 9(5): 1–25.

Bennett, R.E. 2002. Inexorable and inevitable: The continuing story of technology and assessment. *The Journal of Technology, Learning and Assessment*. Retrieved from May 2011: http://escholarship.bc.edu/jtla/.

Bennett, R.E. 2010. Cognitively based assessment of, for, and as learning (CBAL): A preliminary theory of action for summative and formative assessment. *Measurement: Interdisciplinary Research and Perspectives* 8: 70–91.

Bennett, R.E., H. Persky, A.R. Weiss, and F. Jenkins. 2007. *Problem solving in technology-rich environments: A report from the NAEP technology-based assessment project (NCES 2007–466)*. US Department of Education. Washington, DC: National Center for Education Statistics. Retrieved from May 2011: http://nces.ed.gov/nationsreportcard/pdf/studies/2007466.pdf.

Bennett, R.E., H. Persky, A. Weiss, and F. Jenkins, 2010. Measuring problem solving with technology: A demonstration study for NAEP. *Journal of Technology, Learning, and Assessment* 8(8). Retrieved from May 2011: http://www.jtla.org.

Bennett, R. E., and D. H. Gitomer. 2009. Transforming K-12 assessment: Integrating accountability testing, formative assessment and professional support. In *Educational assessment in the 21st century*, eds. C. Wyatt-Smith and J. J. Cumming, 43–61. NY: Springer.

Chudowsky, N., J.W. Pellegrino. 2003. Large-scale assessments that support learning: What will it take?. *Theory Into Practice* 42.1: 75–83.

Johnstone, C., M. Thurlow, J. Altman, J. Timmons, and K. Keto. 2009. Assistive technology approaches for large-scale assessment: Perceptions of teachers of students with visual impairments. *Exceptionality* 17(2): 66–75.

Koretz, D., and L.S. Hamilton. 2006. Testing for accountability in K-12. In, *Educational Measurement* (4th edition), ed. R. L. Brennan, 531–578. Westport. CT: American Council on Education/Praeger.

Kozma, R. 2009. Assessing and teaching twenty-first century skills: A call to action. In *The transition to computer-based assessment: New approaches to skills assessment and implications for large scale assessment*, eds. F. Schueremann and J. Bjornsson, 13–23. Brussels: European Communities. Retrieved from May 2011: http://www.worldclassarena.net/doc/file17.pdf.

Griffin, P., B. McGaw, and E. Care. (eds.) 2011. *Assessment and teaching of twenty-first century skills*. Dordrecht: Springer.

Herman, J., Y. Dai, A.M. Htut, M. Martinez, and N. Rivera. 2011. *Evaluation of the enhanced assessment grants (EAGs) SimScientists program: Site visit findings*. (CRESST Report 791). Los Angeles, CA: University of California, National Center for Research on Evaluation, Standards, and Student Testing (CRESST). Retrived from November 2011: http://www.cse.ucla.edu/products/reports/R791.pdf.

Levi, F. 2010. *How technology changes demands for human skills.* Retrieved from May 2011 OECD iLibrary: http://www.oecd-ilibrary.org/education/how-technology-changes-demands-for-human-skills_5kmhds6czqzq-en.

Linn, R. 2010. A new era of test-based educational accountability. *Measurement: Interdisciplinary Research and Perspectives* 8 (2/3): 145–149. Retrieved from May 2011: http://pdfserve.informaworld.com/373233__926993282.pdf.

Nichols, S.N. and D.C. Berliner. 2007. *Collateral damage: The effects of high-stakes testing on America's schools*. Cambridge, MA: Harvard Education Press.

OECD. 2010. *PISA Computer-based assessment of student skills in science*. Paris: OECD.

Quellmalz, E.S., and J.W. Pellegrino. 2009. Technology and testing. *Science* 323: 75–79.

Quellmalz, E. S., M.J. Timms, and B. Buckley. 2009. *Using science simulations to support powerful formative assessments of complex science learning*. WestEd. Retrieved from May 2011: http://www.simscientists.org/downloads/Quellmalz_Formative_Assessment.pdf.

Quellmalz, E.S., M.D Silberglitt, and M.J. Timms. 2011. How can simulations be components of balanced state science assessment systems?. *Policy Brief*. WestEd. Retrieved from November 2011: http://simscientist.org/downloads/SimScientistsPolicyBrief.pdf.

Sandene, B., N. Horkay, R.E. Bennett, N. Allen, J. Braswell, B. Kaplan, and A. Oranje. 2005. Online assessment in mathematics and writing: Reports from the NAEP technology-based assessment project, *Research and Development Series*. Retrieved from May 2011: http://nces. ed.gov/nationsreportcard/pubs/studies/2005457.asp.

Schleicher, A. 2008. PIAAC: A new strategy for assesing adult competencies. *International Review of Education* 54 (5/6): 627–650.

The Assessment and Teaching of Twenty-First Century Skills (ATC21S). Retrieved 12 June 2012 from: http://atc21s.org/.

Thompson, S., C.J. Johnstone, and M.L. Thurlow. 2002. *Universal design applied to large scale assessments*. Retrieved from May 2011: http://www.cehd.umn.edu/NCEO/onlinepubs/synthesis44.html.

Turmo, A., and L. Svein. 2006. *PISA's Computer-based assessment of science—A gender equity perspective*. AEA-E Annual Conference 2006, Assessment and equity. Naples, Italy. Retrieved from May 2011: http://www.aea-europe.net/userfiles/D1%20Are%20Turmo%20&%20Svein% 20Lie.pdf.

US Department of Education. 2010. *US Secretary of Education Duncan announces winners of competition to improve student assessments*. Retrieved from May 2011: http://www.ed.gov/ news/press-releases/us-secretary-education-duncan-announces-winners-competition-improve-student-asse.

Chapter 4
The Role of International Assessments of Cognitive Skills in the Analysis of Growth and Development

Eric A. Hanushek and Ludger Woessmann

Introduction

Economists have found the concept of human capital to be very useful in explaining not only differences in individual earnings but also aggregate variations in the well-being of nations. Because of the importance of human capital, another strand of research has delved into the determinants of relevant skills that fit into human capital. Both lines of inquiry have advanced markedly with development and expansion of international testing of achievement, particularly in math and science.

Economists are now accustomed to looking at issues of skill development from the vantage point of human capital theory. The simplest notion is that individuals make investments in skills that have later payoffs in outcomes that matter. And, in this, it is commonly presumed that formal schooling is one of several important contributors to the skills of an individual and to human capital. It is not the only factor. Parents, individual abilities, and friends undoubtedly contribute. Schools nevertheless have a special place because they are most directly affected by public policies.

The human capital and investment perspective immediately makes it evident that the real issues are ones of long-term outcomes. Future incomes of individuals are related to their past investments. It is not their income while in school or their income in their first job. Instead, it is their income over the course of their working life.

Much of the early and continuing development of empirical work on human capital concentrates on the role of school attainment, that is, the quantity of schooling. The revolution in the United States during the twentieth century was universal

E. A. Hanushek (✉)
Hoover Institution, National Bureau of Economic Research and CESifo,
Stanford University, Stanford, CA 94305-6010, USA
e-mail: hanushek@stanford.edu

L. Woessmann
Ifo Institute for Economic Research and CESifo, University of Munich, Poschingerstr. 5, 81679 Munich, Germany
e-mail: woessmann@ifo.de

M. von Davier et al. (eds.), *The Role of International Large-Scale Assessments: Perspectives from Technology, Economy, and Educational Research,*
DOI 10.1007/978-94-007-4629-9_4, © Springer Science+Business Media Dordrecht 2013

schooling. This policy goal has spread around the world, encompassing both developed and developing countries. It also has lent itself to regular measurement. Quantity of schooling is easily measured, and data on years attained, both over time and across individuals, are readily available. But quantity of schooling proves to be a poor measure of the skills of individuals both within and across countries.

The growth of standardized measures of achievement has proven extraordinarily valuable in filling out a richer picture of human capital. The research base has expanded significantly through work in the United States and elsewhere that exploits rich school accountability data. The administrative data sets accompanying accountability systems have proven very valuable in understanding the determinants of student achievement.

The research based on the international assessments is perhaps equally important. Importantly, it goes in two different directions. Research designed to understand the underlying determinants of cognitive skills parallels that of the administrative data sets while permitting a range of analyses not possible with the accountability data. Additionally, however, the research based in international data sets has focused on the consequences of skill differences.

By going beyond the use of simple measures of the quantity of schooling, economists have been able to understand better the role of human capital in outcomes and the elements that are important in producing more human capital. International achievement data, developed and refined over the past half century, were not collected to support any specific economic research agenda. But there are a number of research and policy agendas that are uniquely amenable to analysis because of the existence of such data.

This discussion, following the development in Hanushek and Woessmann (2011a), concentrates on the role of achievement as a direct measure of human capital. The international data have distinct advantages over research restricted to single countries or states. The data permit exploitation of variation that only exists across countries. For example, systematic institutional variation between countries—as found with differences in the competitiveness and flexibility of teacher labor markets, forms of accountability systems, the extent of a private school sector, or the structure of student tracking—simply does not exist within most countries. And, even where within-country variation exists, variations across countries in key institutional factors and in characteristics of the schools and population are frequently much larger than those found within any country.

The international achievement data, based on a consistent collection process, provides an opportunity to examine comparable estimates of the determinants and consequences of educational achievement for a diverse set of countries. Such research can thus illuminate whether a result is truly country-specific, applies more generally, or is simply a spurious result from a particular within-country sample. Further, international evidence can identify systematic heterogeneity in effects that differ across countries.

Even where within-country variation exists, for example, in the case of public and private schools operating within the same system, comparisons of student achievement are often subject to severe selection problems. Students who choose to attend a private school may differ along both observable and unobservable dimensions from students taught in neighborhood public schools. While it is possible to control for some differences in student, family, and school characteristics when estimating the effects of institutional structures, such estimates may still suffer from selection on unobserved characteristics (see Chap. 7). At the country level, it is possible to circumvent these selection problems—in effect measuring the impact of, for example, the share of students in a country attending private schools on student achievement in the country as a whole. Such cross-country evidence will not be biased by standard issues of selection at the individual level. (At the same time, as discussed below, international comparisons present their own analytical challenges).

Importantly, uncovering general equilibrium effects is often impossible in a single country but sometimes feasible across countries. For example, the presence of private schools may influence the behavior of nearby public schools with which they compete for students. As a result, simple comparisons of private and public schools may miss an important part of the effects of greater private involvement in education, while aggregation to the country level can potentially solve the problem. By comparing the average performance of systems with larger and smaller shares of private schools, the cross-country approach captures any systemic effect of competition from private schools.

Research into the consequences of differences in cognitive skills has similar advantages. For example, while the implications of human capital development for macroeconomic outcomes—including, importantly, economic growth—can potentially be investigated with time-series data for individual countries, historical data are effectively limited to school attainment with no information on the cognitive skills that we emphasize here. On the other hand, variations in cognitive skills across different economies can, as we describe below, effectively get at such fundamental questions. Similarly, investigating whether features of the structure of economic activity affect the individual returns to skills is very difficult within a single economy with interlocking labor and product markets.

While international achievement data at times substitute for the collection of national data, the discussion here focuses on the use of international tests for cross-country analyses. These studies have different basic designs. One focuses on within-country variations in achievement or the outcomes of achievement but then considers how these within-country relationships differ across countries. The second emphasizes the cross-country relationships per se.

International Testing[1]

International consortia were formed in the mid-1960s to develop and implement comparisons of educational achievement across nations. The first major international test was conducted in 1964 when 12 countries participated in the First International Mathematics Study (FIMS). This and a series of subsequent assessments

---

[1] A more detailed description of historical international testing is found in Hanushek and Woessmann (2011b). This section provides an overview of relevant testing.

involved a cooperative venture developed by the International Association for the Evaluation of Educational Achievement (IEA). Since then, the math, science, and reading performance of students in many countries have been tested on multiple occasions using (at each occasion) a common set of test questions in all participating countries. By 2010, three major international large-scale assessment (ILSA) programs were surveying student performance on a regular basis: the Programme for International Student Assessment (PISA), testing math, science, and reading performance of 15-year-olds on a three-year cycle since 2000; the Trends in International Mathematics and Science Study (TIMSS), testing math and science performance (mostly) of fourth and eighth-graders on a four-year cycle since 1995; and the Progress in International Reading Literacy Study (PIRLS), testing primary-school reading performance on a five-year cycle since 2001. In addition, regional testing programs have produced comparable performance information for many countries in Latin America and sub-Saharan Africa, and international adult literacy surveys have produced internationally comparable data on the educational achievement of adults.

These international testing programs have some common elements. They involve a group of voluntarily participating countries that each pay for their participation and administer the same assessment, translated into their own (official) language(s). The set of participating countries has differed across time and even across tested domains of specific testing occasions. Additionally, the different tests differ somewhat in their focus and intended subject matter. For example, the IEA tests, of which the most recent version is TIMSS, are developed by international panels but are related to common elements of primary and secondary school curriculum, while the Organisation for Economic Co-operation and Development's (OECD) PISA tests are designed to measure more applied knowledge and skills.[2] Until recently testing has been almost exclusively cross-sectional in nature, not following individual students' change in achievement.[3]

Along with the assessments of cognitive skills, extensive contextual information and student background data have been provided by related surveys. The motivation for this is using the international databases to address a variety of policy issues relevant to the participating countries.

The IEA and OECD assessments have the broadest coverage and have also adapted regular testing cycles. Table 4.1 provides an account of their major international tests with an indication of age (or grade level) of testing, subject matter, and participating countries. By 2007, there were 15 testing occasions, most of which include subparts based upon subject and grade level.[4]

---

[2] A separate analysis of coverage and testing can be found in Neidorf et al. (2006).

[3] The Second International Mathematics Study (SIMS) of the IEA did have a one-year follow-up of individual students that permitted some longitudinal, panel information, but this design was not repeated. Recent innovations have permitted development of panel data by individual countries. This comparison over time has been aided by the linking of tests over time—including recent administrations of TIMSS, PIRLS, and PISA.

[4] See Mullis et al. (2007, 2008), and Organisation for Economic Co-operation and Development (2007) for details on the most recent cycle of the three major ongoing international testing cycles. PISA also has conducted a 2009 assessment and both PISA and TIMSS have announced future assessments.

Table 4.1 International tests of educational achievement: IEA and OECD student achievement tests. (Source: Hanushek and Woessmann 2011a)

Abbreviation	Study	Year	Subject	Age[a,b]	Countries[c]	Organization[d]	Scale[e]
FIMS	First international mathematics study	1964	Math	13, FS	11	IEA	PC
FISS	First international science study	1970–1971	Science	10, 14, FS	14, 16, 16	IEA	PC
FIRS	First international reading study	1970–1972	Reading	13	12	IEA	PC
SIMS	Second international mathematics study	1980–1982	Math	13, FS	17, 12	IEA	PC
SISS	Second international science study	1983–1984	Science	10, 13, FS	15, 17, 13	IEA	PC
SIRS	Second international reading study	1990–1991	Reading	9, 13	26, 30	IEA	IRT
TIMSS	Third international mathematics and science study	1994–1995	Math/Science	9(3+4), 13(7+8), FS	25, 39, 21	IEA	IRT
TIMSS-Repeat	TIMSS-repeat	1999	Math/Science	13(8)	38	IEA	IRT
PISA 2000/2002	Programme for international student assessment	2000–2002	Math/Sci./Read.	15	31+10	OECD	IRT
PIRLS	Progress in international reading literacy study	2001	Reading	9(4)	34	IEA	IRT
TIMSS 2003	Trends in Int'l mathematics and science study	2003	Math/Science	9(4), 13(8)	24, 45	IEA	IRT
PISA 2003	Programme for international student assessment	2003	Math/Sci./Read.	15	40	OECD	IRT
PIRLS 2006	Progress in international reading literacy study	2006	Reading	>9.5(4)	39	IEA	IRT
PISA 2006	Programme for international student assessment	2006	Math/Sci./Read.	15	57	OECD	IRT
TIMSS 2007	Trends in international mathematics and science study	2007	Math/Science	>9.5(4), >13.5(8)	35, 48	IEA	IRT

OECD Organisation for Economic Co-operation and development, *IRT* item-response-theory proficiency scale

a Grade in parentheses where grade level was target population

b FS final year of secondary education (differs across countries)

c Number of participating countries that yielded internationally comparable performance data

d Conducting organization: international association for the evaluation of educational achievement (IEA)

e Test scale: percent-correct formal (PC)

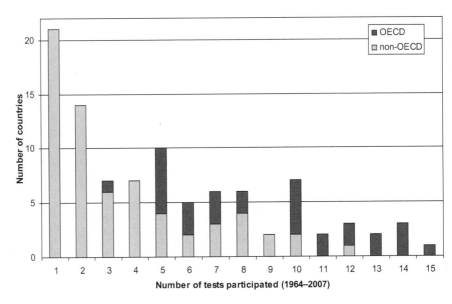

Fig. 4.1 Participation in international student achievement tests of IEA and OECD through 2007. (Source: Hanushek and Woessmann 2011a)

The major IEA and OECD testing programs have expanded dramatically in terms of participating countries. While only 29 countries participated in these large-scale assessments through 1990, a total of 96 countries have participated by 2007. Three additional countries participated in 2009, and another three planned to participate in 2011, raising the total number of countries ever participating in one of these international tests to 102. Only the United States participated in all 15 testing occasions, but an additional 17 countries participated in 10 or more different assessments. Figure 4.1[5], from Hanushek and Woessmann (2011a), shows the histogram of participation on the IEA or OECD tests between 1964–2007, divided by OECD and other countries. From this figure, it is clear that the depth of coverage is much greater for developed than for developing countries. Further, much of the participation in one or two different test administrations occurs after 2000.

At the same time, a number of more idiosyncratic tests, some on a regional basis, have also been developed. These tests have been more varied in their focus, development, and quality, and they have in general been used much less frequently in analytical work. Of the ten additional testing occasions, six are regional tests for Latin America (ECIEL, LLECE, SERCE) or Africa (SACMEQ I and II, PASEC); *see* Hanushek and Woessmann (2011a). One difficulty with these regional tests has been the lack of linkage to the other international tests, implying that any cross-

---

[5] Number of tests in which a country has participated in the following 15 IEA and OECD tests: FIMS, FISS, FIRS, SIMS, SISS, SIRS, TIMSS, TIMSS-Repeat, PISA 2000/02, PIRLS, TIMSS 2003, PISA 2003, PIRLS 2006, PISA 2006, TIMSS 2007. Total number of participating countries: 96.

country analyses must rely exclusively on the within-region variance in institutions, populations, and achievement.

The remaining international assessments and surveys cover a broader set of countries but are somewhat different in focus. The International Assessment of Educational Progress (IAEP) I and II are tests constructed to mirror the National Assessment of Educational Progress (NAEP) that has been used in the United States since 1970 and that aligns to the US school curriculum. The International Adult Literacy Survey (IALS) and the Adult Literacy and Life Skills (ALL) survey have a very different structure involving sampling of adults in the workforce.[6] The IALS survey data in particular have been used in a variety of studies about the consequences of education and cognitive skills.

Interestingly, the TIMSS tests, with their curricular focus, and the PISA tests, with their real-world application focus, are highly correlated at the country level. For example, the correlation coefficients at the country level between the TIMSS 2003 tests of eighth graders and the PISA 2003 tests of 15-year-olds across the 19 countries participating in both are 0.87 in math and 0.97 in science, and they are 0.86 in both math and science across the 21 countries participating both in the TIMSS 1999 tests and the PISA 2000/02 tests. There is also a high correlation at the country level between the curriculum-based student tests of TIMSS and the practical literacy adult examinations of IALS (Hanushek and Zhang 2009). Tests with very different foci and perspectives tend to be highly related at the country level, suggesting that they are measuring a common dimension of skills (see also Brown et al. 2007).

The Explosion of Studies

Economists largely ignored the existence or potential of these international assessments until fairly recently. They made little use of the possibility of comparative studies across countries. But the last decade has seen a tremendous upsurge in research activity on cross-country issues.

As noted, economists have pursued two separate lines of inquiry, each related to notions of human capital. The first subsection considers studies that take the cognitive skills measures from the international tests as a direct measure of human capital and focuses on the determinants of varying levels of human capital. This work, commonly referred to as analyses of education production functions, investigates how various inputs to education affect outcomes. The traditional investigations of how families and school resources influence achievement have been supplemented by a range of studies into economic institutions—accountability, choice, etc.

---

[6] The OECD has currently also embarked on a new endeavor, the Programme for the International Assessment of Adult Competencies (PIAAC), which will update and expand the adult testing, in terms of both the scope of the test and the number of participating countries. This assessment began being administered in 2011.

Table 4.2 Economic studies of the determinants of human capital using international achievement tests (Source: Hanushek and Woessmann 2011a)

Data source	Determinants of student achievement				Achievement equity	Total	Unique studies
	Family background plus school inputs		Institutions				
	Within country	Cross-country	Within country	Cross-country			
IEA	15	2	1	2	1	21	20
OECD	6	4	3	7	2	22	20
Other		2	2	1		5	4
Combined	3	3		4	6	16	16
Total	*24*	*11*	*6*	*14*	*9*	*64*	*60*

The second major line of inquiry has turned to cross-country investigations of the outcomes of human capital and is discussed in the second subsection. The traditional labor market studies of the determination of earnings across individuals have been placed in an international context, permitting some investigation of how different economies reward human capital. Additionally, studies of outcomes have looked at the distribution of earnings within countries and at differences in economic growth across countries.[7]

Studies of the Determinants of Achievement

Table 4.2 summarizes the economic studies found in the review in Hanushek and Woessmann (2011a).[8] A total of 60 unique studies have considered the determinants of cognitive skills across countries. Interestingly, only four of these studies were published before 2000.[9] The recentness of the analysis partially reflects recent expansion in the scope of international testing, but it also derives from more recent appreciation of the kinds of analyses that are possible with the international data.

For the determinants of achievement, a prime distinction from an analytical viewpoint is whether the study uses the between-country variation in performance in the basic estimation. Studies that are labeled "within country" estimate a series of models based on samples stratified by country. The results are then compared across countries. The studies labeled "cross country" use the variations in outcomes among countries in the basic estimation. The within-country analyses always rely

---

[7] Studies of outcome differences related to cognitive skills are reviewed and evaluated in Hanushek and Woessmann (2008).

[8] The primary requirement for inclusion in the review is that the studies are comparative in nature, relying on the comparisons across countries. Some studies relying on the international data sets along with a large number of studies employing single country data sources have maintained a focus simply on the determinants of achievement within an individual country and are not included here.

[9] Heyneman and Loxley (1983), Bishop (1995), Bishop (1997), and Toma (1996).

on the microdata sets from the various international studies, while the cross-country studies include a mixture of those relying on microdata and those using country aggregate data from the international data sets.

The studies of determinants are further subdivided into those primarily considering the role of families and school resources and those that highlight institutional factors. Quite naturally, studies of families and resources tend to rely most on within-country variation, while institutional studies rely more on cross-country variation. Institutions that set the general rules for school operations structure much of what goes on in the schools of every country—but they cause analytical difficulties because they often apply to all schools in a country. Thus, it is difficult to observe any variations of what occurs with different institutions, and it is difficult to understand fully the impact on achievement of both the institutions and other features of the educational system. With educational system level variables such as reliance on accountability systems or reliance on private schools, there is generally limited variation within countries, and the variation that exists is often contaminated by selection factors that make the identification of effects difficult. Therefore, it is necessary to look across countries where the institutional variation exists.

A total of 51 studies investigate differences across countries in the production of achievement.[10] Another nine studies look at the variation in achievement—or equality of achievement—across countries and what factors influence that.[11]

The second element of the table is tracing the data that lies behind each of the studies. The studies to date have been dominated by the various IEA and OECD data collections. Here the importance of the IEA and OECD is clear, with relatively few using other sources. Moreover, the majority of the combined studies employ the various IEA and OECD assessments only.

The international investigations of the determinants of educational achievement have followed a voluminous literature based on data for individual countries.[12] Indeed the data available within individual countries is often superior to that from the international surveys. Specifically, more recent studies tend to rely heavily on panel data sets that follow the achievement of individual students and that can link this achievement growth to characteristics of families, schools, and teachers. With these extensive data sets, identification of separate causal determinants of achievement is frequently much clearer than in the simple cross-sections of data supplied by the international assessments.

What makes the international data valuable in these studies is the chance to observe influences that cannot be readily analyzed within a single country. The most straightforward example is the application of test-based accountability. Since these frequently apply to entire countries, there is no variation within countries that can

---

[10] Three studies appear in more than one column of studies of determinants because they focus equally on institutional factors and on families and schools.

[11] One of these studies also appeared in the tabulation for the four preceding columns, making a total of 60 unique studies of various aspects of the determinants of achievement.

[12] See, for example, the review in Hanushek (2003) and the international perspective in Woessmann (2003).

be used (except perhaps the information about before and after introduction of a system).[13] But systems vary across countries, allowing variation that can be exploited to understand the impacts of accountability. Similarly the impacts of broad-based preschool programs or general choice of schools is subject to selection problems if just program take-up is considered, and any general equilibrium effects (improvements to all schools) are difficult to detect within individual systems.

The clearest and most unique evidence provided by this international work is that the overall set of educational institutions has a significant impact on student achievement. In particular, countries with test-based accountability systems, with more school choice, and with more local decision making or more local autonomy tend to do better (Hanushek and Woessmann (2011a)). Moreover, the work has provided some important, policy-relevant details. For example, having local decision making over teacher salaries only appears to make sense if the country has other supportive institutions such as an accountability system that will focus attention on the appropriate set of outcomes.[14]

The analytical tradeoff, of course, with the international surveys is that it is often difficult to be sure that cultural factors and other systematic differences across countries are satisfactorily dealt with in the analysis. In simplest terms it is generally difficult to be sure that international results are not driven by unmeasured culture, institutions, and the like. Therefore, these international assessments are not a substitute for national data systems but instead are a complement that permits alternative kinds of studies. Moreover, as mentioned, a number of studies cannot be done within the confines of a single country.

The Studies of Outcomes

The outcome studies are quite different. They look at the economic implications of varying achievement. Table 4.3 summarizes the existing studies reviewed in Hanushek and Woessmann (2011a), all but one of which has been published from 2000 onwards.

The studies that have been conducted have each addressed issues that cannot be studied with data on an individual country. They specifically rely on the cross-country variation in measured skills.

Because the benefits of investment in human capital necessarily come over time, the standard international data collection at a given school age does not provide di-

---

[13] The United States with varying state accountability systems prior to No Child Left Behind has similarities to the international differences—where there is no institutional variation within states but there is variation between states. See Carnoy and Loeb (2002) and Hanushek and Raymond (2005).

[14] Hanushek et al. (2011) Combine all of the PISA data into a country-level panel. With this, they investigate how school autonomy in various areas affects achievement. They find that developed countries, particularly those with high performing school systems and with text-based accountability tend to perform better with local decision making. However, less developed countries appear to do worse when there is more autonomy in decision making.

Table 4.3 Studies of the economic consequences of human capital using international achievement tests. (Source: Hanushek and Woessmann 2011a)

Data source	Economic consequences			Total
	Individual earnings	Equity	Aggregate outcomes	
IEA		1	1	2
OECD				
Other	6	3	1	10
Combined			13	13
Total	*6*	*4*	*15*	*25*

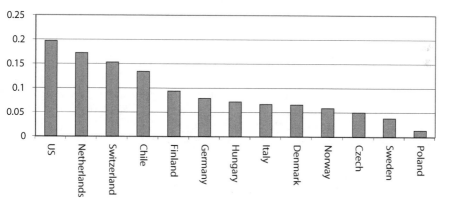

Fig. 4.2 Returns to cognitive skills, international adult literacy survey. (Source: Hanushek and Zhang 2009)

rect information on the value of cognitive skills for individuals in the labor market. Indeed this has been a general problem in looking at wage determination even within countries, because general census data and other surveys do not follow individuals over time. As a result, studies of individual earnings never use the IEA or PISA data but instead have relied on the IALS because that survey collects information on individuals of varying ages along with their earnings.[15]

One of the most interesting results from the international studies of that different economies appear to value cognitive skills to quite different degrees. Hanushek and Zhang (2009) trace the returns to higher cognitive skills across 11 countries participating in IALS.[16] Figure 4.2, which plots of proportional increase in earnings associated with a one standard deviation increase in achievement, shows that the US economy appears to reward skills more than any of the other countries observed. Some countries, like Poland and Sweden, however, provide little labor market

---

[15] The only exception to use of IALS data is Bedard and Ferrall (2003), which combines observations of Gini coefficients with early IEA data.

[16] The analysis follows what is commonly referred to as a Mincer earnings function in which differences in individual earnings are related to school attainment and labor market experience. These estimates simply add the IALS measure of cognitive skills to such a relationship.

reward to higher skills. (The explanation of the causes of these differences awaits further research).

The most unique use of the international tests—and in many ways the most important—has related to aggregate economic performance of nations. Economists have spent considerable effort over the past two decades trying to understand why some countries grow faster than others. This is an extraordinarily important question because it is economic growth that determines the long run well-being of societies.

Much of the initial work by economists recognized that the economic performance of a nation had to relate to the human capital of the nation, but it was hampered by measurement issues. In particular, the only readily available information on skills was school attainment. But use of school attainment for nations requires an assumption that learning in a year of schooling is the same across countries—an almost ludicrous assumption.

The international achievement measures provide a much more defensible way to measure skill differences. This approach was first pursued in Hanushek and Kimko (2000)) and has subsequently been reproduced and extended elsewhere (see the review in Hanushek and Woessmann (2008)). The underlying idea is to combine test from the various existing international assessments. These ILSA programs have included a varying group of participating countries, and the tests are (until recently) not linked to each other. But, we develop a comparable scale for them by noting that the US has participated in all of the assessments *and* the US has a linked national assessment in the National Assessment of Educational Progress (NAEP). By using the scores on NAEP to adjust the US scores on comparable international exams (by age and subject), it is possible to create a time-consistent series of performance of the US We then develop an estimate of the appropriate variance for each international test by using the variance within a set of comparison countries from those with well-developed schooling systems at the time of the earlier tests. This variance estimate allows us to put all countries who ever participate in an international assessment onto a common scale. For most purposes, then, we take the simple average of all observed scores for a country as a measure of the achievement that is relevant for the labor force. (For details on the construction of the comparable test data over time, see Hanushek and Woessmann (2009)).

The power of these measures is easy to see. Figure 4.3[17] shows the relationship between achievement and average annual economic growth in GDP per capita from 1960–2000 for 50 countries with the necessary data.[18] The strength of the relationship between skills and growth is apparent from this figure. Behind this figure is a

---

[17] Added-variable plot of a regression of the average annual rate of growth (in percent) of real GDP per capita in 1960–2000 on the initial level of real GDP per capita in 1960, average years of schooling in 1960, and average test scores on international student achievement tests.

[18] This plot is an added-variable plot where the other estimated underlying regression model also includes initial level of gross domestic product (GDP) per capita. In simplest terms it is easier for a low-income country to grow faster because it only needs to imitate the technologies in more advanced countries while advanced countries must develop innovations in order to grow.

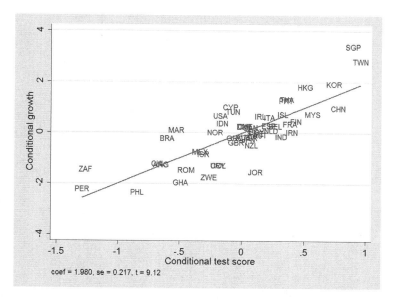

Fig. 4.3 Cognitive skills and economic growth. (Source: Hanushek and Woessmann 2008)

simple statistical relationship that relates annual growth rates to GDP per capita in 1960 and our calculation of achievement for each country.

It is also possible in a parallel manner to show the traditional story based on school attainment. Figure 4.4[19] describes the simple relationship of school attainment and growth (taking into account initial income levels). As the top panel shows, attainment is correlated with growth——but much less closely than we saw for cognitive skills. But, once cognitive skills are included, there is no relationship between school attainment and growth (bottom panel). In other words, only school attainment that translates into learning and achievement has an impact.

There are of course many caveats and qualifications to this. Perhaps the most important is worry about whether the relationship can be assumed to represent a causal relationship and not merely an association in this particular sample. Hanushek and Woessmann (2009) provide a variety of tests that support a causal interpretation, although it remains difficult in a small cross-sectional of countries to obtain conclusive evidence.[20]

If we use the underlying estimates of the growth relationship, we can vividly see the importance of achievement. Hanushek and Woessmann (2011b) simulate the impact of the US economy (and other OECD economies) for a series of scenarios

---

[19] Added variable plot of a regression of the average annual rate of growth (in percent) of real GDP per capita in 1960–2000 on the initial level of real GDP per capita in 1960 and average years of schooling in 1960. The bottom panel additionally controls for average test scores on international student achievement tests, whereas the top panel does not.

[20] That study also discusses in detail the construction of the underlying data series along with a variety of interpretive issues.

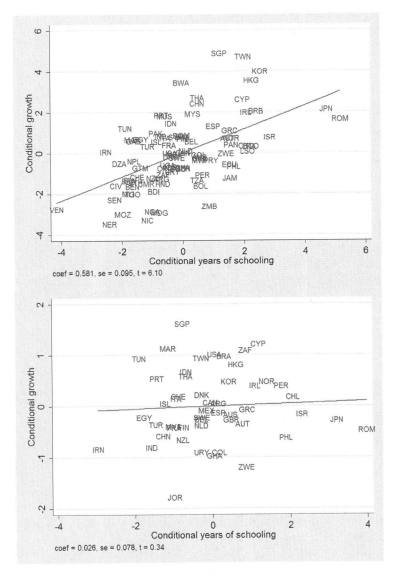

Fig. 4.4 Years of schooling and economic growth without and with test-score controls. (Source: Based on Hanushek and Woessmann 2008)

representing different school improvement programs. In each, it is assumed that the United States takes 20 years to reach new achievement levels. The three scenarios are as follows: (1) a gain of 25 points (1/4 S.D.) on the PISA tests; (2) a movement up to the level of Finland, the world leader on PISA; and, (3) movement of all students scoring below 400 (one standard deviation below the OECD mean, or generally Level 1). The simulations presume that the cognitive skills-growth relationship

Table 4.4 Estimated long run impact of improvement in achievement. (Source: Hanushek and Woessmann 2011b)

	Scenario I: Increase avg. performance by 1/4 S.D.	Scenario II: Bring each country to Finnish level of 546 points on PISA	Scenario III: Bring all to minimum of 400 points on PISA
	(1)	(2)	(3)
OECD Aggregate Improvement in trillion US$	123.1	275.4	226.3
United States Improvement in trillion US$	43.8	111.9	86.1

Discounted value of future increases in OECD GDP until 2090, expressed in trillion US$ (PPP)

observed across the past half-century hold into the future, and this permits estimating how much higher gross domestic product (GDP) would be with added achievement compared to the current levels.

The implications for the economy of these differences are truly astounding. Economic growth is projected over an 80-year period (the expected life of somebody born today), and then the present value of the gains is calculated.[21] Table 4.4 summarizes estimates of the three scenarios for all of the OECD countries and for the United States by itself. A 25-point improvement (something obtained by a number of other countries in the world) would have a present value of US$ 44 trillion for the United States (and US$ 123 trillion for the entire OECD). Reaching the performance levels of Finland would add US$ 112 trillion in present value to the US economy. Just bringing everybody up to basic skills (400 points on PISA)—something akin to achieving No Child Left Behind—would, however, yield a striking US$ 86 trillion.

From a policy point of view, these calculations underscore the need for aggressive (and successful) policies aimed at improving achievement and skills. From a research point of view, the ability to uncover such fundamental relationships highlights the enormous value of the underlying large scale international surveys.

Some Things to be Addressed

The existing literature has produced a number of interesting and useful results. But it also has faced a number of continuing problems and challenges. Here we simply list some of the biggest issues.

---

[21] The present value weights economic gains closer to today more heavily than those in the future. It is easiest to interpret as the amount of money that, invested at an assumed return of 3 % per year, could produce the projected GDP pattern over time.

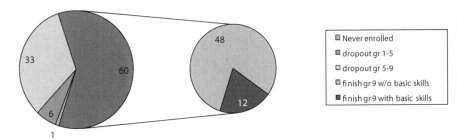

Fig. 4.5. School performance in Peru. (Source: Based on Hanushek and Woessmann 2008)

Some Measurement Issues

The international assessments meet a variety of purposes for the individual countries and for development organizations. One important purpose is to provide individual countries with a benchmark both of what is possible and of where the country stands.

These issues are important for all countries, but they are especially important for developing countries. And here the story is not very pretty. Look for example at schooling in Peru (Fig. 4.5). Peru has a high level of school attainment—but few of its students appear to be learning much when in school. Only one-fifth of the students are achieving at the basic 400-point level on PISA. From a measurement viewpoint, one has to wonder if the PISA test is even giving meaningful information about the skills of students in Peru and other countries similarly situated in terms of performance. An obvious direction in the testing evolution is developing tests that provide meaningful information within and across developing countries while also providing linking information to show relative standings in the world. This could be accomplished, for example, by continuing regional tests that were aimed at specific populations while including meaningful linking items to the PISA and TIMSS tests.

A second issue is the ability to link assessments to earlier experiences or to ones that were originally conducted in parallel, such as TIMSS and PISA. The ideal approach involves including linking items on all tests and, for parallel tests, going to large-scale studies administering both assessments to equivalent samples of students. Statistical adjustments such as the one described by Hanushek and Woessmann (2009) may be used, but rely on strong assumptions. All of the repeated international assessments have recently made progress on linkages of assessment cycles over time. Further work, including linkages between PISA and TIMSS, would have substantial pay-offs. These issues are relevant both for studies of educational production functions and for studies of the economic outcomes.

Issues of Causation

A prime difficulty in the existing analyses is being confident about the identification of causal effects. Almost all of these studies are concerned with policy issues— either improving achievement or using achievement to obtain improved economic outcomes. It is obviously difficult to produce randomized experiments in a number of these areas. Pushing forward on causal issues is frequently quite difficult.

One of the key issues, particularly when looking at the determinants of individual achievement, is to follow the growth trajectories of students over time. The importance of collecting panel data on student performance is that it facilitates isolating the impact of specific interventions on achievement. Of course, as discussed above and elsewhere, other approaches such as exploiting natural experiments for exploring causal influences should also be pursued. The use of panel data simply provides a broadly applicable way to going deeper into the policy questions that are important. This conclusion, for example, comes out of the extensive work on administrative data bases within individual countries. With the exception of the IEA in the Second International Mathematics Study (SIMS), this has not been pursued in the main assessments. Interestingly, however, several countries have developed their own national follow-on studies, beginning with the sampled students for the PISA assessment. This kind of activity should clearly be encouraged.

Understanding Individual Economic Outcomes

As noted, there has already been preliminary work done on adult assessments and surveys that permit investigation of labor market outcomes. These surveys have been very important for research into the determinants of earnings. Expansion of these would permit research into the deeper question of what aspects of an economy drive the demands for human capital and skills. While there have been a few attempts to get at these issues, the work to date is quite rudimentary.[22]

Looking in the opposite direction, validating the importance of measured tests for economic outcomes could provide valuable information about the tests themselves. A variety of people have criticized current testing systems because of potential problems such as teaching to the test or outright cheating.[23] If on the other hand the scores on these achievement assessments prove to be closely related to economic outcomes that we care about, we would have less concern about focusing on such test performance.

---

[22] See, for example, the innovative attempt to understand supply and demand for skills in Leuven et al. (2004).

[23] See, for example, Hout and Elliott (2011). Although, the evidence behind these critiques has been extraordinarily limited and weak, indicating that other approaches to validating the tests are necessary (Hanushek 2012).

Conclusions

The development of international testing and assessments has been quite extraordinary. From humble beginnings, when the question was more, "Can it be done?", assessments have become embedded in the international world.

Much of the development of these assessments has been driven by a general notion that having comparisons across countries is a good idea—without much explicit consideration of how these assessments might be used in a larger research and policy context.

The burgeoning literature that considers both what factors contribute to score differences and what impacts scores have on economic outcomes shows the larger value of these assessments. It is perhaps time to consider how these large-scale international assessments could be made even more useful through direct linkage to the larger research activities.

References

Bedard, Kelly, and Christopher Ferrall. 2003. Wage and test score dispersion: some international evidence. *Economics of Education Review* 22 (1):31–43.

Bishop, John H. 1995. The impact of curriculum-based external examinations on school priorities and student learning. *International Journal Of Educational Research* 23 (8):653–752.

Bishop, John H. 1997. The effect of national standards and curriculum-based examinations on achievement. *American Economic Review* 87 (2):260–264.

Brown, Giorgina, John, Micklewright, Sylke V., Schnepf and Waldmann, Robert. 2007. International surveys of educational achievement: How robust are the findings? *Journal of the Royal Statistical society A* 170 (3):623–646.

Carnoy, Martin, and Loeb, Susanna. 2002. Does external accountability affect student outcomes? A cross-state analysis. *Educational Evaluation and Policy Analysis* 24 (Winter 4):305–331.

Hanushek, Eric A. 2003. The failure of input-based schooling policies. *Economic Journal* 113 (February 485):64-98.

Hanushek, Eric A. 2012. Grinding the anti-testing ax: The national research council's accountability report. *Education Next* 12 (Spring 1):68–73.

Hanushek, Eric A., and Kimko, Dennis D. 2000. Schooling, labor force quality, and the growth of nations. *American Economic Review* 90 (December 5):1184–1208.

Hanushek, Eric A., Link, Susanne and Ludger, Woessmann. 2011. Does school autonomy make sense everywhere? panel estimates from PISA. *NBER Working Paper* 17591 (November). Cambridge: National Bureau of Economic Research.

Hanushek, Eric A., and Raymond, Margaret E. 2005. Does school accountability lead to improved student performance? *Journal of Policy Analysis and Management* 24. (Spring 2):297–327.

Hanushek, Eric A., and Woessmann, Ludger. 2008. The role of cognitive skills in economic development. *Journal of Economic Literature* 46. (September 3):607–668.

Hanushek, Eric A., and Woessmann, Ludger. 2009. Do better schools lead to more growth? cognitive skills, economic outcomes, and causation. NBER Working Paper 14633. (January). Cambridge: National Bureau of Economic Research.

Hanushek, Eric A., and Woessmann, Ludger. 2011a. The economics of international differences in educational achievement. In *Handbook of the economics of education, Vol. 3*. eds. Eric A, Hanushek, Machin, Stephen, and Woessmann, Ludger, 89–200. Amsterdam: North Holland.

Hanushek, Eric A., and Woessmann, Ludger. 2011b. How much do educational outcomes matter in OECD countries? *Economic policy* 26 (67):427–491.

Hanushek, Eric A., and Zhang, Lei. 2009. Quality-consistent estimates of international schooling and skill gradients. *Journal of Human Capital* 3 (Summer 2):107–143.

Heyneman, Stephen P., and Loxley, William. 1983. The effect of primary school quality on academic achievement across twenty-nine high and low income countries. *American Journal Of Sociology* 88 (May 6):1162–1194.

Hout, Michael, and Elliott, Stuart W. eds. 2011. *Incentives and test-based accountability in education.* Washington, DC: National academies press.

Leuven, Edwin, Hessel, Oosterbeek and van Ophem, Hans. 2004. Explaining international differences in male skill wage differentials by differences in demand and supply of skills. *Economic Journal* 114 (April 495):466–486.

Mullis, Ina V.S., Michael. O. Martin, and Foy, Pierce. 2008. *TIMSS 2007 International mathematics report: Findings from IEA's trends in international mathematics and science study at the fourth and eighth grades.* Chestnut Hill: TIMSS & PIRLS International Study Center, Lynch School of Education, Boston College.

Mullis, Ina V. S., Michael. O, Martin, Ann M., Kennedy and Foy, Pierce. 2007. *PIRLS 2006 international report: IEA's progress in international reading literacy study in primary schools in 40 countries.* Chestnut Hill: TIMSS & PIRLS International Study Center, Lynch School of Education, Boston College.

Neidorf, Teresa S., Marilyn, Binkley, Kim, Gattis and Nohara, David. 2006. *Comparing mathematics content in the national assessment of educational progress (NAEP), Trends in international mathematics and science study (TIMSS), and program for international student assessment (PISA) 2003 assessments* (May). Washington: National Center for Education Statistics.

Organisation for Economic Co-operation and Development. 2007. *PISA 2006: Science competencies for tomorrow's world* Vol. 1 Analysis Paris: OECD.

Toma, Eugenia F. 1996. Public funding and private schooling across countries. *Journal of Law and Economics* 39 (1):121–148.

Woessmann, Ludger. 2003. Schooling resources, educational institutions, and student performance: the international evidence. *Oxford Bulletin of Economics and Statistics* 65 (2):117–170.

Chapter 5
The Utility and Need for Incorporating Noncognitive Skills Into Large-Scale Educational Assessments

Henry M. Levin

Introduction

International comparisons of educational systems have become increasingly common as nations explore the potential of education for improving their citizenry and economic productivity. It is not unusual to see headlines in the news for any particular country on how it ranks on the periodic surveys of the Programme of International Achievement (PISA), International Adult Literacy Survey (IALS), Trends in International Mathematics and Science Study (TIMSS), and the Progress in International Reading Literacy Study (PIRLS). Countries take their rankings very seriously, and the media either praise their country's performance or decry it, calling for major educational reforms. At the same time, national and regional assessments compare different regions and educational entities on the quality of their educational systems, primarily using the metrics of student achievement as the guide.

It is hardly surprising that the notion of a good school or good educational performance is viewed through the prism of student achievement as represented by standardized test scores. In the United States, real estate brokers use achievement results to suggest the desirability of a particular residential neighborhood. School districts feel pressed to raise their test scores as the primary indicator of their educational quality. Parents view the educational promise of their children in terms of how well they do on such tests. And, of course, governments set out accountability standards on the basis of test results as well as sanctions for poor test performance such as those of the No Child Left Behind law. Correspondingly teachers and principals seek ways to focus on raising achievement, even if it means narrowing the curriculum to the subjects being tested and teaching primarily through strategies that put instruction in the form of test formats and test practice. Clearly, there are many advantages to the use of standardized testing, whether domestically or internationally. What students learn should be assessed, and few would question that knowledge, and abilities to use that knowledge, are essential for human function.

H. M. Levin (✉)
Teachers College, Columbia University, 525 West 120 Street, New York, NY 10027, USA
e-mail: HL361@columbia.edu

M. von Davier et al. (eds.), *The Role of International Large-Scale Assessments:*
Perspectives from Technology, Economy, and Educational Research,
DOI 10.1007/978-94-007-4629-9_5, © Springer Science+Business Media Dordrecht 2013

But, at least some of the attractiveness of cognitive test scores is due to the fact that the assessment of cognitive skills has developed to the point where they are relatively easy to measure. A relatively small sample of test performance can be obtained at low cost and with what appears to have predictive validity for individuals, at least for further academic performance and occupational placement and earnings. Of course, this type of psychological testing has a long history of development. In contrast, systematic assessment of other personality characteristics that may also predict both academic and economic productivity is far less developed in educational assessments. Such social and behavioral aspects or measures of personality, or what are commonly called noncognitive measures, are more complex in terms of their underlying definitions, structure, and measurement, and there are many more of these dimensions suggested in the literature. For these reasons, they are likely to be more difficult to measure in the streamlined way—conventional testing—that is used for cognitive outcomes. Unfortunately, even their terminologies differ among disciplines and authors. In some cases they are called noncognitive, and in others, affective, or social, behavioral, and emotional. For purposes of parsimony, I will use these terms interchangeably, even though I recognize they may have very different meanings in different contexts. My main concern will be to differentiate them from the knowledge and skills that we normally measure with the use of cognitive test scores.

This chapter argues that both domestic and international educational assessments should expand their measures of educational outcomes to take account of the development of noncognitive student attributes that are required for productive economic and democratic participation and personal development. Some would assert that the main ingredient for productive adulthood is the knowledge and abilities acquired, and that these are best measured through cognitive testing. However, that view is countered by the fact that microeconomic studies show that such tests explain only a relatively small portion of the variance in earnings and supervisory ratings and a minor portion of the statistical relation between schooling attainments and economic outcomes. This is not to argue the irrelevance of what is measured by the test scores to adult outcomes and economic results, but only that they account for much less power in molding adult outcomes than is normally assumed and should not be used exclusively as a statistical measure to evaluate the educational merit or quality of educational systems. Cognitive achievement is important and should continue to be assessed. But it is a highly incomplete category for measuring student and adult success. This chapter sounds an appeal to consider the potential importance of noncognitive skills and dimensions of human behavior as they comprise important adult competencies and the role of schools in developing them. But first we must acknowledge them, conceptualize their roles and identities, and measure them. The latter is where large-scale assessment ultimately enters the picture. What follows is designed to make the case.

Consider the following presentation by Alex Inkeles, one of the foremost social psychologists of personality, in his study of individual and societal productivity. Inkeles (1966) relied on a functionalist framework to identify the requirements of competent adulthood and the "socialization of competence":

To perform effectively in contemporary society, one must acquire a series of qualities I believe to be developed mainly in the socialization process. Effective participation in a modern industrial and urban society requires certain levels of skill in the manipulation of language and other symbol systems, such as arithmetic and time; the ability to comprehend and complete forms; information as to when and where to go for what; skills in interpersonal relations which permit negotiation, insure protection of one's interests, and provide maintenance of stable and satisfying relations with intimates, peers, and authorities; motives to achieve, to master, to persevere; defenses to control and channel acceptably the impulses to aggression, to sexual expression, to extreme dependency, a cognitive style which permits thinking in concrete terms while still permitting reasonable handling of abstractions and general concepts; a mind which does not insist on excessively premature closure, is tolerant of diversity, and has some components of flexibility; a conative style which facilitates reasonably regular, steady, and persistent effort, relieved by rest and relaxation but not requiring long periods of total withdrawal or depressive psychic slump; and a style of expressing affect which encourages stable and enduring relationships without excessive narcissistic dependence or explosive aggression in the face of petty frustration. This is already a long list and surely much more could be added. (Inkeles 1966, pp. 280–281)

What is striking about this list is the complexity of an expert's view on what needs to be developed in the human personality for adult competence in modern life and the relatively limited role of standardized tests for shedding light on these competencies.

In subsequent work, Inkeles and Smith (1974) developed an index of modernism composed of many items, reflecting the following: informed citizenship; personal efficacy; independence and autonomy relative to traditional sources of influence in making personal decisions; and openness to new experience and ideas constructed with 19 subscales. These scales were used to measure "modernity" among almost 6,000 men in six developing countries—Argentina, Bangladesh, Chile, India, Israel, and Nigeria—using a stratified sample to obtain representation of distinct occupations and rural and urban populations. The researchers also formulated a range of socialization variables that could influence modernity attitudes: education, work experience, contact with mass media, consumer goods possessed, father's education, urbanism of residence, skill level, length of urban residence, modernity of workplace, modernity of home, and school background. This combination of variables was able to explain statistically between 32–62 % of the variance in modernity scores, considerably higher than most earnings equations among individual adults, even today. In all six countries, education was the most powerful statistical influence, at least two to three times more powerful than any other influence in standardized coefficients (Inkeles 1975).

The sheer breadth of both the underlying theory and empirical findings of the Inkeles framework highlight the narrowness of the measures of educational outcome on which our international surveys are focusing. That is, schools have far more impact on important components of human formation that matter in the workplace, community, and home than just what is measured by test scores. In this chapter I will not attempt to develop new empirical information, largely because there already exists an impressive pattern of evidence that suggests: (1) schools influence personality traits that are determinants of both achievement and work productivity; and (2) by limiting attention only to the cognitive test scores dimension of educational outcomes, we are influencing the establishment of educational policies that are likely to restrict social and economic productivity.

I will recommend that large-scale assessments, both international and domestic, move beyond the focus on cognitive test scores to embrace a larger set of potential educational outcomes including student attitudes, behaviors, and other noncognitive measures that are important for explaining valuable individual and social outcomes including economic productivity. I recognize that there is no simple dividing line between so-called cognitive and noncognitive educational results or skills imparted by the educational system. Although we may refer to noncognitive attributes or skills as social and behavioral attributes, it is clear that they can be heavily bound up with cognitive knowledge. As a working distinction we can distinguish the cognitive attributes that are measured by test scores, a category limited to knowledge in particular test domains or subjects, and modes of measuring these domains or subjects as the cognitive focus of schools. In contrast this chapter refers to noncognitive skills essentially as those that are generally viewed as attitudes, behaviors, and values that contribute to adult competencies.[1] We should keep in mind that some of these interact with cognitive skills such as problem-solving ability, where modes of analytic and relational thinking must draw upon a knowledge base. While the distinctions between cognitive and noncognitive will not be sharply delineated, they will be sufficiently differentiated to understand the thrust of the arguments.

The Test Score Image and Reality

- Few college educated individuals will forget their college entrance scores (e.g., SAT) or test scores for graduate or professional school admissions, even after many decades.
- Academics have fought bitterly over the origins of IQ (phenotype or genotype), but few question the importance and social value of IQ as they take pride and ownership in their own high IQs.

Cognitive testing has an impressive history. Its development and sophistication have far outpaced assessment in noncognitive areas of performance in its precision, statistical analysis, and widespread adoption. The test score illusion is that we tend to overstate the importance of tests in accounting for human productivity. At both individual and societal levels, they carry considerable influence. But, their importance is greater in the popular imagination than the evidence supports. The advent of human capital theory in economics had important and deservingly profound effects on the thinking about the link between education and economic output. Educational investments became viewed as investments in human beings that increased

---

[1] The most ambitious and encyclopedic review of personality characteristics as they relate to economic outcomes is found in the comprehensive and magisterial treatment by Almlund et al. (2011). Also see Borghans et al. (2008a).

productive skills, leading to greater productivity and economic output. Little was said about the nature of such skills. In his pioneering work on human capital, Gary Becker (1964) provides almost no analysis of the skills that are encompassed by human capital. And the vacuum on precisely what skills were developed through human capital investments—and the vacuum filler of educational attainment data—combined to make the years of education attained as the standard measure of human capital. The most comprehensive and widely used sources of data such as the US Census or household surveys on earnings of workers reported the amount of education attained, but not test results.

Measures of educational attainment in terms of number of years of schooling are highly errorful measures. These are self-reported and lack information on areas of study, educational quality, rigor of courses, and student effort. As a result it was logical to seek data sources that had more direct measures of academic attainment, and test results were a more direct verification of skills than the amount of time spent in schools. It seemed reasonable that most of what was learned in schools could be measured by test scores.

This perspective was first questioned by Gintis (1971) and Bowles and Gintis (1976) in the decade following the human capital revolution in their attempt to show that school organizations reflect the practices of employers in student development where many similar noncognitive demands are placed on both students and workers. More recently, Bowles et al. (2001) summarized much of the ensuing research that has addressed this phenomenon. One of their most salient findings is that only a small portion of the overall statistical impact of schooling on earnings can be explained by test scores per se. A summary of 25 studies over a period of four decades (late 1950s to early 1990s) provided 58 estimates of earnings functions where test scores were available. Starting with the conventional human capital formulation in which demographics, socioeconomic status, and schooling are used as explanatory variables for predicting earnings, they estimate the coefficient for the schooling contribution to earnings (usually measured by years of education). They then posit that if the schooling variable is a just a rough proxy for achievement, it is highly errorful relative to a direct measure of what is learned and contributes to productivity, a measure of test scores. By adding the test score to the equation, they can test "how much" of the "naïve" schooling effect indicated by monetary returns to years of schooling is reduced by a direct measure of cognitive skill created through education. Across the 58 estimates they find that the schooling coefficient retains about 82 % of its "naïve" value, suggesting that most of the effect of schooling on earnings is due to factors other than those measured by standardized tests (Bowles et al. 2001, pp. 1147–1150)

It is almost an article of faith among policymakers and the general public that the impact of cognitive skills in labor markets is rising. Much of the support for this view comes from the evidence of one well-constructed study that compares test score impacts on earnings between 1978 and 1986 and finds that there was a rise in hourly wage over those years based on returns to mathematic scores (Murnane et al. 1995). But an analysis of a wider range of studies finds no such trend among 65 estimates from 24 studies reflecting a 30-year period (Bowles et al. 2001, pp. 1154–1156). This study not only found no rising trend, but relatively small estimated impacts of mathematics achievement on wages. A standard deviation in test score was associated with a 10 % increase in wages, equal to about one year of schooling. Of special pertinence is that no existing educational intervention has shown effects even close to one standard deviation. Of the relatively few that seem to improve mathematics achievement, it is rare to find results that exceed one-fifth of a standard deviation. A study for the United Kingdom finds no increase in the returns to cognitive skills for the period 1995–2004, the most recent period found for these studies (Vignoles et al. 2011). The overall support for the rising effect of cognitive skills is absent or mixed in other research studies and is beset with methodological issues (Cawley et al. 2001), which should at least raise a caution flag in asserting rising returns.

The exaggeration of cognitive impacts of workers on worker productivity has also been a feature of the literature on using test scores directly for worker selection. The most important public use was that by the US Employment Service, which used the General Ability Test Battery (GATB) to rank workers for referral to employer requests for candidates. The GATB includes subtests of intelligence, verbal aptitude and numerical aptitude as well as a range of other measures. State employment services informed prospective employers that they would refer the most productive applicants for consideration on the basis of the GATB rankings. However, there was considerable controversy over the practice of norming the rankings separately within race so that two individuals of different races with different raw scores might have the same percentile ranking. Because blacks had considerably lower scores on the GATB, the normalized rankings for blacks had a much lower GATB score than a white with the same ranking. The National Research Council of the National Academy of Sciences and National Academy of Engineering formed a panel that was asked to focus especially on the validity claims for GATB and other employee tests that were asserted to have predictive validities of .6–.7 on supervisory ratings of worker productivity according to leading advocates (Hartigan and Wigdor 1989). The study panel found that the estimated predictive validities were vastly inflated by questionable procedures, so the best estimate of validity was about .25, a dramatic reduction from the claims. Thus, the tests used to refer workers to employers accounted for only about 6 % of the variance in performance, leaving 94 % to be explained by *other* characteristics of workers. More recent summaries of the empirical literature across many different studies and measures support this modest finding (Sackett et al. 2001).

Even well-specified earnings functions that include more than one direct measure of cognitive skill and many other covariates show low total explained variance, typically one third or less (Murnane et al. 2001). And the cognitive measures in themselves show "modest" relations to earnings (Murnane et al. 2000). Clearly cognitive abilities are important for many important dimensions of adult performance, including economic, civic, and personal demands upon individuals. But they are far from dominant in explaining economic and social outcomes and are probably considerably less important than commonly believed. Yet the domestic and international comparisons of educational achievement focus almost exclusively on these.

In the next section we address what is known about noncognitive aspects of schooling and work performance.

Multiple Sources of Support for Noncognitive Measures

When one reviews many different sources of information, the importance of social and behavioral competencies beyond cognitive skills is apparent. In this section, I will provide brief glimpses of a number of these sources.

Employer Needs

It is common for employers to explain that they seek workers both with good cognitive skills and social/behavioral competencies to qualify for employment. This is not a new phenomenon. Almost three decades ago, the National Research Council convened a panel to set out the competencies that employers desired (National Research Council 1984). The panel, composed almost entirely of employers from a large range of business sectors and a few government agencies, was charged with studying and formulating the set of core competencies that they would want among the high school graduates they employ.[2] The motivation of the NRC for forming the panel was to recognize the knowledge needs of the changing workplace for high school graduates. Panel members were asked to work closely with supervisors in their human resources departments to get a ground-level view of worker requirements.

The panel developed a comprehensive list that was heavy on cognitive requirements such as command of the English language, reasoning, reading, writing, computation, and knowledge of basic science and technology. But the panel found the same level of concern by human resource supervisors for a substantial list of behavioral and social worker characteristics on "Interpersonal Relationships" and "Personal Work Habits and Attitudes." These included such attributes as interacting in a socially appropriate manner; demonstrating respect for the opinions, customs, and individual differences of others; handling conflict maturely; and participation in reaching group decisions. They also included a realistic positive attitude toward one's self; self-discipline, including regular and punctual attendance and dependability; ability to set goals and allocate time to achievement of them; and capacity to accept responsibility (National Research Council 1984). To the degree that national testing such as the National Assessment of Educational Progress (NAEP) and the international comparisons of educational achievement are motivated by preparation for the workplace and economic productivity, their results largely ignore these perspectives in providing information on educational preparation.

---

[2] In the spirit of full disclosure, I was the "token academic" on this panel.

The Employer Employment Survey in the early 1990s, sponsored by the US Department of Education, surveyed more than 4,000 employers "to identify employers' practices and expectations in their search for a skilled and proficient work force." When asked to identify the recruitment characteristics that they used to make hiring decisions on a scale of 1–5 (with 5 being the highest), applicant's attitude was 4.6 and communication skills were 4.2, the two highest in the survey. Tests administered by the firm, academic grades in school, and reputation of applicant's school were at 2.5 or 2.4, at the bottom of the list (Zemsky and Iannozzi 1995).

The latest National Employer Skills Survey for England 2009 (Shury et al. 2010) is notable for its lack of discussion of academic skills. The survey finds that about one fifth of the enterprises are affected by a skills gap, but for 71 % of these, the "main cause" is lack of experience and recent recruitment. Thus, it is no surprise to find that 64 % of employers were concerned with a lack of technical, practical, or job-specific skills. A third of employers implicated a lack of motivation on the part of workers. Employers also were concerned about such skills as customer-handling (41 %), problem-solving (38 %), and team-working (37 %), with literacy and numeracy further down the list. That is, social and behavioral skills were important challenges for UK employers in this recent study.

It seems obvious that from the perspective of employer concerns, both in the past and more recently, there is at least as much concern for the noncognitive attributes of workers as for the cognitive ones. Indeed, the former may even be a stronger source of concern.

Cognitive or Noncognitive Effects

The Perry Preschool is best known for its role as the earliest study showing substantial long-term effects of preschool. The study followed the lives of 123 persons who had been randomly assigned as 3–4-year-olds to experimental treatment and control groups where the experimental group was enrolled in the preschool program. The subjects were black inner-city children from poverty families. Study participants were followed up to the age of 40 for their educational results and life experiences. The experimental students showed initial intellectual and literacy gains over the students in the control group, but the differences faded out in the early elementary years. Yet when comparisons were made of life accomplishments, the Perry Preschool participants did substantially better than the control group in terms of educational attainments, reduction in crime, earnings, employment, and welfare costs (Schweinhart 2010, p. 161). For example, 28 % of the Perry participants had been convicted of a crime by age 40, relative to 52 % of the control group, and earnings were about one third higher. High school graduation rates were higher for the Perry group, and their attitudes toward school were more positive. Evaluations of the investments in Perry Preschool show a high return (Heckman et al. 2010). These types of outcomes are important to both the individuals who benefited and society, even though they do not seem to be attributable to the early test results. One interpretation is that Perry mainly had an influence on school readiness and other noncognitive behaviors that contributed to the increase in school and life success.

A different challenge is the puzzle of the findings on the economic success and social experience of students who acquire the General Education Development (GED) credential in lieu of graduating from high school. The purpose of the GED is to credential dropouts as equivalent to high school graduates if they succeed on the GED examination. Heckman and Rubinstein (2001) found that they do about as well on a cognitive test as high school graduates who do not enroll in college. But their earnings patterns are considerably below high school graduates, and when adjusted for their cognitive performance, are even lower than those of high school dropouts who do not take the GED. In addition, their ultimate education attainment also lags behind that of dropouts who did not take the GED. The authors conclude that the GED recipients have lower noncognitive skills that count in employment, and this interpretation is buttressed by a measure of illicit activity that is higher for the GED students than for the non-GED dropouts or high school graduates.

A third potential example is that of the Tennessee Class Size or Star experiment in which students in grades from kindergarten to grade three were assigned to large classes (23–25 students) or small classes (13–17 students) at random in the schools chosen for the experiment. Students could receive from one to four years of the small-class treatment or none. In his review of the study, distinguished statistician Fred Mosteller called the study "…one of the most important education investigations ever carried out" (Mosteller 1995). Test results showed moderate achievement advantages in reading, word study, and mathematics that increased with the duration of the treatment. But perhaps what is most surprising is the substantial difference in graduation rates almost a decade later. This was particularly so for the disadvantaged students—those eligible for a free or reduced cost lunch. Disadvantaged students with smaller classes for four years had graduation rates 18 % points higher than similar students who had attended only regular size classes, 88–70 %. This was found to be well beyond the predictive effect of the early academic achievement that was experienced, suggesting that noncognitive effects accounted for at least a portion, and perhaps a large portion, of the higher graduation performance (Finn et al. 2005). Insights into a mechanism for explaining this noncognitive effect is found in a recent study that linked class size reduction to improving student learning behaviors (Dee and West 2011).

An intriguing study (Lindqvist and Vestman 2011) from Sweden evaluated cognitive and noncognitive dimensions of military enlistees (enlistment is a mandatory requirement for all Swedish males). All enlistees filled out an extensive questionnaire with 70–80 questions. A certified psychologist was provided with this information as well as measures of cognitive ability and other attributes. Following a specified set of procedures, the enlistee was interviewed by the psychologist and evaluated according to the perceived ability of the conscript to cope with the psychological requirements of military service. Each conscript was given a score according to the same distribution used for the cognitive ability score. Using a random sample of men born between 1965–1984, the authors evaluated the impact of cognitive and noncognitive measures on wages, unemployment, and annual earnings.

They found that men who do poorly in the labor market lack noncognitive abilities. In contrast, cognitive ability is a stronger predictor of wages and earnings for workers with earnings above the median.

Schools and Noncognitive Outcomes

One question that might arise is whether schools can actually change noncognitive outcomes. Relatively little attention has been devoted to systematic consideration of this question and its measurement because there is not the body of rigorous research available that exists for cognitive measures. However, considerable attention has been devoted to this subject in early childhood education, where attempts have been made to see if students are "school ready."

Cognitive control, self-regulation, or executive function (EF) is the focus of a study testing directly whether a noncognitive skill can be taught effectively. Diamond et al. (2007) evaluated The Tools of the Mind curriculum, a framework that contains 40 EF-promoting activities. Students and teachers were assigned randomly to The Tools of the Mind curriculum and an alternative. The Tools of the Mind curriculum not only had significant effects in promoting greater EF, but the higher EF in itself was associated with higher standardized measures of reading. The importance of this finding is magnified by the fact that EF has been more strongly linked to school readiness than cognitive measures (Blair and Razza 2007). A more extensive, recent randomization study confirms the findings on the educational effects of The Tools of the Mind curriculum, and particularly its impact on social development of the child and improvement of classroom experience (Barnett et al. 2011). Distinguished psychologist Albert Bandura (1997) has also maintained that there is an impressive knowledge base showing that self-efficacy (the belief that one can influence a personal outcome) can be conditioned in the young in his extensive lifelong study of self-efficacy.

Clearly, not all prekindergarten experiences contribute to children's school readiness, as evidenced by a more general study that focused on prekindergarten impacts on school cognitive outcomes and behavior problems without examining the program specifics (Magnuson et al. 2007). In contrast, The Tools of the Mind studies highlight that the specific goals of the preschool program are central in determining whether they improve noncognitive functioning in the school environment as applied to preschool experiences of any type. Program design matters in exploring the impacts of educational programs.

Overall summaries of the literature also confirm the importance of early childhood interventions on behavioral or socioemotional change. Nores and Barnett (2010) summarized a total of 38 studies reviewing 30 interventions in 23 countries that had applied quasiexperimental or random assignment designs. They took into consideration the type of intervention, sample size, study design and duration, country, target group, subpopulations, and dosage of interventions. They found both cognitive benefits and behavioral benefits. Camilli et al. (2010) undertook a meta-analysis of 123 comparative studies of early childhood interventions. The evaluation of all programs in the review had been designed using experimental principles. Although the largest effects were found for cognitive outcomes, preschool experience was also found to be associated with student's social skills and school progress.

Duncan and associates (2007) used six longitudinal data sets to estimate the links between academic, attention, and socioemotional skills at school entry and subsequent school reading and math achievement. Attention-related skills refer to task persistence and self-regulation or EF. We do not know the content of the preschool experience, so these measures are recorded at school entry. They found math skills to show the greatest predictive power, followed by reading and attention skills. As with the Magnuson et al. (2007) study, the focus was on participation in preschool, but not on specific programs that focus on noncognitive skill development, as did The Tools of the Mind curriculum. Duncan and Magnuson (2011) also find important relations between both early childhood cognitive scores and social behavior on later educational outcomes and criminal involvement.

The most extensive evaluation of the direct study of the teaching of social and emotional skills and their impact is found in Durlak et al. (2011). This work is based upon a meta-analysis of 213 school-based social and emotional learning (SEL) programs from kindergarten through high school, studies encompassing 270,000 children overall from ages 5–18. Only intervention studies that had control groups were included. Outcomes included six criteria:

- *Social and emotional skills*—includes evaluations of different types of cognitive, affective, and social skills related to such areas as identifying emotions from social cues, goal setting, perspective taking, interpersonal problem solving, conflict resolution, and decision making.
- *Attitudes toward self and others*—includes positive attitudes about the self, school, and social topics, including self-perceptions (e.g., self-esteem, self-concept, and self-efficacy), school bonding (e.g., attitudes toward school and teachers), and conventional (i.e., prosocial) beliefs about violence, helping others, social justice, and drug use.
- *Positive social behavior*—includes outcomes such as getting along with others derived from the student, teacher, parent, or an independent observer on the basis of daily behavior as opposed to hypothetical situations.
- *Conduct problems*—includes measures of different types of behavior problems, such as disruptive class behavior, noncompliance, aggression, bullying, school suspensions, and delinquent acts.
- *Emotional distress*—includes internalized mental health issues. These included reports of depression, anxiety, stress, or social withdrawal, which could be provided by students, teachers, or parents.
- *Academic performance*—includes standardized reading or math achievement test scores from such measures as the Stanford Achievement Test or the Iowa Test of Basic Skills, and school grades in the form of students' overall grade point average (GPA) or their grades in specific subjects (usually reading or math). Only data drawn from school records were included.

Meaningful effect sizes were found for all six criteria: social and emotional skills, 0.57; attitudes, 0.23; positive social behavior, 0.24; student conduct problems, 0.22; emotional distress, 0.24; and academic performance, 0.27. Thirty-three of the academic performance studies had follow-up evaluations of at least six months after the intervention ended, with a median follow-up time of about one calendar year. All effect sizes continued at statistically significant levels, with the effect size for academic performance at 0.32 for the subgroup, suggesting that development of social and emotional skills have particular salience for improving student achievement.

A reasonable summary of this literature is that noncognitive skills can be taught through purposive interventions and that they can make a difference for many valuable social/behavioral outcomes and for student achievement. The latter is an important conclusion because not only are these outcomes important in themselves, but they also appear to have a positive impact on achievement. In the Durlak et al. (2011) study, the average effect size among studies is adequate to raise standardized student achievement scores by 11 percentiles. This is equivalent to an increase of PISA scores by about 30 points—the difference between the United States and higher-scoring Canada, and a rise in rankings from 17th to 5th place, or from 14th to 3rd place if we exclude cities or city-states Shanghai, Hong Kong, and Singapore. While this may not be a simple matter of policy, it does provide a framework for considering the potential of noncognitive interventions.

Schooling and Labor Market Effects

Without question, the scholar who has done the most to develop an understanding of the role of noncognitive skills in educational and economic outcomes is James Heckman of the University of Chicago, aided by his colleagues.[3] Heckman has not only called attention to the importance of noncognitive skills, but has worked with psychologists and neurologists to estimate optimal time patterns of investment between development of the different types of skills and their impact on labor market returns (Knudsen et al. 2006). His masterful article with Flavio Cunha is considered to be the most ambitious and sophisticated attempt to both formulate a theory of optimal investment between cognitive and noncognitive skills from birth to the labor force, but also to apply the model to a specific longitudinal data set to measure the impact of cognitive and noncognitive skill development on earnings (Cunha and Heckman 2008). The authors create a battery of noncognitive scores

---

[3] Heckman has produced most of the important scholarship on this subject and has continued his program to deepen understanding of the role of noncognitive skills. It would take pages to list all of his contributions. However, it would be helpful to review the citations to Heckman and colleagues in the bibliography of the masterful article by Borghans et al. (2008a). Heckman's role is central to the content of the symposium on "The Noncognitive Determination of Labor Market and Behavioral Outcomes," XVII (4).

from their data set focused on an antisocial construct using student anxiety, head-strongness, hyperactivity, and peer conflict to go along with cognitive test scores in this analysis. Based upon the psychological, neurological, social, and other aspects of child development, they model the developmental path and estimate the impact of investments in cognitive skill and noncognitive skill on high school graduation and earnings (at age 23) at three different periods during the span from age 6–13. As the child ages, the impact of investment returns shifts markedly from cognitive skills at the earlier ages (6–9) to noncognitive skills during the later period.

Clearly, this analysis, if it stands up to replication, has profound implications for school policy and the construction of educational programs. The work of Heckman and his students stands as a milestone in considering the optimal mix of interventions and policy implications for enhancing human development through a combination of appropriate strategies of both cognitive and noncognitive skills. This work also seems to correspond in many of its assumptions with the attempt to create a unified theory of child development by Sameroff (2010), suggesting that the leading edge of this research is moving in similar directions. As with the program of Heckman, Sameroff has developed a conceptual approach that interconnects the individual and context in a dynamic manner.

Perhaps the best single source on the role of noncognitive skills and the economy is the symposium on "The Noncognitive Determinants of Labor Market and Behavioral Outcomes" (2008).[4] This unusually focused volume contains an article by Borghans et al. (2008a) that analyzes tradeoffs in roles of caring and directness in jobs that have different interpersonal requirements. Caring requires cooperation, whereas directness requires clear communication. The returns to these attributes depend upon relative supply and demand. The authors find that returns to these roles, which are held in different combinations by different individuals, match their assignment models. Articles by Fortin (2008), Krueger and Schkade (2008), Segal (2008), and Urzua (2008) address other labor market consequences related to noncognitive skills and roles of workers as well as impacts of noncognitive skills of students.

Noncognitive Variables

There exist so many concepts, constructs, and names for the personality and social and behavioral characteristics that are referred to as noncognitive that I will not allocate much space to attempting to list them or categorize them. The most comprehensive analysis of personality and its roles in labor markets, health, crime, and civic behavior is that of Almlund et al. (2004).[5] However, it is important to provide

---

[4] Also see the papers presented at the recent IZA Workshop: Cognitive and Non-Cognitive Skills, January 25–27, Bonn, Germany. Available at: http://www.iza.org/link/CoNoCoSk2011.

[5] This is an overwhelmingly ambitious exercise to map personality traits into economic modelling.

at least a glimpse of how they have been referred to and used in the psychological literature.

The Five-Factor Model

For at least the last two decades, the five-factor model of personality has been used to relate noncognitive skills to academic achievement, educational attainment, and other outcomes. The history is one in which an accumulation of different hypotheses and empirical studies were used to create statistical factor analytic dimensions by independent researchers (Digman 1990). The consolidation of many different dimensions of personality into the five-factor model was an attempt to find a basic structure for what was a highly disorganized and idiosyncratic set of measures and constructs. Accordingly, these have been considered to be the basic structure underlying all personality traits and have been used to integrate a variety of findings in personality psychology.

The Big Five factors are:

1. *Openness*—inventive and curious as opposed to consistent and cautious
2. *Conscientiousness*—efficient and organized as opposed to easygoing and careless
3. *Extraversion*—outgoing and energetic as opposed to solitary and reserved
4. *Agreeableness*—friendly and compassionate as opposed to cold and unkind
5. *Neuroticism*—sensitive and nervous as opposed to secure and confident

These categories have been used in many studies to predict behavior and are prominent in the massive review by Almlund et al. (2011). An example of a study that explores the relation between the Big Five and academic outcomes is Noftle and Robins (2007). Four different university student samples were used in the study. After controlling for high school GPA and SAT scores, the Big Five were tested, but only the dimension of "conscientiousness" was found to predict college GPA. SAT verbal score was predicted by "openness." The researchers also found that academic effort and perceived academic ability served to mediate the conscientiousness-SAT relationship, independent of academic achievement.[6] An example of the use of the Big Five for a measure of workplace productivity is the study of Neuman and Wright (1999). These authors studied the relation between personality characteristics of 316 full-time human resource representatives at local stores of a large wholesale department store enterprise. They found that "agreeableness" and "conscientiousness" predicted peer ratings of team member performance beyond controls for job-specific skills and general cognitive ability.

Promising work on the further development of noncognitive constructs and measures is being undertaken by the Research Division of Educational Testing Ser-

---

[6] From an economist's perspective, there would be concern for problems of endogeneity in use of some of the explanatory variables.

vice (Kyllonen et al. 2008) in Princeton, NJ. This work focuses on both personality characteristics and motivation, reviewing studies that link them to educational outcomes. Their work considers various measurement approaches and also documents particular interventions in developing certain personality facets that lead to higher achievement. The report develops an approach to implement a comprehensive psychosocial skills assessment at middle school and high school levels. At this time, this report is protected as proprietary and its specific contents and findings cannot be cited, although I expect that it might be released in modified form in the near future.

Summary and Implications for Educational Assessments

Modern societies demand much of their members, and fostering competence in meeting these demands must be a high social priority. Among all of the vehicles for socializing the young, schools are a very powerful one because of the considerable time spent there and the peculiar functions of schools to prepare the young in many ways for adulthood. Clearly knowledge and cognitive functioning are an important goal of schools and provide crucial skills for creating productive workers and citizens. But noncognitive or behavioral/social skills and attitudes are also crucial and of at least the same level of importance. Even with the same cognitive achievement, differences in effort, self-discipline, cooperation, self-presentation, tolerance, respect, time management, and other noncognitive dimensions form both healthy character and contribute to productive relations in workplaces, communities, families, and politics.

To a large degree, the almost singular focus on test score performance in educational assessments at both domestic and international levels is not without foundation. The cognitive domains tested are important determinants of both educational outcomes and life chances, the measurement technologies are well developed, and the process of assessment of cognitive skills is parsimonious in that a valid sample of cognitive knowledge and behavior can be obtained and evaluated at low cost. But I have emphasized that the assumptions that cognitive skills are all that counts, and that they have singular influence on producing healthy and productive adult personalities, goes well beyond the evidence. Although they are important determinants of productivity and income at both individual and societal levels, empirical studies show that their measurable influence is far more modest than generally assumed. Moreover, their impact does not seem to be rising despite the conventional wisdom. Employers who indicate skill shortages place as much or more emphasis on getting workers with proper attitudes and social behaviors as cognitive competencies. The studies of Heckman and colleagues show that the connections between noncognitive skills and workplace productivity are of comparable importance overall and of even greater importance than cognitive skills in the productive development and influence on wages and graduation of older children.

Cunha and Heckman (2010, p. 401) conclude that the noncognitive variables contribute to the impact of cognitive variables on earnings, but there is weak evidence of the reverse.[7] Thus, there are at least three reasons that the singular use of academic achievement measures to predict economic productivity and growth are overstated when noncognitive measures are omitted. The first is that academic achievement is correlated with noncognitive attributes and serves as a proxy for them when predicting economic outcomes, overstating purely cognitive effects when noncognitive variables are omitted. The second is that noncognitive attributes are not merely correlated with cognitive attributes, but contribute to cognitive outcomes. The third is that aggregated attempts to connect academic test scores with economic growth at the country level suffer the same kind of upward bias that Hanushek et al. (1996) stress when criticizing upward bias in aggregate estimates of educational production functions. On this basis it appears that the dramatic and highly publicized extrapolations by Hanushek and Woessman (2008) of contributions to economic growth of international achievement results among countries overstate the impact of the tests on economic output, possibly by a large magnitude.[8] Unfortunately, the promise of massive gains in economic output of even modest gains in test scores have been disseminated widely and taken seriously; even though those administering policy are not aware or knowledgeable about the degree to which upward bias is present in the reported results and their policy extrapolations.

Far from being harmless, the obsessive focus on test scores and the omission of the noncognitive impact of schools can provide far-reaching damage. In recent years, in the United States and other countries, there is an attempt to marshal evidence-based policies. But the evidence that is presented is limited to test score comparisons with the explicit or tacit implication that test scores are the crucial determinant of labor force quality. This message places pressure on schools by citizens and government to focus exclusively on raising test scores. In particular, pressures are placed on the schools through accountability sanctions to raise test scores in the limited domains and measures used in the national and international assessments, usually test scores in reading, mathematics, or sciences. Schools are pressed to use their time and resources to improve scores on these subjects at the expense of other activities and subjects including noncognitive goals. Yet other goals may be as important or more important in the long run in terms of creating productive, equitable, and socially cohesive societies and economic growth (Gradstein and Justman 2002).

The "evidence-based" arguments have led to a singular focus on a cognitive achievement gap in the No Child Left Behind legislation, leading schools to nar-

---

[7] As a more general proposition I would leave this as an open question. Some four decades ago I used the Coleman data to estimate the determinants of multiple school outcomes in a model that allowed for simultaneous equations estimation (Levin 1970). The results of that model estimation suggested reciprocal relationships where motivation and sense of efficacy influence student achievement and are also influenced by student achievement.

[8] Hanushek has responded that even if this is true, the magnitude of the gains in income are so large that even enormous biases still leave very large unrealized gains.

row their curriculum and focus on test preparation as a major instructional strategy (Rothstein et al. 2008). It is difficult for an evidence-based policy to embrace noncognitive measures when the assessment practices exclude them from national and international studies. Even the obsession with the test score gap among races obscures the potential noncognitive impacts of schooling. For example, Fortin (2008) found the effects of noncognitive ability to be stronger for blacks than whites on labor market outcomes and a particularly strong predictor of the black-white gap for males in their incarceration rates.

Singular focus on the cognitive test scores can also introduce teacher policies that ignore the importance of noncognitive skills and fail to value roles of teachers and schools in the noncognitive domain. For example, many states and local school districts in the United States have adopted a value-added approach for teacher policy where student test score gains associated with individual teachers are the basis for hiring, retaining, and remunerating teachers. With the recent cuts in public funding, school districts are considering layoffs of teachers based upon the value-added metric. But in addition to the serious methodological issues surrounding the calculation of value-added for each teacher (Corcoran 2010; Harris 2009), there is an even more fundamental question. Why has the purpose of schooling and teacher productivity been reduced to the gains on narrowly construed math and verbal tests if there are so many other results that we expect of schools, including noncognitive outcomes? Even if there is a tradeoff between teacher effectiveness on cognitive and noncognitive skill production, both must be taken account of in educational policy. That is the case for incorporating noncognitive skill measurement in both large-scale and small-scale assessments.[9]

Next Steps

To incorporate noncognitive skills into assessments is a major challenge. As Heckman and Rubinstein (2001) concluded in their study of the GED 10 years ago:

> We have established the quantitative importance of noncognitive skills without identifying any specific noncognitive skill. Research in the field is in its infancy. Too little is understood about the formation of these skills or about the separate effects of all of these diverse traits currently subsumed under the rubric of noncognitive skills (p. 149).

Fortunately, the research has exploded on this topic. Just seven years after the publication of this bleak statement, Cunha and Heckman (2008) were able to identify and employ specific noncognitive measures in existing data sets that could be used for analysis followed by an exceedingly productive exploration emerging from Almlund et al. (2011) and Borghans et al. (2008a). As mentioned above, Kyllonen et al. (2008) have developed rich literature reviews of noncognitive skills, including their

---

[9] This has been recognized increasingly on both sides of the Atlantic. See Brunello and Schlotter (2010) for a report prepared for the European Commission.

measurement and predictive values, and linked these to specific school interventions that might raise noncognitive performance in key areas.

My recommendation is to build on these efforts by selecting a few noncognitive skill areas and measures that can be incorporated into research on academic achievement, school graduation, postsecondary attainments, labor market outcomes, health status, and reduced involvement in the criminal justice system in conjunction with the standard academic performance measures. The Big Five are certainly leading candidates, with guidelines already suggested in the review by Almlund et al. (2011). Structural models and quasiexperimental designs might be used to understand the interplay of cognitive and noncognitive skills in explaining particular outcomes for specific demographic groups. At some point, we should learn enough to incorporate specific noncognitive measures into both small-scale and large-scale assessments that can lead to a deeper understanding of school effects and school policy.

References

Almlund, M., A. L. Duckworth, J. Heckman, and T. Kautz. 2011. *Personality Psychology and Economics,* NBER Working Paper 16822 (Cambridge, MA: National Bureau of Economic Research). http://www.nber.org/papers/w16822.pdf. Accessed 1 June 2012.

Bandura, A. 1997. *Self-efficacy: The exercise of control.* New York: Macmillan.

Barnett, W. S. et al. 2008. Educational effects of the tools of the mind curriculum: A randomized trial. *Early childhood research quarterly* 23(3):299–313.

Blair, C., and R. P. Razza. 2007. Relating effortful control, executive function and false belief understanding to emerging math & literacy in kindergarten. *Child Development* 78(2):647–663.

Becker, G. 1964. *Human capital: A theoretical and empirical analysis, with special reference to education.* Chicago: University of Chicago.

Borghans, L., A. L. Duckworth, J. J. Heckman, and B. ter Weel. 2008a. The economics and psychology of personality traits. *The Journal of Human Resources* 43(4):972-1059.

Borghans, L., ter Weel, B. and Weinberg, B. A. 2008b. Interpersonal styles and labor market outcomes. *The Journal of Human Resources* 43(4):815–858.

Bowles, S., Gintis, H., and Osborne, M. 2001. The determinants of earnings: A behavioral approach. *Journal of Economic Literature* 39(4):137–1176.

Bowles, S., and Gintis, H. 1976. Schooling in Capitalist America: Educational Reform and the Contradictions of Economic Life. New York: Basic Books.

Brunello, G., and M. Schlotter. 2010. *The effect of noncognitive skills and personality traits on labour market outcomes,* analytical report for the european commission prepared by the european expert network on economics of education. http://ftp.iza.org/dp5743.pdf. Accessed 1 June 2012.

Camilli, G., S. Vargas, S. Ryan, and W. S. Barnett. 2010. Meta-analysis of the effects of early education interventions on cognitive and social development. *Teachers College Record* 112(3):579–620.

Cawley, J., Heckman, J., and Vytlacil, E. 2001. Three observations on wages and measured cognitive ability. *Labour Economics* 8(4):419–442.

Corcoran, S. 2010. *Can teachers be evaluated by their students' test scores? should they be? the use of value-added measures of teacher Effectiveness in policy and practice.* Providence: The Annenberg Institute for School Reform, Brown University.

Cunha, F., and Heckman, J. J. 2008. Formulating, identifying and estimating the technology of cognitive and noncognitive skill formation. *The Journal of Human Resources,* 42(4):738–782.

Cunha F., and Heckman, J. J. 2010. Investing in our young people. In *Childhood programs and practices in the first decade of life,* eds. Reynolds, A. J., Rolnick, A. J., Englund, M. M., and Temple, J. A., 381–414. New York: Cambridge University Press.

Dee, T., and West, M. R. 2011. The non-cognitive returns to class size. *Educational Evaluation and Policy Analysis* 33(1):23–46.

Diamond, A., Barnett, W. S., Thomas, J., and Munro, S. 2007. Preschool program improves cognitive control. *Science* 318(5855):1387–1388.

Digman, J. 1990. Personality structure: Emergence of the five-factor model. *Annual Review of Psychology* 41: 417–440.

Duncan, G. J. et al. 2007. School readiness and later achievement. *Developmental Psychology.* 43(6): 1428–1446.

Duncan, G. J., and Magnuson, K. (2011). The nature and impact of early achievement skills, attention and behavior problems. In *Whither opportunity: Rising inequality and the uncertain life chance of low-income children,* eds. Duncan, G and Murnane, R. New York: Russell Sage Press.

Durlak, J. A., Weissberg, R. P., Dymnicki, A. B., Taylor, R. D., and Schellinger, K. B. 2011. The impact of enhancing students' social and emotional learning: A meta-analysis of school-based universal interventions. *Child Development* 82(1):405–432.

Finn, J. D., Gerber, S. B., and Boyd-Zaharias, J. 2005. Small classes in the early grades, academic achievement and graduating from high school. *Journal of Educational Psychology* 97(2):214–223.

Fortin, N. M. 2008. The gender wage gap among young adults in the United States: The Importance of Money vs. People. *The Journal of Human Resources* 43(4):884–918.

Gintis, H. 1971. Education, technology, and the characteristics of worker productivity. *American Economic Review* 61(2):266–279.

Gradstein, M., Justman, M. 2002. Education, social cohesion, & economic growth. *American Economic Review* 92(4):1192–1204.

Hanushek, E., Rivkin, S., and Taylor, L. 1996. Aggregation and the estimated effects of school resources. *Review of Economics and Statistics* 78(4):611–627.

Hanushek, E., Woessmann, L. 2008. The role of cognitive skills in economic development. *Journal of Economic Literature* 46(3):607–668.

Harris, D. 2009. Would accountability based on teacher value-added be smart policy? an examination of the statistical properties and policy alternatives. *Educational Finance and Policy* 4(4):319–350.

Hartigan J., and Wigdor A. 1989. *Fairness in employment testing: Validity generalization, minority issues, and the general aptitude test battery.* Washington: National Academy Press.

Heckman, J., Moon, S. H., Pinto, R., Savelyev, P., and Yavitz, A. 2010. A new cost-benefit and rate of return analysis for the perry preschool program: A summary. In *Childhood programs and practices in the first decade of life,* eds. Reynolds, A. J., Rolnick, A. J., Englund, M. M., and Temple, J. A., 366–380. New York: Cambridge University Press.

Heckman, J.,Rubenstein, Y. 2001. The importance of noncognitive skills: Lessons from the GED testing program. *American Economic Review* 91(2): 145–149.

Inkeles, A. 1966. The socialization of competence. *Harvard Educational Review* 36(3):265–283.

Inkeles, A. 1975. Becoming modern: Individual change in six developing countries. *Ethos* 3(2):323–342.

Inkeles, A., and Smith, D. 1974. *Becoming modern: Individual changes in six developing societies.* Cambridge: Harvard University Press.

Knudsen, E. I., Heckman, J. J., Cameron, J. L., and Shonkoff, J. P. 2006. Economic, neurobiological, and behavioral perspectives on building America's future workforce. *PNAS* (Proceedings of the National Academy of Sciences) 103(27):10155–10162.

Krueger, A., and Schkade, D. 2008. Sorting in the labor market: Do gregarious workers flock to interactive jobs? *The Journal of Human Resources* 43(4):859–883.

Kyllonen, P. C., Lipnevich, A. A., Burrus, J., and Roberts, R. D. 2008. *Personality, motivation, and college readiness: A prospectus for assessment and development.* Princeton: Educational Testing Service.

Levin, H. M. 1970. A new model of school effectiveness. In *Do teachers make a difference?* ed. Mood A. M. 55–78 Washington: Office of Education, U.S. Department of Health, Education and Welfare. http://eric.ed.gov/ERICWebPortal/search/detailmini.jsp?_nfpb=true&_&ERICExtSearch_SearchValue_0=ED04025. Accessed June 1, 2012.

Lindqvist, E., and Vestman, R. 2011. The labor market returns to cognitive and noncognitive ability: Evidence from the Swedish Enlistment. *American Economic Journal: Applied Economics* 3:101–128.

Magnuson, K. A., Ruhm, C., and Waldfogel, J. 2007. Does prekindergarten improve school preparation and performance? *Economics of Education Review* 26:33–51.

Mosteller, F. 1995. The Tennessee study of class size in the early school grades. *The Future of Children* 5(2):113–127.

Murnane, R., Willett, J., and Levy, F. 1995. The growing importance of cognitive skills in wage determination. *The Review of Economics and Statistics* 77(2):251–266.

Murnane, R., Willett, J., Bratz, M., Duhaldeborde, Y. 2001. Do different dimensions of male high school students' skills predict labor market success a decade later? evidence from the NLSY. *Economics of Education Review* 20:311–320.

Murnane, R., Willett, J., Duhaldeborde, Y., and Tyler, J. 2000. How important are the cognitive skills of teenagers in predicting subsequent earnings? *Journal of Policy Analysis and Management* 19(4):547–568.

National Research Council. 1984. *High schools and the changing workplace: The employers' view.* Report of the Panel on Secondary School Education for the changing workplace Washington, DC: National Academy Press.

Neuman, G. A., and Wright, J. 1999. Team effectiveness: Beyond skills and cognitive ability. *Journal of Applied Psychology* 84(3):376–389.

Noftle, E. E., and Robins, R. W. 2007. Personality predictors of academic outcomes: Big five correlates of GPA and SAT scores. *Journal of Personality and Social Psychology* 93(1):116–130.

Nores, M., and Barnett, W. S. 2010. Benefits of early childhood interventions across the world: (Under) Investing in the very young. *Economics of Education Review* 29:271–282.

Reynolds, A. J., Rolnick, A. J., Englund, M. M., and Temple, J. A. 2010. *Childhood programs and practices in the first decade of life.* New York: Cambridge University Press.

Rothstein, R., Jacobson, R., Wilder, T. 2008. *Grading education: Getting accountability right.* New York: Teachers College Press.

Sackett, P. R., Schmitt, N., Ellingson, J. E., and Kabin, M. B. 2001. High stakes testing in employment, credentialing, and higher education: Prospects in a post-affirmative action world. *American Psychologist* 56(4):302–318.

Sameroff, A. 2010. A unified theory of development: A dialectic integration of nature and nurture. *Child development* 81(1):6–22.

Schweinhart, L.J. 2010. The challenge of the highscope Perry preschool study. In *Childhood programs and practices in the first decade of life.,* eds. Reynolds, A. J., Rolnick, A. J., Englund, M. M., and Temple, J. A., 366–380. New York: Cambridge University Press.

Segal, C. 2008. Classroom behavior. *The Journal of Human Resources* 43(4):783–814.

Shury, J., Winterbotham, M., and Oldfield, K. 2010. *National employer skills survey for England 2009: Key findings report.* South Yorkshire: UK Commission for Employment & Skills.

ter Weel, B. 2008. Symposium on the noncognitive determinants of labor market and behavioral outcomes. *The Journal of Human Resources* 43(4).

Urzua, S. 2008. Racial labor market gaps: The role of abilities and schooling choices. *The Journal of Human Resources* 43(4):919–971.

Vignoles, A., De Coulon, A., and Marcenaro-Gutierrez, O 2011. The value of basic skills in the British labour market. *Oxford Economic Papers,* 63(1):27–48.

Zemsky, R., and Iannozzi, M. 1995. *A reality check: First finding from the EQW national employer survey (10).* Philadelphia: National Center on the Educational Quality of the Workforce, University of Pennsylvania. http://www.eric.ed.gov/PDFS/ED398385.pdf. Accessed June 1, 2012.

Chapter 6
The Contributions of International Large-Scale Studies in Civic Education and Engagement

Judith Torney-Purta and Jo-Ann Amadeo

International large-scale assessments (ILSAs) have the potential to make contributions at least at three levels. They can contribute at the macro level (to a general understanding of countries' educational goals), at the meso level (to the needs of education policy specialists and those such as journalists who communicate information about education to the public), and at the micro level (to improve processes of teaching and learning). Examining a range of these international studies and their interpretation at the beginning of the second decade of the twenty-first century suggests that these potential contributions to constructive change are not being fully realized. The enhancement of studies of civic education and engagement in the portfolio of ILSAs can play a unique positive role in this process. A short history of one of the organizations deeply involved in this area, the International Association for the Evaluation of Educational Achievement (IEA)—which launched its studies in civic education in the early 1970s during the Cold War, a time of broad disagreement on what constituted legitimate civic education—provides a context for these issues in general. It also provides a context for discussing education (and assessment) relating to civic engagement and citizenship in particular.

History of ILSAs and of IEA in Relation to Civic Education

A small group of scholars in the late 1950s envisioned an empirically based science of comparative education research. Some Europeans were interested in recently broadened access to upper secondary education; in the United States, competition

J. Torney-Purta (✉)
Department of Human Development and Quantitative Methodology,
University of Maryland, College Park, MD 20742, USA
e-mail: jtpurta@umd.edu

J.-A. Amadeo
Department of Psychology, Marymount University, Arlington, 22207 VA, USA
e-mail: jamadeo@marymount.edu

M. von Davier et al. (eds.), *The Role of International Large-Scale Assessments:*
Perspectives from Technology, Economy, and Educational Research,
DOI 10.1007/978-94-007-4629-9_6, © Springer Science+Business Media Dordrecht 2013

with the Soviet Union due to the launch of Sputnik had raised concern. Mathematics was chosen as the topic for the first IEA cross-national study because it was universally valued (Husen 1967).

In the late 1960s, IEA conducted surveys in six subject areas, including civic education. The *Nation at Risk* commission in the United States in the early 1980s requested one paper on the civic values learned in schools (Torney-Purta and Schwille 1986). Its full report, however, only used data from the IEA science and mathematics studies as it lamented the performance of students in the United States. Raising an alarm seemed to be the only role for international studies of achievement in debates on excellence (Torney-Purta 1987). This missed a potential contribution of international studies in identifying effective practices, the context of these practices, and the extent to which they might be adapted for use internationally (Torney-Purta 1990), a topic that is still a matter of debate (Luke 2011).

In the mid-1980s, the National Education Goal of making the United States first in the world in science and mathematics was announced, and IEA's leadership was asked to move quickly into international large-scale assessments of these two subjects. At about this time, a program officer at the National Academy of Sciences called together a small interdisciplinary group to discuss how to ensure that the planned studies were rigorous enough to be persuasive to policymakers. The Board on International Comparative Studies in Education's (BICSE) first report, *Framework and Principles for International Comparative Studies in Education* (Bradburn and Gilford 1990), called for international studies "addressing a range of content areas and grade levels" and "encompassing quantitative survey research studies as well as more intensive studies that use a range of qualitative methods" (p. 9–10).

BICSE encouraged attempts to unpackage the processes of science and math education in participating countries through video studies and case studies associated with the Trends in International Mathematics and Science Study (TIMSS). Thousands of hours of observations of mathematics classrooms and interviews with students, teachers, and parents took place in Germany, Japan, and the United States, often showing inconsistencies between intended curricula and observed educational practices (LeTendre 1998). Although these studies were consistent with IEA's original aims to understand processes of education, beginning in about 2002, trend studies in science and mathematics began to garner the major attention. This focus has been predicated on the belief of many economists and educational policymakers that high science and mathematics achievement is a major precondition for economic success.

The "hand-wringing response" by US journalists when TIMSS results are released is predictable. It used to be Japan that anchored the top spot; now it is often Finland. However, a few scholars are beginning to raise questions. Some argue that there are substantial groups of students in the US who show excellent performance, but pervasive inequity in schooling means that many other students have low performance (often related to lack of home or neighborhood educational resources as well). Recently some are arguing that what are variously called noncognitive attributes influenced by schooling (Levin, Chap. 5) or Twenty-first Century Competencies (National Research Council 2010) are products of schooling that are important to economic growth.

Perhaps the focus in the policy debate on testing in order to produce country rankings in science and mathematics has resulted in looking at a relatively easily measured but too narrowly defined domain. The old joke about the man who looked under the lamp post for his keys may be a relevant analogy. It was easier to see in the strong light, even though his keys were lost blocks away. Large-scale assessments in mathematics may be easier to design than assessments about engagement in one's studies (Brophy 2008; Marsh et al. 2000) and less expensive to administer than assessments of the ability to participate effectively with others in cooperative groups (Johnson and Johnson 2009). Attending to outcomes beyond cognitive achievement could be useful in predicting economic productivity and might also send a signal to school leaders that it is safe to move some attention to activities more motivating than test preparation (see a recent Rand Corporation report by Schwartz et al. 2011). In this context, what is the place of civic education studies, and what do they have to offer?

International Studies in Civic Education and Engagement

Knowledge of one's government and how it works, attitudes conducive to engagement in democracy and positive intergroup attitudes have been themes in research for several decades. Studies in the field known as political socialization research began in the 1960s when political scientists and psychologists began to study the ways in which young people become involved in the political systems and communities in which they live (reviewed by Jennings 2007). Within the last 15 years, increasing use of the term "civic engagement" recognizes the multiple ways citizens can participate in the civic sphere (Sherrod et al. 2010). The name for the construct changed because there were problems both with the term "political" (emphasizing partisan politics) and with "socialization" (emphasizing a top-down process). In international comparative research that includes a cognitive component, "civic education" is the term that has been used to describe many studies in this area, and more recently, "civics and citizenship education."

In general civic education studies conceptualize competent democratic citizenship as encompassing knowledge, skills, attitudes, values, and behaviors (current and expected). Responsible citizens have fundamental knowledge of democratic processes, an awareness of issues in their nations and communities, and an understanding of ways to obtain and analyze information. They also participate in their communities (including volunteer activity) and in organizations (at school and in their neighborhoods), possess basic civic-related skills (such as cooperation in groups and effective and respectful communication), are concerned for the rights of others (as well as themselves), and are predisposed to find democratic methods to bring about change.

Why and How the Civic Domain Is Important to ILSAs

There are a number of reasons that studies in the civic domain are valuable for inclusion in ILSAs. First and most obviously, studies of civic-related topics make a unique contribution to understanding young people's preparation to live in democracy and willingness to respect human rights (including their attitudes toward ethnic minorities and immigrants in their societies) and their willingness to vote and to participate in activities that further democratic processes (Coley and Sum 2012). It is no longer the case that only adults who are eligible to vote have extensive opportunities to participate in political and social action, however. Scholars' and citizens' interest in human rights has burgeoned over the last several decades in policy-related as well as education-related discourse (Ramirez et al. 2011) during the same period that studies of civic education have grown in importance. Daily headlines are reminders that political and civil rights are among the aspirations of young people as well as adults in many countries. The capacity to assess whether and how to be involved along with the motivation to fulfill roles as responsible and active citizens are usually acquired by the end of adolescence. Assessing the nature and quality of these capacities and motivations comparatively is an important contribution of ILSAs in civic education.

A second contribution of civic education studies is that outcomes broader than knowledge are conceptualized and measured, providing a more satisfying view of students and their learning than studies limited to cognitive outcomes. This is true of both the Civic Education Study (CIVED, conducted by IEA in 1999) and the International Civics and Citizenship Study (ICCS, conducted by IEA in 2009). Taking an even broader perspective, the DeSeCo project of the Organisation for Economic Co-operation and Development (OECD) formulated a wide-ranging set of competencies needed for a successful life (Rychen and Salganik 2001) with consultation from multiple disciplinary perspectives and involving scholars from several countries. Although these competencies were never instantiated in measures for a comparative study, the DeSeCo project together with IEA's experience in civic education show that students' outcomes broader than knowledge can be conceptualized and agreed upon.

Third, many of the competencies falling under the rubric of civic education are aspects of readiness for adapting to the workplace and participating in community life. These include the ability to decode and understand media presentation and experience in understanding and respecting individuals who have different ideas and perspectives. If one wished to raise a country's reputation in the world using arguments about the excellence of the workforce, achievement of these competencies would be an advantage. In other words reliable measures developed for international civic education studies cover a wide a variety of competencies (corresponding to many of those Levin identifies in this volume). Many of these competencies are valuable in the workplace and can make an independent contribution to economic growth.

For twenty years groups of scholars and policy advisors who have looked in depth at international comparative assessments (for example, the National Academy's BICSE Board) have been calling for a portfolio of international studies in different areas, defining a balanced range of competencies, and including studies of different types to look at ways of improving the educational process in a range of subject areas (Bradburn and Gilford 1990; Gilford 1993). Recently a workshop sponsored by the Board on Science Education at the Academy explored twenty-first century skills and called for further research and elaboration (National Research Council 2010). Studies in the civic domain have the potential to fill many of these needs.

A fourth contribution is the opportunity that studies in areas such as civic education provide to investigate the context in which learning takes place. This is especially true when analytic models that are able to investigate aspects of the social and cultural context are utilized. We will refer later to the process of unpacking of international findings, a concept used in cross-cultural psychology studies (Vaughn 2010). Analyses with a small grain size allow inferences about specific factors that might account for high (or low) performance, for scores with normal (or bimodal) distributions, or for strong (or weak) associations between variables. To put it in another way, what are the educational and developmental processes that lie behind different patterns of achievement? How does the national context (for example, historical political factors or current problems with government corruption) set parameters for these processes? To realize this contribution requires a period of time after the collection of data by IEA (or any comparable organization) to allow secondary analysis. This is the reason that most of the examples given in this chapter come from the CIVED study (testing in 1999), although we also consider a few ICCS results (testing in 2009). The fact that the United States did not participate in ICCS makes that study of somewhat less value for purposes of illustration, however.

To summarize, studies in the civic domain should remain a part of ILSAs (and even be strengthened) for the insights about global, national, economic, and community issues and the methodological innovations they can provide (especially in measuring attitudes and skills in large samples). The importance of studies such as these has been recognized by a number of groups (including the National Research Council) over a period of two decades. IEA's CIVED and ICCS projects have established a strong foundation on which to build.

IEA's Role in Civic Education

IEA has a history of work in civic education that extends over more than four decades. This entry in the *International Encyclopedia of Education* reflects on the atmosphere of the 1970s in IEA when this first civic education study was conducted:

> It is difficult to recapture today the concerns that surrounded this domain in the midst of the Cold War. What counted as legitimate civic education in one country was not what counted in countries with different ideologies. Measurement was daunting in the civic education domain, where attitudes were important as desired outcomes of civic education, and where model standards for measurement of knowledge were rare. In other words, this study was a bold move with risks both for the researchers and for IEA as an organization (Torney-Purta et al. 2010b, p. 656).

The first civic education study, including measures of content knowledge, attitudes (anti-authoritarian, trust in government, support for women's political rights) and participatory behavior (discussion of political issues) tested in 1971. The results from this survey of about 30,000 students were published in the six-subject series (Torney et al. 1975). The fact that endorsement of democratic values was high in what was then West Germany, 25 years after the end of World War II, or that students in the United States had relatively low scores on support for women's rights, received little public attention, however. Results showed that an open classroom climate for discussion was one of the central predictors of both civic knowledge and civic engagement. This was an early and successful attempt to connect classroom processes to students' outcomes in an ILSA. However, from the late 1970s until the mid 1980s, IEA did not repeat a study in civic education but began to focus on science and mathematics, and on reading literacy. A general classroom environment study was launched but did not attract as much attention as subject matter studies in these three areas (Anderson et al. 1989).

However, during this period, groups in the United States became interested in assessments of political socialization and civic education. During the late 1980s, the National Assessment of Educational Progress (NAEP) tested the civic knowledge of representative samples 4th, 8th, and 12th graders. Political scientists Niemi and Junn (1998) reanalyzed the 1988 NAEP data and suggested that current education was inadequate in this area. Similar discontent with the effectiveness of civic education and the level of youth participation was voiced in England and Australia during this time (reviewed in Arthur et al. 2008).

The most important event during this period was the fall of the Berlin Wall in 1989 and the collapse of Communism across Central and Eastern Europe. Questions about the extent to which the educational systems of these countries were prepared to teach young people about democracy and human rights were raised. Would it be possible to replace Marxism with democratic theory? Could teachers be asked to teach in a new way and cover material about political rights with which they had limited familiarity? What about young people who had been warned by their families never to state their views about social and political issues outside their homes?

In 1993 the General Assembly of IEA (its governing body) requested a proposal for a civic education study, with part of the impetus from Eastern European delegates who saw the relevance of the comparative methodology for studying how their next generation of citizens could be prepared for democracy. Declining levels of political interest and participation among young people motivated some delegates from Western Europe and the United States to support a civic education study. An innovation was a two-phased design in which the first phase of the study was a set of structured national case studies (a qualitative approach). The guidelines for the case studies recognized that conceptions of civic education could vary more across countries than in subjects like mathematics and science. Each participating country's team wrote a case study responsive to a list of general and specific questions about the nature of civic education in the country, reviewed by the international steering committee. Although the materials in the case studies were diverse, it was possible to identify domains that could be addressed across countries (Torney-Purta et al. 1999). There was considerable consistency across the case studies about the challenges that schools face (Schwille and Amadeo 2002).

Developing plans for social science studies by consensus among researchers from different countries is often difficult, as a survey of 26 projects by Torney-Purta (2008) has documented. At the first meeting of the CIVED National Research Coordinators in the Netherlands in 1994, considerable mistrust existed and a collaborative atmosphere had to be nurtured. All those in attendance voted on a list of topics that might be covered in a test and survey. There was enough agreement that the group agreed to go ahead (with IEA support). To assure that no one country's perspective was dominant, actual quotations from the case study documents of several countries were incorporated in test specifications covering the following domains and subdomains: "Democracy and its Defining Characteristics," "Institutions and Practices in Democracy," "Citizenship Rights and Duties" (including topics relating to human rights), "National Identity," "International Relations," and "Social Cohesion and Diversity."

The information collected during this early phase of the study contributed to the design of the instruments. Approximately 90,000 14-year-old students from 28 countries were administered tests of civic knowledge and skills and surveys of civic attitudes, activities, and anticipated actions in 1999. Findings were released in 2001 and reported in *Citizenship and Education in Twenty-eight Countries: Civic Knowledge and Engagement at Age Fourteen* (Torney-Purta et al. 2001; see also Baldi et al. 2001). Fourteen-year-olds in the United States performed well in many areas. Overall civic knowledge scores and scores on several attitude scales placed them in the group of countries with scores above the international mean.

In the following year, over 50,000 upper secondary school students from 16 countries received a similar test of civic knowledge and skills (and also economic literacy items not given to the 14-year-olds) and the same survey of civic attitudes and behaviors (Amadeo et al. 2002). Details about the scales can be found in Husfeldt et al. (2005) and Schulz and Sibberns (2004).

The theoretical framework of this IEA Civic Education Study (CIVED) conceptualized the ways in which "the everyday lives of young people in homes, with peers and at school serve as a 'nested' context for young people's thinking and action in the social and political world" (Torney-Purta et al. 2001, p. 20). This theoretical model has its roots in Bronfenbrenner's ecological theory (covered in Wilkenfeld et al. 2010) and Lave and Wenger's ideas about situated cognition (covered in Torney-Purta et al. 2010a). Recently, the idea of a developmental niche for emergent participatory citizenship has been employed (Torney-Purta and Amadeo 2011). In short, these models posit that adolescents' engagement in the community and the development of an identity within the group, together with classroom instruction and the everyday experience of a climate for open and respectful discussion of issues, facilitate learning about citizenship and democratic processes.

In 2009, IEA conducted the International Civics and Citizenship Study (ICCS). A more elaborated conceptual framework guided this test's development, including "Civic Society and Systems," "Civic Principles," "Civic Participation," and "Civic Identities." A larger pool of cognitive items was developed (many accompanied by introductory explanatory material) and matrix sampling was used. Data were collected in 38 countries, with the findings released in late 2010 (Schulz et al. 2010). Of the 17 countries that participated in both 1999 and 2009, only Slovenia showed a significant increase in civic knowledge (on a set of items developed in CIVED 1999 and reserved to test trends over time). An innovation in this study was the implementation of regional modules for Asia, Europe, and Latin America (Kerr et al. 2010).

In the period from 1990 to 2010, in summary, major steps were taken in IEA comparative studies, including those in civic education. At the same time it has become clear that science, mathematics, and literacy studies will continue to be repeated on a regular schedule. The preponderant method of presenting these results to the public and to educators is likely to remain rankings of countries, relying on the shock value of the relatively low position of countries like the United States to get attention for mathematics and science education. Civic education studies have not become part of official cycles and trend studies. In fact, these studies have enormous but unrecognized potential. The next two sections will illustrate specific contributions of studies in the civic education area by presenting some secondary analysis of material not included in the original reports (and therefore not well known internationally):

• Patterns in multiple aspects of student outcomes that include but go beyond knowledge
• Positive values and attitudes relating to democratic engagement
• Attitudes toward ethnic groups and immigrants
• Skills and attitudes important in the workplace

The emphasis will be on analyzing the data in order to unpack contexts and processes and on relating the findings to recently expressed interest in outcomes of education other than knowledge.

Studies of Civic Education as Opportunities to Study Multiple Aspects of Student Outcomes

Most of the reports of the comparative large-scale mathematics and science studies are devoted to cognitive achievement results. The civic education studies conducted under IEA auspices have had multiple outcome measures balanced between cognitive and noncognitive assessment items. In CIVED each student has a knowledge score based on 38 items. This knowledge score has strong psychometric properties across countries and was also designed to be decomposed into knowledge and skills items (Torney-Purta et al. 2001). Each student also answered a number of attitudinal items (formed into about 20 different scales with strong psychometric properties, ranging from support for different types of citizenship activities to attitudes toward women's political rights or trust in government).

Because of the diversity of civic education experiences across the world, we did not expect that any country would perform uniformly well on all aspects of the test (cognitive) and survey (attitudes). In fact, it turned out to be appropriate to rank countries' student performances only on total civic knowledge scores. The basic reports contain tables of the attitudinal scores with the countries in alphabetical order (Torney-Purta et al. 2001; Amadeo et al. 2002). No country or region appears to be superior on all potentially valuable aspects of civic engagement and citizenship. The ICCS findings are similar, and not markedly different on a regional basis from the findings of CIVED 10 years earlier (Schulz et al. 2010). The multidimensionality of the civic instruments means that there are many possibilities for secondary analysis. The next sections present three examples.

Cognitive Diagnostic Models of Conceptual Knowledge and Skills

To illustrate the power of conceptualizing educational outcomes in a multidimensional way, three types of analysis conducted with CIVED data will be described. The first example uses the cognitive test data to look at civic-related cognitive capacities in a single nation at a smaller grain size than the original reports. Zhang et al. (2012) took a model-based cognitive diagnosis approach to analyze IEA CIVED test items administered to US students. A distinction was made in CIVED between conceptual or content knowledge (for example, asking what is usually contained in a country's constitution)[1] and skills items (for example, asking a student to interpret a political cartoon or to distinguish between a fact and an opinion). We decomposed targeted cognitive components into a still smaller grain size and analyzed four multidimensional components through an advanced psychometric mode called cognitive diagnostic modeling (CDM). This approach allows researchers to test hypotheses about the nature of students' response processes when they answer assessment items. By using CDM, one can classify students into different profile groups based on their item responses. Cognitive diagnostic models have been used in the past in secondary analysis of data from large-scale assessments such as TIMSS, PIRLS, and NAEP to obtain information about students' cognitive capacities (Chiu and Seo 2009; Tatsuoka et al. 2004; von Davier 2007; Xin et al. 2004; Xu and von Davier 2008).

The IEA CIVED data had not previously been analyzed to identify the abilities underlying students' performance using the cognitive diagnosis approach. Matrix sampling was not used in CIVED, and each respondent answered all 38 test questions, making this analysis somewhat less complex than in ILSAs where test-lets and matrix sampling are used (Rutkowski et al. 2010). Four cognitive attributes describing the content and process skills underlying the CIVED test items were identified (Zhang et al. 2012): basic conceptual knowledge, advanced conceptual

---

[1] No questions specific to any given country's political structure were included in the international test.

knowledge, media-based skills, and advanced interpretive skills. Based on mastery of each attribute, students were classified into four different cognitive profiles. Examining these cognitive profiles suggests that basic conceptual knowledge is prerequisite for more advanced conceptual knowledge. It appears that in the United States a substantial group of students acquires civic skills without having basic conceptual knowledge and some acquire these skills outside of school.

Then, using multilevel analysis contextual factors such as characteristics of civic education experience were linked to the specific cognitive profiles. Results showed that students' possession of particular civic-related attributes are associated with their socioeconomic backgrounds, experience with an open discussion climate, and with conceptually based traditional teaching.

Zhang and Torney-Purta (2010) extended the model-based cognitive diagnosis approach to CIVED data from Australia and Hong Kong. The four cognitive attributes identified through the analysis described above were consistent across the three countries. However, Hong Kong students were strong in basic conceptual knowledge but weak in analyzing and synthesizing skills. A considerable proportion of US students were strong in analyzing and synthesizing skills and deficient in conceptual knowledge. In general evidence from the analyses supported the hypothesis that basic conceptual knowledge of civic topics is prerequisite for more advanced conceptual knowledge but to a lesser extent for skills. This secondary analysis looking at the data in a relatively small grain size shows the value of cognitive modeling as a technique for understanding different aspects of performance on a test of cognitive civic knowledge and skills within and across nations.

Examining Countries' Positions on Multiple Dimensions of Attitudes

Another illustration of the value of comparisons of multiple dimensions that are possible in studies in the civic domain is shown in Table 6.1, which contains about a dozen countries' means on three attitudinal scales from CIVED. The first column contains means on support for the norms of conventional citizenship (e.g., voting), and in the second column on support for the norms of social movement citizenship (e.g., joining a human rights or volunteer organization). Finland, which is always strong in achievement test scores (well above the mean in international civic knowledge, for example), has an unaccustomed place at the bottom of the country rankings for two measures of attitudes toward civic engagement. This discrepancy between achievement and attitudes scores suggests that placing extensive emphasis on countries whose students excel in cognitive achievement can distort policy debates (as Takayama 2010, has suggested in the case of Japan).

Results on attitudes toward ethnic and minority groups are found in the third column of Table 6.1. The post-Communist countries, plus Germany and Italy, are toward the bottom, with the Nordic and Anglo-Saxon countries at or above the mean. Note that no country is substantially above the international mean on all three

Table 6.1 Twelve countries' means on three attitudinal measures. (Sources: Torney-Purta et al. (2001) and Husfeldt et al. (2005))

Mean	Support for norms of conventional citizenship	Support for norms of social-movement citizenship	Support for rights of ethnic groups
10.5–10.8		Portugal	US, England, Portugal
10.1–10.4	US, Italy, Portugal	US, Italy, Norway	Finland, Norway, Sweden
10.0	Latvia		Australia
9.6–9.9	Germany	Germany, Sweden, Czech Rep.	Czech Rep., Estonia, Italy
9.2–9.5	Australia, Sweden, England, Norway, Estonia, Czech	Latvia, Australia, England, Estonia	Latvia, Germany
8.8–9.1	Finland	Finland	

scales in Table 6.1 (though Portugal and the United States rank fairly high). Positive scores on these attitude scales are also associated with aspects of schooling outside the content of the formal curriculum, for example, positive contacts between immigrants and non-immigrants in the school setting and opportunities in the classroom to discuss issues on which individuals have different points of view (Torney-Purta et al. 2008).

Country means on these attitude scales from the study of upper secondary students in a smaller number of countries (Amadeo et al. 2002) show almost identical results. Furthermore, in the 2009 ICCS study, Finland once again scored significantly below the international average on both the norms of conventional citizenship and on social movement-related citizenship scales (Schulz et al. 2010).

The guidelines developed by the CIVED national representatives and other advisory groups in this subject area have always distinguished between different types of participation (here the more and the less conventionally political). Furthermore, young people's attitudes toward immigrant groups and ethnic groups have been of nearly as much interest as cognitive outcomes in many countries. This is especially true because the testing of school-based samples allows the analysis of factors associated with positive or negative attitudes (for example, the proportion of immigrant students in the school or the extent to which intergroup relations or community issues are seen as an appropriate topic for discussion). In short, the ability to analyze non-cognitive dimensions (including attitudes) has been especially important to educators who teach in increasingly diverse communities and in policy debates on how to prepare young people who will seek employment in increasingly diverse work settings.

Person-Centered Approaches to Understanding Patterns of Civic Attitudes

A second approach used in the CIVED analysis with potential for dealing with multiple dimensions is the person-centered approach to analysis. This contrasts with the variables-centered approach. Person-centered analysis has a relatively long history in developmental psychology, especially exemplified in the work of Swedish psychologists (Bergman et al. 2003; Mahoney et al. 2001). Person-centered analysis (in this case K-mean cluster analysis) is especially useful for large-scale studies where there are multidimensional outcomes. Instead of looking at mean differences on variables, in this approach one looks for clusters or groups of persons who have similar patterns or profiles of attitudes.

In this CIVED analysis about 30,000 students in ten countries were clustered using their responses on 12 attitudinal scales. One cluster analysis included the United States, Australia, and three Western Europe countries; the other analysis included five countries in Eastern Europe.[2] For details of the analysis and the results see Torney-Purta (2009) and Torney-Purta and Barber (2011). The purpose was to identify distinct clusters of individuals who differed in systematic ways in their civic and social attitudes. To decide the cluster names we looked at the pattern of means on the 12 attitudinal scales of each cluster group in comparison to those of other cluster groups. We also have suggested a label for each cluster in the form of a "motto" that expresses the particular characteristics of each profile of attitudes. This makes it easier for a general audience to interpret than designations of proficiency levels, especially when the method used to set the proficiency cut-points is often not transparent and sometimes arbitrary. This labeling of clusters can represent the results of sophisticated analysis of attitudinal data and produces a presentation that can be understood by audiences with little statistical expertise. Below is a description of the five clusters extracted in these ten countries and then the distributions of cluster membership by country.

Adolescents who are found in the *Social Justice* cluster in these ten countries endorse immigrants' rights, the rights of minority/ethnic groups, and women's rights (average of about one standard deviation above the mean). Students in this cluster have relatively low scores on scales measuring belief in the importance of citizens participating in action, either in the conventional political domain or through social action in communities or nongovernmental organizations, however. For the *Social Justice* cluster, the motto is, "I believe in rights for everyone but do not feel obligated to do much about it."

Adolescents in the *Conventionally Oriented* cluster in these countries show high levels of trust in governmental institutions and are patriotic (both in the sense of having positive national feelings and protectionist attitudes toward their nation). Adolescents in this cluster have high levels of political self-efficacy and believe that adults should be active in socially oriented activities (e.g., volunteering to help the community or joining human rights organizations) as well as in conventional political activities such as voting. In Australia, the United States, and the three Western Europe countries, members of this cluster also have relatively high social justice attitudes. In describing this cluster for these countries (but not for the Eastern European countries), it is appropriate to use the term *Conventional/Inclusive*. For the

---

[2] Australia, England, Finland, Sweden, United States, Bulgaria, Czech Republic, Estonia, Hungary, Latvia.

Conventional cluster across the ten countries an appropriate motto is, "I believe in my country and will support the status quo with political and civic actions that are expected of me."

The *Indifferent* cluster in both regions contains individuals who have attitudes very close to the mean on the large majority of the attitudinal scales. Adolescents in the *Indifferent* cluster are willing to do the minimum as citizens. They are inclined to obey the law and may vote, but there are many nonpolitical activities that interest them more. In the Nordic countries, they may correspond in some respect to the "stand-by citizens" identified by Amnå and Zetterberg (2010). The *Disaffected* cluster is similar to the *Indifferent* cluster but with more negative beliefs about norms of citizenship related to both conventional political activities and involvement in the community. The *Indifferent* and the *Disaffected* clusters can be described by the same motto: "I have better things to do with my time than be active in politics, but I won't do anything rash."

The fifth cluster in these ten countries shows an *Alienated* profile including negative attitudes almost uniformly across the scales. For this cluster group, scores on trust in government averaged between one and two standard deviations below the international mean. Their attitudes toward rights of immigrants, minorities, and women were also extremely negative when compared with those of students in the other clusters.

The proportion of students in this *Alienated* cluster who think it is "not important for citizens to obey the law" ranges from more than 30 % in Australia and the United States, to 23 % in Sweden, 16 % in Finland and 10 % in England. This compares with between 1 and 3 % of students in the *Social Justice, Conventional* and *Indifferent* clusters who do not believe in obeying the law. Willingness to protest by actions such as occupying buildings or blocking traffic were common only among the *Alienated* cluster, not among those supporting social justice, for example. The motto for the *Alienated* cluster is, "I'm angry about the immigrants and minority groups in my country, and I don't trust the government. I have the right to do what I want." The remainder of this section will devote attention to clusters of students in Australia, the United States, and the three Western European countries, with special attention to the alienated group of students.

This clustering suggested that in 1999 there was already a significant amount of anti-immigrant feeling and xenophobia among adolescents in Australia, the United States, and several European countries and that this group seemed willing to act on these attitudes in ways that may be against the law. This age cohort turned 26 years old in 2011. These findings shed some light on recent increases in the strength of anti-immigrant feeling among adults in these countries (Vertovec and Wessendorf 2010) and on recent instances of violent action against immigrants or those perceived to support immigrants' rights.

Civic knowledge scores are highest among the *Social Justice* and *Conventional* clusters (Table 6.2). In the United States and Australia, *Indifferent* students have civic knowledge scores that are quite similar to *Conventional* cluster group members. In England, Finland and Sweden the *Indifferent* students have lower average

Table 6.2 Average total civic knowledge score in each cluster (by country)

	Australia	England	Finland	Sweden	United States
Social justice	108.94 (1.25)	105.31 (1.00)	116.19 (1.13)	105.25 (1.14)	112.47 (1.48)
Conventional	106.06 (1.66)	105.55 (1.87)	116.57 (1.21)	104.74 (1.05)	109.09 (1.35)
Indifferent	103.05 (1.02)	99.58 (1.11)	109.32 (0.91)	96.35 (1.14)	107.08 (1.92)
Disaffected	98.94 (0.93)	95.64 (0.91)	105.64 (0.86)	95.74 (1.11)	103.28 (1.43)
Alienated	90.23 (1.70)	92.33 (1.27)	99.58 (1.29)	90.47 (1.77)	94.54 (1.95)

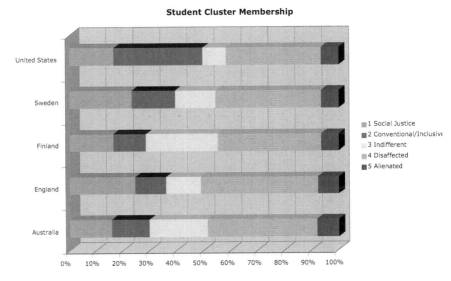

Fig. 6.1 Distributions of cluster membership in five countries

knowledge scores than the *Conventional* students. In all countries the students in the *Alienated* cluster have the lowest knowledge scores.

Distributions of the clusters in the CIVED data across the Western European countries (Fig. 6.1) shows that the most prevalent pattern is *Disaffected*, while about 7 % of the students are *Alienated*. In the United States there are approximately equal numbers of students in the *Conventional/Inclusive* and the *Disaffected* group, while about 7 % are *Alienated*. A study 20 years ago of attitudinal clusters among adults in the United States also found substantial proportions in categories such as Disaffected, Bystanders, and Followers (Ornstein et al. 1988).

The second most prevalent cluster among English and Swedish students (after *Disaffected*) is about a quarter of the students in the *Social Justice* group. Remember, however, that these students are not particularly interested in taking action in support of rights and justice. In Australia and Finland, in comparison, *Disaffected* and *Indifferent* students are frequent. Across all five countries focused on here, about 7–8 % of the students show the alienated pattern of negative attitudes toward immigrant and ethnic groups and also low trust in government institutions. The country patterns of clusters within the post-Communist countries show *Disaffected* and *Indifferent* students are a majority. The proportion of student in the *Alienated* cluster ranges from 7 % in the Czech Republic to 20 % in Bulgaria.

To summarize this secondary analysis of CIVED, there are many students who are positively disposed toward social justice (nearly half in the United States and more than 30 % in England and Sweden in the social justice or conventional/inclusive clusters). It is sobering to note, however, how few students seem motivated by positive social justice attitudes to join relevant organizations or participate in non-violent protests. Furthermore, in *all* ten of these countries substantial proportions of the adolescents surveyed are indifferent, disaffected, or alienated. The alienated group is a small but worrisome minority in both new and old democracies.

The school appears to have a role in reducing the likelihood of belonging to the cluster characterized by anti-immigrant attitudes and lack of trust in institutions (the Alienated Cluster). The IEA CIVED Study contained two school-based measures of the climate in school, one focused on adolescents' sense that they can have an effect in the school setting (Confidence in the Value of School Participation) and the other measuring adolescents' sense that their classrooms are places where respectful discussion of different opinions takes place (Openness of Classroom Climate for Discussion). Those adolescents who report that their school climate and classroom climate are positive are less likely to belong to the *Alienated* cluster. These results (from a logistic regression) are parallel in the two regions (Torney-Purta 2009 and Torney-Purta and Barber 2011).

In summary, after extensive variable-oriented analysis of the CIVED data (modeled on the ILSAs in other subject areas) this exploratory analysis attempted to identify groups of adolescents sharing similar attitudes and provided several insights. Adopting a cluster-based analytic strategy has theoretical roots and also a practical advantage for presentations to nonacademic audiences. Identifying profiles that characterize individuals within and across countries aids in interpreting the information gained from cross-national summary statistics. When it is possible to see a cluster of individual adolescents who remind them of young people they know, adults are much more likely to understand the strengths and weaknesses found in patterns of civic engagement than when they are told only about averages and statistical trends. Particularly when there is a problematic group, such as the alienated adolescents, it is important for educators and policymakers to know the extent of its membership and nature of their views.

Cluster analysis could be conducted with rating scales in ILSAs other than CIVED. Using the ICCS data from 2009, it would be informative to cluster individuals according to their responses on the items dealing with national identity, identity within Europe, and global identity. How many students identify with none of these groups, for example? Or how many are strongly nationalistic and lack a sense of membership in other levels of the system? This would be more informative for policymakers than reporting that the mean score on a national identity item is higher than on a European identity item (Kerr et al. 2010). Likewise, the clustering approach could be helpful in suggesting how young people relate to their communities and to associational groups within and outside of school. This could be more informative than comparing average rates of participation (Schulz et al. 2010). Finally, if psychometrically strong scales on classroom environment were included in all large-scale comparative studies it would be possible to cluster these perceptions of learning environments across subject areas (as Tapola and Niemivirta 2008, have done in their study of Finnish students).

In summary, person-centered analysis of data from civic engagement studies has the potential to provide researchers, educators, and policymakers with a wide range of information on students' knowledge, attitudes, and actions. Cognitive diagnostic modeling enables us to better understand profiles of students' learning in the cognitive domain of civic education with implications for classroom practice. Cognitive diagnostic modeling was facilitated in CIVED because every student answered all the items. The cluster analysis was facilitated because of the range of reliably scaled attitudinal items included in the CIVED instrument. This person-centric cluster analyses along multiple dimensions allowed us to examine trends and patterns both within and across several countries.

Studies in Civic Engagement as Opportunities to Study Contexts

International studies contribute to a variety of discourses and at a variety of levels. For example, studies producing country rankings in mathematics and science have contributed to debates about entire countries and their potential economic competitiveness as the next generation comes of age. Citing poor student performance on international tests is often a way to stimulate interest in educational reform. The results of international comparative studies can contribute much more than this, however. Studies in civic education provide evidence of this.

National and School Level Contexts in Relation to Civic Knowledge and Attitudes

What does it mean to unpack international comparative results at different levels (vom Hau 2009)? What characteristics of countries and their macro level policies are related to their strong or weak performances? Our first insights about the possibilities of looking at specific aspects of national context came when examining CIVED item responses from Chile, Colombia, Portugal and the United States for a report to the Organization of American States (Torney-Purta and Amadeo 2004). These countries showed strong support for several aspects of citizens' action. However, in addition to attitudinal scales, the CIVED survey included a number of questions such as the following: "Is it good or bad for democracy when citizens have the right to elect leaders freely" or "when everyone has the right to express opinions?"

There was little variation across the 28 countries in agreement with these positive statements. More interesting were the responses to more contentious statements like these: "Is it good or bad for democracy when courts and judges are influenced by politicians" or "when wealthy business people have more influence on the government than others?" Students in Chile (and to some extent in Portugal) were less likely than those in other countries to see these conditions as bad for democracy (Torney-Purta and Amadeo 2004). This raised the possibility that experiencing a dictatorship in the country's recent past might be associated with young people being less alert to possible threats to democracy, or that some of the problematic characteristics of such governments are difficult to eradicate even after a democracy is established.

Once we began using HLM (Hierarchical Linear Modeling), a new set of possibilities opened for analyzing characteristics of countries in relation to young people's responses contained in the CIVED dataset. This type of secondary analysis would be appropriate for ICCS and other ILSAs as well. Analytic methods such as hierarchical linear modeling analysis are well designed for IEA data because of the nested nature of the sample (students sampled within schools). These methods are especially useful for looking at how countries' contexts and practices influence achievement or attitudes. Torney-Purta et al. (2008) examined knowledge, support, and practice of human rights among adolescents in relation to national policies and conditions. As the previous section indicated, the CIVED study has data from 14 year olds drawn from nationally representative samples of schools. We collected several pieces of information from other databases about citizenship and human rights policies at the country level: first, the extent to which the country referred to human rights in its international discourse on education (Suarez and Ramirez 2007) and second, its ratings by the Freedom House (a New York-based organization that serves as an independent watchdog on issues of human rights) indicating support for civil rights. These were available in 27 of the 28 countries (not Hong Kong).

The outcome variables at the student level included responses on two CIVED knowledge items that dealt explicitly with international human rights and on 36 other items dealing with other civic topics. We also used scores for each student on support for the norms of social movement-related citizenship and positive attitudes toward immigrants' rights. In addition we had information from students about their home literacy resources, about the extent to which the classroom climate was open for respectful discussion of different opinions, whether the student believed that student participation made a difference in school, how often the teacher discussed international issues, and how often the student read international news (this could include online reading, though that was not frequent in 1999) (Amadeo 2007).

We looked at two analyses, one of knowledge (two items) and one of attitudes (three scales). These were carefully controlled HLM analyses (Torney-Purta et al. 2008). Here we present results for one knowledge item and two attitude scales, first looking at the country level. For knowledge, students who were more likely to correctly answer the question about the U.N. Declaration on the Rights of the Child than one would predict on the basis of their overall civic knowledge were especially likely to come from countries where the government frequently referred to human rights in intergovernmental discourse (Suarez and Ramirez's count of mentions of human rights in governments' submission to the International Bureau of Education published in 2007). We also looked at individual level predictors and found that those who correctly answered the children's rights question were more likely to read international news and more likely to have experience with student democracy at school.

For attitudes we found that accurate knowledge demonstrated in answering the item about the Declaration of the Rights of the Child was a positive predictor of both positive attitudes toward immigrants' rights and of the belief that citizens *should* be active in social movement organizations (such as environmental or human rights groups). Reading the international news, confidence in student democratic participation at school, and an open climate for discussion in the classroom were also positively related to immigrant rights attitudes and social movement support at the individual level. Home literacy resources were not significantly related to either attitude scale. We did not find country-level policy effects on these two attitude scales.

This analysis is a first step in unpacking aspects of the country and school level contexts, in particular what it means for a country to have a favorable climate for teaching about human rights and what it means for a school to give students an everyday experience of democracy, embodied in an open climate for classroom discussion and opportunities for students to form groups to take action on school problems.

Similar analysis of CIVED data has been undertaken of support for immigrants' rights with country level predictors such as policies regarding how many years an immigrant must wait before applying for citizenship. Intergroup attitudes are an especially important area for analysis in depth because, as the previous section showed, there are substantial proportions of young people characterized by a pattern of negative attitudes. Further, the sense of national identity seems to be based on exclusion of ethnic groups or immigrants for many young people. Finally, there is evidence from the ICCS testing in 2009 that few teachers think that anti-racism education is part of their responsibility (Schulz et al. 2010). In short, there are a number of opportunities for investigating the relation of characteristics of national context to students' attitudes (see also Amnå 2011).

Classroom and School Contexts in Relation to Civic and Workplace Competencies

Another aim of CIVED secondary analysis has been to unpack the meaning of specific factors within the school context, in particular the climate for respectful discussion in the classroom (see also Hess 2009). Beginning with the first civic education study in the 1970s and continuing with the basic reports from CIVED and from ICCS, open classroom climate for discussion has been a powerful predictor of both knowledge and participation outcomes. For example, across countries, Barber and Torney-Purta

(2009) showed the extent to which having an open classroom climate for discussion was especially effective in promoting male students' support for women's rights. Few of the other ILSAs have such a thread of common findings about aspects of classroom processes extending across several decades. Trzesniewski et al. (2011) argue in their book about secondary analysis for psychologists that constructs such as these are especially fruitful areas for study.

Another part of recent secondary analysis of CIVED has attempted to understand students' preparation for the workplace as well as for citizenship. In the United States, this area has recently been called twenty-first century competencies (or non-cognitive skills) and includes outcomes such as the ability to understand communications in a variety of media (media literacy), ability to understand the economic system and global issues, skill in cooperating with diverse others, and innovative problem solving. These outcomes fit well into the general theme identified in a recent National Research Council Workshop (2010), which enumerated complex problem solving, self-management, and systems thinking as part of twenty-first century skills.

Educators have expressed concern that it will be several years before tests can be developed to assess these competencies internationally. But we realized that the CIVED instruments administered to students already included many of these outcomes. Beginning in 2008 we looked within the US dataset (and later within other countries) to see what aspects of social studies, history and civics classrooms were associated with the achievement of several twenty-first century workplace competencies.

First, we focused on two dimensions of the students' perceptions of educational activities within their classrooms. One was the extent to which there was an open and respectful climate for class discussions, measured by a five-item scale including items such as: "the teacher encourages us to discuss issues about which there are different opinions." A parallel scale, with four items, assessed the extent to which students' classrooms were characterized by traditional teaching activities such as lectures and textbook use.

Four groups of students were identified. The group above the median on both the open class climate scale and the traditional teaching scale was called the *Both* group; the group below the median on the open class climate and the traditional teaching scale was called the *Neither* group. The group above the median on open classroom climate but below the median on the traditional teaching scale was called the *Interactive* group. The group above the median on the traditional teaching scale but below the median on the open classroom climate scale was called the *Lecture* group. In the United States although the *Neither* and *Both* groups were large (700–850), there were also substantial numbers of students found in the *Interactive* and *Lecture* groups (400–550).

Comparing these four education groups on mean levels of workplace competencies is another way to unpack the CIVED findings. Details of the analysis are in Torney-Purta and Wilkenfeld (2009), and Table 6.3 summarizes these findings. There are significant differences between the four educational groups on media literacy skills, with the interactive group the highest and the group who reported receiving

Table 6.3 Twenty-first century competencies: summary of students' scores based on type of civic education instruction

Traditional teaching in civic education classes	Open classroom climate in civic education classes	
	Low	High
High	*Lecture group is higher* than Neither and *lower* than Both or Interactive on all 12 competencies	*Both group is highest* on follows the news; learned to understand others, to cooperate, to have global concern; believes that good citizen works hard, obeys the laws, votes, attends to media; *equal to Interactive* on ethnic attitudes and efficacy
Low	*Neither group is lowest* on all 12 competencies	*Interactive group is highest* on economic knowledge, media literacy skills; *equal to Both* on ethnic attitudes and efficacy

Notes: The designations of Neither, Interactive, Lecture, and Both correspond to the four groups identified in this section. Summary of results in Torney-Purta and Wilkenfeld (2009) based on an analysis of 2,542 US ninth graders tested in the IEA Civic Education Study

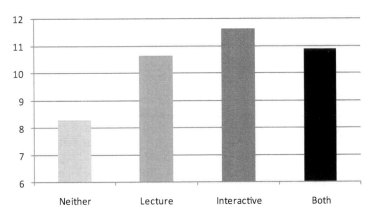

Fig. 6.2 Media literacy skills by educational experience

neither interactive nor traditional education the lowest (Fig. 6.2). A similar pattern appears for economic knowledge (not shown). For positive attitudes toward ethnic groups, the *Interactive* group and the *Both* group are the highest (and not significantly different from each other). A similar pattern appears for a self-efficacy scale (not shown). In summary, for skills and intergroup attitudes, the interactive experience of an open classroom climate for discussion appears to be vital either by itself or in combination with traditional teaching.

CIVED also has measures of the kinds of experience students report in learning to understand others who hold different opinions and in cooperative groups. In this set of outcomes we observe a "stair step" pattern. The group with both interactive and traditional experience is the highest, the interactive group the second highest, followed by the lecture and the neither groups. A similar pattern characterized the

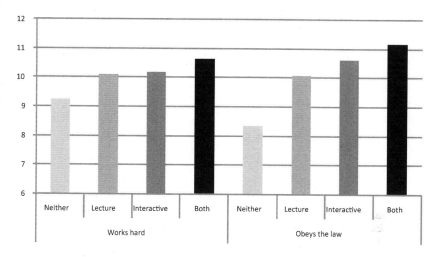

Fig. 6.3 Norms of responsibility: mean scores by educational experience

students' endorsement of responsibility, for example, willingness to obey the law and work hard (Fig. 6.3).

It was striking that the interactive and lecture-based experiences were compatible and together led to the achievement of both civic and workplace competencies. On none of the measures was the group that only experienced Lectures (and other traditional activities) superior to the *Interactive* or to the *Both* group. In all of the comparisons, the group with *Neither* kind of experience had the poorest outcomes.

A civic educator who was designing programs for post-Communist countries asked whether the same results could be expected in those contexts. Using the CIVED data from Estonia, Latvia, and the Russian Federation, the same four groups were formed (within each country) based on their perceptions of whether their classrooms had a positive classroom climate for discussion (above the median) or a low climate for discussion (Torney-Purta and Wilkenfeld 2009, 2010). Also these groups were divided according to whether they were above or below the median in reporting that traditional teaching (lecture, textbook use) was characteristic of their classrooms. The results in these post-Communist countries were almost identical to those in the United States (previously shown in Table 6.3 and Figs. 6.2 and 6.3). Again the group that had only the traditional/lecture-based experience was not superior to the *Both* or *Interactive* group on any of the outcomes examined. In other words, interactive classroom climate seems to be effective for civic and workplace outcomes both in the United States and in newer democracies. The group receiving neither type of civic education always had the lowest scores.

There is increasing interest in research about students' perceptions of the learning conditions and climates of their classrooms. In a study of six countries (four of which overlap with those in the IEA studies), Gorard and Smith (2010) arrive at much the same conclusions as the CIVED study (Torney-Purta et al. 2001; Amadeo et al. 2002) and ICCS (Schulz et al. 2010). For example, students surveyed and interviewed by Gorard and Smith in Italy and England were more likely than those in Belgium (French) to perceive that teachers encouraged them to make up their own mind and respected their opinions even if they disagreed. Students in the Czech Republic were least likely to hold this point of view. Gorard and his colleagues looked broadly at the practice of equity in the classroom. They wanted to know how students themselves experienced injustice, for example, whether they ever felt humiliated by a teacher, whether they felt that less able students or students who put forth less effort deserved extra help. According to these authors, equity can be addressed convincingly only if student perceptions as well as actual socioeconomic gaps are taken into account. The IEA data in civic education include items that would allow this issue to be more fully addressed in secondary analysis.

Both the IEA studies in the civic education area and research conducted outside of IEA suggest that strong scales measuring students' perceptions of classroom climate and instructional processes ought to be part of ILSAs across subject areas. There is a growing consensus that documenting social gradients of achievement and proposing generalized solutions (such as requiring more qualified teachers to teach in schools with poor students) are unlikely to be successful unless the perspectives of the students about quality and equity in their education are also taken into account.

Conclusions

Should civic and citizenship subjects be included in the cycle of comparative studies? We answer an emphatic yes for several reasons. Because both cognitive and noncognitive variables are assessed, civic education ILSAs can contribute to an in-depth understanding of young people's current civic knowledge, attitudes, and activities as well as their expectations for the future. Stated another way, civic and citizenship studies go beyond country rankings of achievement scores and examine citizenship from multiple dimensions and viewpoints, providing information that is important to strengthening democracies and national economies. Further, studies in civic education and engagement can provide balance to the predominantly negative view of adolescents in the United States (and elsewhere). For example, in CIVED in 1999, US students performed well on the test of civic knowledge and civic skills. In the person-oriented cluster analysis, the distribution of US students showed a high proportion of students in the Conventional/Inclusive Citizen cluster. These findings counter the view that all adolescents are apathetic, disengaged, and unreliable—negative portrayals of adolescents that can become self-fulfilling prophecies. That is an important lesson for adults (parents, teachers, and politicians), who may underestimate what most young people are capable of as citizens and members of their communities.

Advocacy for a cycle of studies in civic education (or as part of a broader study including noncognitive outcomes in general) and widespread participation in these studies would help to track the extent to which students continue to understand

and support democratic principles and practices in times of global change and uncertainty.

Also, there is some evidence that the often discussed (and also sometimes criticized) *twenty-first century competencies* believed to be necessary in the workforce bear considerable similarity to civic knowledge, attitudes, and skills (an argument supported by analysis in Torney-Purta and Wilkenfeld 2009). Measuring these competencies will help educators and employers know where to focus teaching and teachers' professional development. We cannot expect young people to use effective workforce strategies and skills if we do not help them learn to do so.

More broadly, if democracies are to survive and thrive, all citizens need to reach a minimum threshold of knowledge and participation in each succeeding generation. Everyone, of course, also needs basic literacy and numeracy; math and science knowledge is essential in everyday life. But relatively few young people go on to mathematics- or science-related careers. Decisions to specialize in these subjects are based on a variety of factors that include but are not limited to cognitive achievement. Some longitudinal studies in the United States in fact show the importance of attitudes developed in the early years of college rather than in high school in solidifying the choice of mathematically related careers (Musu-Gillette 2010). Efforts to prepare citizens begin in middle childhood, should involve every young person, and can be tested reliably by age 14.

In addition, researchers in the civic and citizenship area have been innovative in their modes of testing and have been early adopters of new methodologies of analysis (especially HLM). This area of inquiry (and also the way the measures were designed) is especially well suited to studying the effects of national contexts and also the effects of classroom or school contexts. These studies have a record of contributing to thoughtful unpacking of context issues, for example, the value of participation in civil deliberative discussion. The civic-related studies have provided empirical evidence about controversial but important topics such as attitudes toward equality for women and immigrants.

To give one example relating to the study of contexts, although the World Values Survey and the European Social Survey of adults each deal with attitudes toward immigrants and immigration, these data collections are based on limited sets of questions and do not assess the everyday contexts in which attitudes are acquired and expressed in behavior. Using nationally representative samples of schools, it is feasible to investigate the contexts in which adolescents' attitudes about immigrants' rights and civic engagement develop. Imagine the situation if we believed that attitudes toward immigrants were only acquired after the age of 20. In order to examine the context in which these attitudes developed, we would need representative samples of places of work as well as college and universities. Because we know that these attitudes have roots in adolescence, having nationally representative samples of schools (as international comparative studies do) provides a feasible way to study the process.

Ensuring that civic-related studies appear in the cycle of ILSAs at approximately 10-year intervals (either on their own or as part of studies of noncognitive factors) is necessary but not sufficient to capitalize on the strengths of these studies. Greater reflection is also needed, about how we collaborate most effectively to address country differences and policy-related issues, about how we bring the next generation of researchers into the process, about how to look simultaneously at national and international perspectives, and about how to incorporate new methodologies and constructs. This would mean maintaining an innovative edge in the system of international studies by reestablishing a committee, perhaps with foundation support and certainly with interdisciplinary membership and individuals from other nations as well as the United States.

This committee might resemble the Board on International and Comparative Studies in Education (BICSE). Oversight is not needed now (as was BICSE's role two decades ago). What is needed is a group of scholars and policymakers charged with reflecting on the potential for secondary analysis and innovative measurement of ILSAs of different types and in different subject areas. These studies need to become less expensive to conduct. Better ways to present their results to policy-oriented audiences and journalists (as well as those who are more academically oriented) need to be developed. Suggestions made earlier about the use of cluster analysis and labels that are transparent are relevant here. Further there is a need to articulate the practical implications of these findings to teachers and others who work directly with youth. This would require more attention to both educational processes and contexts than is currently found in reports that focus on country rankings.

A redesigned BICSE could also encourage and suggest support for further secondary analysis, especially of projects like ICCS. This is needed for several reasons. The reports issued by IEA are inherently complex and are not always easy for those outside the projects to interpret. The IEA organization is not allowed by its policies to make recommendations about educational reform to its member countries. Many researchers lack the resources to use the existing data fully to investigate important hypotheses having to do, for example, with process, with equity, and with context (topics to which the CIVED study has made particular contributions).

When ILSAs have been completed, they should be examined regarding their implications for future design issues. For example, ICCS developed a cognitive test of civics that had a great deal more introductory reading material than was used in CIVED. Females outperformed males on the ICCS cognitive test, perhaps because females tend to be better readers than males. The advisability of retaining or changing this approach to cognitive civics measure in future cycles should be examined. Further investigation of a topic such as intolerance or anti-immigrant feeling, measured in both CIVED and ICCS, could mobilize the interest of many researchers from a cross-section of disciplines and could suggest the collection of additional information to aid in the interpretation of results (Barber and Torney-Purta 2012). Examples could be found in other subject matter assessments as well.

Finally, classroom process measures with both common items and items tailored to specific subjects could be developed based on the successful model in the civic studies. Mixed methods, for example, case studies and videos that are integrated and appropriately sequenced into large-scale data collections, would make enormous contributions.

In short, civic-related subjects should remain in the regular cycle of ILSA studies. CIVED and ICCS are not optional niche studies but central in showing an appropriately multidimensional picture of adolescents and their preparation for adulthood at a time when the large proportion are still in school. These studies have the potential to help policymakers understand the development of civic-related skills and attitudes (both positive and negative). For example, secondary analysis of the CIVED uncovered the roots in adolescence of xenophobic attitudes of 14-year-olds and a small group of deeply alienated youth. Studies of adults' attitudes in this area such as the World Values Survey can never give the rich contextual information about the everyday settings in which intergroup relations occur that is available in studies sampling schools, as ILSAs in education do. Opportunities for extensive interactive civil discussions of issues about which people disagree have been shown to have a positive role to play. One of the first places that most young people encounter opportunities for such discussion is in schools (Hess 2009).

In conclusion, the profile and contributions of large-scale international studies in education would be seriously diminished if assessments in fields such as civic education, civic learning, and civic engagement were no longer included. These studies make contributions at the macro level (to a fuller picture of countries' education system), and at the micro level (to understanding classroom climate and practices). Studies in this area meet a number of the criteria set out by Bogenschneider and Corbett (2010) in their discussion of ways to further evidence-based policy. Civic-related research is salient to the democratic process to which elected officials and those who work with them are committed. It is possible to make the results in this area accessible in everyday language and transparent in a way that complex statistical presentations of educational data often are not. Many policymakers or members of their staffs are ready to hear information that counteracts the superficial analysis of country rankings that often appears in the media, and they are interested in innovative ways of looking at educational achievement that unpacks its implications for educators.

References

Amadeo, J. 2007. Patterns of internet use and political engagement among youth. In *Young citizens and new media: Learning for democratic participation,* ed. P. Dahlgren, 125–146. London: Routledge.

Amadeo, J., J. Torney-Purta, R. Lehmann, V. Husfeldt, and R. Nikolova. 2002. *Civic knowledge and engagement. An IEA study of upper secondary students in sixteen countries.* Amsterdam: IEA.

Amnå E. 2011. *Discussion.* Princeton: ETS Conference on ILSAs.

Amnå, E., and P. Zetterberg. 2010. A political science perspective on political socialization research: Young Nordic citizens in a comparative light. In *Handbook of research on civic engagement in youth,* eds. L. Sherrod, J. Torney-Purta and C. Flanagan. Hoboken: Wiley.

Anderson, L., D. Ryan, and B. Shapiro, eds. 1989. *The IEA classroom environment study.* Oxford: Pergamon Press.

Arthur, J., I. Davies, and C. Hahn, eds. 2008. *Sage handbook of education for citizenship and democracy.* Los Angeles: Sage.

Baldi, S., M. Perle, D. Skidmore, E. Greenberg, and C. Hahn. 2001. *What democracy means to ninth graders: U.S. results from the International IEA Civic Education Study.* Washington: U.S. Department of Education.

Barber, C., and Torney-Purta, J. 2009. Gender differences in political efficacy and attitudes to women's rights influenced by national and school contexts: Analysis for the IEA civic education study. In *Gender equality and education from international and comparative perspectives, eds.* D. Baker and A. Wiseman, 357–394. Bingley: JAI/Emerald Group Publishing. (*International Perspectives on Education and Society* 10)

Barber, C., and J. Torney-Purta. 2012. Comparing the 1999 and 2009 international civic education studies of IEA: Opportunities and limitations illustrated in five countries. *Journal of Social Science Education* 11(1):47–74.

Bergman, L., D. Magnusson, and B. El Khouri. 2003. *Studying individual development in an inter-individual context: A person oriented approach.* Mahwah: Erlbaum Associates.

Bogenschneider, K., and T.J. Corbett. 2010. *Evidence-based policy making: Insights from policy-minded researchers and research-minded policy makers.* New York: Routledge.

Bradburn, N., and G. Gilford. 1990. *A framework and principles for international comparative studies in education.* Washington: National Academy Press.

Brophy, J. 2008. Developing students' appreciation for what is taught in school. *Educational Psychologist* 43(3):132–141.

Chiu, C., and M. Seo. 2009. *Cluster analysis for cognitive diagnosis: An application to the 2001 PIRLS reading assessment. IERI Monograph Series: Issues and Methodologies in Large-scale Assessment* 2:137–159.

Coley, R.J. and A. Sum. 2012. *Fault lines in our democracy: Civic knowledge, voting behavior, and civic engagement.* Princeton: Educational Testing Service.

Gilford, D. 1993. *A collaborative agenda for improving international comparative studies in education.* Washington: National Academy Press.

Gorard, S., and E. Smith. 2010. *Equity in education: An international comparison of pupil perspectives.* London: MacMillan.

Hess, D. 2009. *Controversy in the classroom: The democratic power of discussion.* New York: Routledge.

Husen, T., ed. 1967. *International study of achievement in mathematics: A comparison of twelve countries.* Stockholm: Almqvist & Wiksell.

Husfeldt, V., C. Barber, and J. Torney-Purta. 2005. *New scales for the IEA Civic Education Study Data.* Retrieved from www.terpconnect.umd.edu/~jtpurta/. edu/~iea and also CEDARS CD-ROM with IEA data.

Jennings, M.K. 2007. Political socialization. In *The Oxford handbook of political behavior,* eds. R.J. Dalton and H.D. Klingemann, 29–44. New York: Oxford University Press.

Johnson, D., and R. Johnson. 2009. An educational psychology success story: Social interdependence theory and cooperative learning. *Educational Researcher* 38(5):365–3779.

Kerr, D., L. Sturman, W. Schulz, and B. Burge. 2010. *ICCS 2009 European report: Civic knowledge, attitudes and engagement among lower-secondary students in 24 European countries.* Amsterdam: IEA.

LeTendre, G. 1998. *The educational system in Japan: Case study.* Washington: U.S. Department of Education.

Luke, A. 2011. Generalizing across borders: Policy and the limits of educational seicne. *Educational Researcher* 40(8):367–377.

Mahoney, J., H. Stattin, and D. Magnusson. 2001. Youth recreation center participation and criminal offending: A 20 year longitudinal study of Swedish boys. *International Journal of Behavioral Development* 25:509–520.

Marsh, H., K-T. Hau, C. Artelt, J. Baumert, and J. Peschar. 2000. OECD's brief self-report measure of educational psychology's most useful affective constructs: Cross-cultural, psychometric comparisons across 25 countries. *International Journal of Testing* 6(4):311–360.

Musu-Gillette, L. 2010. *How students' expectancies and values in math predict their choice of college major.* College Park: University of Maryland.

National Research Council 2010. *Exploring the intersection of science education and 21st century skills: A workshop summary*. Washington: The National Academies Press.

Niemi, R., and J. Junn. 1998. *Civic education: What makes students learn*. New Haven: Yale University Press.

Ornstein, N., A. Kohut, and L. McCarthy. 1988. *The press, the people, and politics*. Reading: Addison-Wesley Publishing.

Ramirez, F.O., P. Bromley, and S. Russell. 2011. The valorization of humanity and diversity. *Multicultural Education Review* 1:29–54.

Rutkowski, L, E. Gonzalez, M. Joncas, and von M. Davier. 2010. International large-scale assessment data: Issues in secondary analysis and reporting. *Educational Researcher* 39(2): 142–151.

Rychen, D., and L. Salganik, eds. 2001. *Defining and selecting key competencies*. Seattle: Hogrefe & Huber.

Schulz, W., and H. Sibberns, eds. 2004. *IEA Civic Education Study technical report*. Amsterdam: IEA.

Schulz, W., Fraillon, Ainley, D. Kerr, and B. Losito. 2010. *ICCS 2009 international report: Civic knowledge, attitudes, and engagement among lower-secondary students in 38 countries*. Amsterdam: IEA.

Schwartz, H., L. Hamilton, B. Stecher, and J. Steele. 2011. *Expanded measures of school performance*. Santa Monica: The Rand Corporation.

Schwille, J., and J. Amadeo. 2002. Elusive and yet ubiquitous: Paradoxes and puzzles of civic education in school. In *New paradigms and recurring paradoxes in education for citizenship*, eds. G. Steiner-Khamsi, J. Torney-Purta and J. Schwille, 105–136. Amsterdam: Elsevier Science.

Sherrod, L., J. Torney-Purta, and C. Flanagan, eds. 2010. *Handbook of research on civic engagement in youth*. Hoboken: Wiley.

Suarez, D., and F. Ramirez. 2007. Human rights and citizenship: The emergence of human rights education. In *Critique and utopia: New developments in the sociology of education*, ed. C. Torres, 43–64. Lanham: Rowman and Littlefield.

Tapola, A., and M. Niemivirta. 2008. The role of achievement goals orientations in students' perceptions of and preferences for classroom environment. *British Journal of Educational Psychology* 78:291–312.

Tatsuoka, K., J. Corter, and C. Tatuoka. 2004. Patterns of diagnosed mathematical content and process skills in TIMSS-R across a sample of 20 countries. *American Educational Research Journal* 41(4):901–926.

Takayama, K. (2010). Politics of externalization in reflective times: Reinventing Japanese education reform discourses through "Finnish PISA success." *Comparative Education Review* 54: 51–75.

Torney, J.V., A.N. Oppenheim, and R.F. Farnen. 1975. *Civic education in ten countries: An empirical study*. New York: Wiley.

Torney-Purta, J. 1987. The role of comparative education in the debate on excellence. In *Education and social concern: An approach to social foundations*, eds. R. Lawson, V. Rust and S. Shafer. Ann Arbor: Prakken Publications.

Torney-Purta, J. 1990. International comparative research in education: Its role in educational improvement in the U.S. *Educational Researcher* 19: 32–35.

Torney-Purta, J. 2008. Results of a survey of international collaborative research in psychology: Views and recommendations from twenty-six leaders of projects. In *International collaborations in the behavioral and social sciences: Report of a workshop*, ed. National Research Council, 64–78. Washington: The National Academies Press.

Torney-Purta, J. 2009. International psychological research that matters for policy and practice. *American Psychologist*, 64(8):825–237.

Torney-Purta, J., and J. Amadeo. 2004. *Strengthening democracy in the Americas through civic education: An empirical analysis highlighting the views of students and teachers*. Washington: Organization of American States.

Torney-Purta, J., and J. Amadeo. 2011. An international perspective on participatory niches for emergent citizenship in early adolescence. In *The Annals of the American Academy of Political and Social Science, "The child as citizen"*, ed. F. Earls, 180–200. Sage.

Torney-Purta, J., and C. Barber. 2011. Fostering young people's support for participatory human rights through their developmental niches. *American Journal of Orthopsychiatry* 81(4):473–481.

Torney-Purta, J., and J. Schwille. 1986. Civic values learned in school: Policy and practice in industrialized countries. *Comparative Education Review* 30:30–49.

Torney-Purta, J., and B. Wilkenfeld. 2009. *Paths to 21st century competencies through civic education classrooms: An analysis of survey results from ninth-graders.* Chicago: Division for Public Education, American Bar Association. (http://www.civicyouth.org)

Torney-Purta, J., and B. Wilkenfeld. 2010. Experience in civic education classrooms associated with student achievement in three post-Communist countries. Paper presented at the IEA's Fourth International Research Conference, Gothenburg, Sweden, July 2010.

Torney-Purta, J., J. Schwille, and J. Amadeo. 1999. Mapping the distinctive and common features of civic education in twenty-four countries. In *Civic education across countries: Twenty-four national case studies from the IEA civic education project,* eds. J. Torney-Purta, J. Schwille and J. Amadeo, 11–35. Amsterdam: IEA.

Torney-Purta, J., R. Lehmann, H. Oswald, and W. Schulz. 2001. *Citizenship and education in twenty-eight countries: Civic knowledge and engagement at age 14.* Amsterdam: IEA.

Torney-Purta, J., B. Wilkenfeld, and C. Barber. 2008. How adolescents in 27 countries understand, support and practice human rights. *Journal of Social Issues* 64(4):857–880.

Torney-Purta, J., J. Amadeo, and M. Andolina. 2010a. A conceptual framework and multi-method approach for research on political socialization and civic engagement. In *Handbook of research on civic engagement in youth,* eds. L. Sherrod, J. Torney-Purta and C. Flanagan. 497–523. Hoboken: Wiley.

Torney-Purta, J., J. Amadeo, and J. Schwille. 2010b. IEA study in civic education. In *International encyclopedia of education,* 3rd ed., 4 vols., eds. P. Peterson, E. Baker and B. McGaw, 656–662. Oxford: Elsevier.

Trzewniewski, K., M. Donnellan, and R. Lucas, eds. 2011. *Secondary data analysis: An introduction for psychologists.* Washington: American Psychological Association.

Vaughn, L. 2010. *Psychology and culture: thinking, feeling, and behaving in a global context.* Hove: Psychology Press.

Vertovek, S., and S. Wessendorf, eds. 2010. *The multiculturalism backlash: European discourses, policies and practices.* New York: Routledge.

vom Hau, M. 2009. Unpacking the school: Textbooks, teachers and the construction of nationhood in Mexico, Argentina and Peru. *Latin American Research Review* 44: 127–154.

von Davier, M. 2007. *Hierarchical general diagnostic model* (Research report no. RR-07–19). Princeton: Educational Testing Service.

Wilkenfeld, B., J. Lauckhardt, and J. Torney-Purta. 2010. The relation between developmental theory and measures of civic engagement in research on adolescents. In *Handbook of research on civic engagement in youth,* eds. L. Sherrod, J. Torney-Purta and C. Flanagan, 193–220. New York: Wiley.

Xin, T., Z. Xu, and K. Tatsuoka. 2004. Linkage between teacher quality, student achievement, and cognitive skills: A rule-space model. *Studies in Educational Evaluation* 30:205–223.

Xu, X., and von M. Davier. 2008. *Fitting the structured general diagnostic model to NAEP data* (Research report no. 08–27). Princeton: Educational Testing Service.

Zhang, T., and J.V. Torney-Purta. 2010, July. *Assessing student's cognitive content and process skills in IEA CIVED: A cross-country analysis.* Paper presented at the 4th IEA International Research Conference (IRC-2010), Gothenburg, Sweden.

Zhang, T., J. Torney-Purta, and C. Barber. 2012. Students' conceptual knowledge and process skills in civic education: Identifying cognitive profiles and classroom correlates. *Theory and Research in Social Education* 40:1–34.

Chapter 7
The Role of Large-Scale Assessments in Research on Educational Effectiveness and School Development

Eckhard Klieme

Goals and Limitations of (International) Large-Scale Assessments

The Role of International Assessments in Educational Policymaking and Effectiveness Research

ILSAs establish a monitoring structure that provides reliable comparative information on education systems, describing system structures as well as the functioning and the productivity (i.e., the gross outcome or "yield") of education systems. The studies also contribute to our *knowledge base on educational effectiveness,* observing patterns of relationships between inputs, processes, and outcomes of education. Thus, they help to understand how educational outcomes are "produced." First, ILSAs allow for a decomposition of variation of student performance by individual, school, and system levels. Moreover, they provide data about multiple factors covering these three levels, which, according to previous research, are expected to impact student performance in specific domains like reading, mathematics, or science. In addition to describing these factors, ILSAs allow us to estimate their direct and indirect relationships to student performance and other outcomes. Statistical models, using multilevel ILSA data, help to reconstruct and understand the complex relationships between input and process factors, and how they interact in "producing" student outcomes. If data on resources and costs are available, ILSAs may also help to understand efficiency, i.e., effectiveness in relation to investments. Large representative samples allow for the generalization of findings both within and across countries.

ILSAs provide a data source for the study of educational contexts in general (e.g., how family, school, and out-of school education interact in the development of life skills). For example, Trends in International Mathematics and Science Study

E. Klieme (✉)
Center for Research on Educational Quality and Evaluation,
German Institute for International Educational Research (DIPF), Goethe University,
Schloßstraße 29, 60486 Frankfurt am Main, Germany
e-mail: klieme@dipf.de

M. von Davier et al. (eds.), *The Role of International Large-Scale Assessments:*
Perspectives from Technology, Economy, and Educational Research,
DOI 10.1007/978-94-007-4629-9_7, © Springer Science+Business Media Dordrecht 2013

(TIMSS), Progress in International Reading Literacy Study (PIRLS), and PISA data are increasingly used by economists and social scientists to examine broader issues such as the impact of human capital on economic growth (Hanushek and Woessmann 2009, see also the chapter by Hanushek and Woessmann in this volume) or how to predict successful integration of migrant families (Stanat and Christensen 2006). The database will become even more informative once these studies move into further cycles, making trend data available that cover more than a decade.

Thus, ILSAs offer three types of "products": (1) *indicators* that monitor the functioning, productivity, and equity of education systems; (2) *knowledge* on factors that determine educational effectiveness; and, (3) a reliable, sustainable, comparative *database* that allows researchers worldwide to study scientific as well as policy-oriented questions.

Policymakers are mainly interested in No. 1. The policy relevance of this system-monitoring enterprise is based on (a) defining and operationalizing cognitive and noncognitive *outcome measures* that inform the selection and prioritization of educational goals within participating countries, (b) examining and reporting *factors that may be subject to control by policy and professional practice* (so-called malleable factors), and (c) providing *international benchmarks* that allow policymakers to ascertain what they may learn from other countries. The selection of indicators is generally guided by policy demands. Educational policymaking must deal with the functioning of the school system (i.e., operational characteristics such as resources allocated to schools), productivity (such as the gross level of student outcomes) and, last but not least, equity (e.g., how resources are distributed).

For example, several indicators based on PISA context data can be found in recent editions of the OECD's Education at a Glance reports (OECD 2007a, 2008, 2009a), such as:

- Relationship between immigrant background and student performance (2007, indicator A6);
- Profiles of top performing students, including their attitudes and motivation (2009 A4/A5);
- Relationships between resources and outcomes in education (2007 and 2008 B7), especially with regard to class size (2008 D2);
- Outcomes of vocational versus general educational programs (2007 and 2008 C1);
- Use of evaluation and assessment in education systems (2008 D5);
- Relationship between student background and access to (or motivation to participate in) higher education (2007 A4/A7, 2008 A3/A7).

Limitations of Large-Scale Assessments as School Effectiveness Research Tools

Researchers are mainly interested in the "products" described above under items 2 and 3. They tend to perceive ILSAs as multigroup (i.e., multicountry) educational effectiveness studies. Besides *describing* strengths and challenges with regard to the students' performance and the conditions of teaching and schooling in participating countries, researchers—but to some extent also policymakers—intend to understand *why* students reach certain levels of performance.

Although the analysis of ILSA data can make important contributions to the knowledge base for educational policy and practice (see the section below on "How large-scale assessments may contribute to our knowledge of educational effectiveness and school development" for details and examples), there are limits that have to be taken into account. As Baker (2009) notes, the history of policymaking informed by international comparative studies has seen a number of short-cut conclusions, based on too simple hypotheses as to the causes of performance differences at the system level. Also, econometricians have studied a number of issues in educational productivity, but much of this work remains descriptive, rather than estimating causal effects, because data are cross-sectional, and important explanatory variables—such as cultural factors—remain unmeasured (Hanushek and Woessmann 2010).

For example, PISA is a yield study, assessing literacy and skills that have been accumulated over the lifespan, from early childhood through different levels of schooling until the age of 15 years. PISA does not ascertain how much learning has taken place in the secondary school where a student is presently enrolled. Such an assessment would require that the student's performance level was measured at the time of entering his or her present school and compared with present performance. In so doing, one would obtain a measure of progress or "value-added" in performance associated with educational experiences in the particular school. However, the PISA design does not provide any baseline measure. Teacher quality and its impact on student performance cannot be judged in PISA, either. At least, this is not feasible with the design that has been in place for over a decade. That is because a random sample of 15-year-olds is taken in each school rather than assessing intact classes, precluding the measurement of instructional strategies and effects at the classroom level. Finally, in one out of five countries that participated in PISA 2006, the majority of the students had only recently been allocated to the schools in question, prohibiting direct conclusions on school effects within these countries.

It is extremely difficult to draw causal inferences such as concluding that a particular educational policy or practice has a direct or indirect impact on student performance based on an observational survey and the kind of assessment data collected in ILSAs (Gustafsson 2007). If, for example, links were found between high student performance and rendering school evaluation data accessible to the public (as a school level policy)—as has been the case in PISA 2006—the design of the study would not allow for causal interpretation. This is because data on at least some potentially important factors, such as prior student performance, can hardly be collected in cross-sectional ILSAs. As a consequence, such potentially important factors cannot be included in the analyses. There is no way of assuring statistical control—neither by modeling the factors that predict outcomes, as in Analysis of Co-Variance (ANCOVA), nor by modeling the treatment assignment process, as in propensity score matching. The data needed for those models are simply left unobserved in current ILSAs. Controlling for student background, such as socioeconomic status (SES), migration status, and gender—as is regularly done in ILSAs—is an inadequate substitute for baseline achievement data. Thus, currently available analyses cannot tell if the policy of making school evaluation data available to the public happens to be applied in high achieving schools, or whether the policy actually results in higher student performance.

The OECD, however, reports that, "Students in schools posting their results publicly performed 14.7 score points better than students in schools that did not, and this association remained positive even after the demographic and socioeconomic background of students and schools was accounted for" (OECD 2007b, p. 243) and concludes "that the impetus provided by external monitoring of standards, rather than relying principally on schools and individual teachers to uphold them, can make a real difference to results" (p. 276). Thus, public posting of achievement data is recommended as a strategy for school improvement. This is just one of many examples of policymakers overinterpreting available data.

The example is noteworthy because it shows that the way out of the dilemmas of causal inference recently proposed by Kröhne (2010) does not help either, at least in this case. Kröhne argued that problems with unobserved predictors arise on the individual level only, e.g., when we want to determine if participation in extracurricular activities has an effect on student learning. However, when analyzing school policies, he considered these policies to be treatments on the school level, introducing propensity score matching on the school level rather than the student level. Based on data from the German national language study DESI (see below), this procedure allowed him to conclude that so-called bilingual instruction (teaching subjects like geography in a foreign language to a certain subgroup of students within the school) had a positive school level effect on students' foreign language competencies (see Fig. 7.1). Had he done the propensity score matching on the individual level, he would have failed to catch the treatment assignment process for individual students within schools because no data were available on student achievement at the time when students were assigned to bilingual instruction. There were, however, good reasons to assume that the implementation of bilingual instruction as a school level policy can be explained from stable variables that we know or can truly estimate, like school type, school size, average parent SES, or percentage of immigrant students. Therefore, in the case of Kröhne's analysis of bilingual instruction, causal inference may be feasible. The same may be true for school policies on truancy and their effect on student absenteeism—an issue that probably will be covered in PISA 2012. However, for many other school level policies, including public reports on evaluation results, the assumption of no relation to prior achievement (both on the individual and on the school level) seems unrealistic.

The main problem with causal inferences in ILSAs is not a statistical or methodological one. The conditions for causal inference from quasiexperimental or survey-type data are well-known, based, e.g., on the Rubin-model of causality. Rather, the problem is substantial. The sociological theory of schooling as well as pedagogical concepts state that student achievement is the core of school education, i.e., the school expects students to strive for achievement, and its main "product" is student

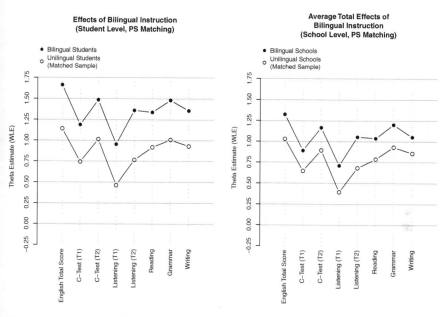

Fig. 7.1 Average total effect of bilingual instruction for eight achievements in English as a Foreign Language, estimated with propensity score matching on the student level (*left*) or on the school level (*right*); data from the German language study DESI, *n*=ca. 10.000 (taken with permission from Kröhne 2010)

achievement. The process of education (*Bildung* in German) can be defined as finding an appropriate individual pathway to knowledge, competency, and expertise. Pedagogical interventions (*Erziehung* in German) need to adapt to the preconditions of learning, especially to prior achievement. In their daily practice, professional educators need to monitor student achievement and change interventions accordingly. When assigning tasks, forming groups for collaborative learning, giving feedback, deciding on grade retention/promotion, and other aspects of educational careers, teachers will inevitably take students' prior achievement into account. Thus, effects of these interventions can hardly be estimated from cross-sectional data alone without knowing prior achievement, the most salient factor that drives the assignment to interventions. There might be ways to approximate prior achievement, e.g. by asking about prior grades, or more valid quasi-experimental designs, such as exploiting variation between two subjects assessed for the same group of students (Schwerdt and Wuppermann 2011). In general, it is difficult to draw causal inference in education without longitudinal achievement data.

Nevertheless, a productive interplay between ILSAs and effectiveness research may be established. ILSA studies do have an impact on educational research, even if strict causal inference cannot be assumed (see the below section on "How large scale assessments may contribute to our knowledge of educational effectiveness and school development"), and this impact can be greatly increased if the design of ILSA studies is enhanced beyond the traditional cross-sectional survey kind of

Table 7.1 Basic elements of the CIPO model of school effectiveness (adapted from Scheerens and Bosker 1997)

Input	Process	Output
Teacher-student-rate, qualification of teaching staff, student population, parent commitment	Quantity of instruction, school curriculum, leadership, teacher cooperation and collaboration, professional development, cohesion, school culture (norms and values), school climate, internal and external evaluation	*School level*
Students per class, teacher competencies	Instructional quality—opportunity to learn, clear, well-structured classroom management, supportive, student-oriented classroom climate, cognitive activation with challenging content	*Classroom level*
SES, social and cultural capital, family support, gender, language and migration background, general intellectual ability, pre-knowledge	Time invested, self regulation, motivation and interest, self concept, learning strategies	*Individual level*

Context: School structure, curriculum, pedagogical traditions and orientations, teacher education, budgeting and regulation, socio-economic and cultural context

design (see the section on "Examples of enriched (longitudinal) designs integrating LSA and EER"). The inverse impact is even more important, i.e., the impact of educational effectiveness research on ILSAs (see the below section on "How Can Educational Effectiveness Research Inform ILSAs? The PISA Design as an Example"). Before we can elaborate on these links, we have to take a closer look at educational effectiveness studies.

Goals and Research Design of Educational Effectiveness Studies

The Basic Model of School Effectiveness (CIPO-Model) and Instructional Quality

Standard models of school and teaching research conceptualize the school as a system wherein the characteristics of the context, input variables, school and instruction processes interact in "producing" student outcomes. The basic structure of this Context-Input-Process-Outcome (CIPO-) model was developed in the 1960s to inform the design of ILSAs undertaken by the IEA (Purves 1987). Addressing the multilevel-structure of the educational systems, current versions of the framework (see Table 7.1) allocate input, process, and outcome characteristics at respective levels of action (i.e., system level, school level, instruction/class/teacher level, individual level).

The main goal of educational effectiveness research (EER) is to identify "factors in teaching, curriculum, and learning environment at different levels such as the classroom, the school, and the above-school levels (that) can directly or indirectly explain the differences in the outcomes of students, taking into account background characteristics, such as ability, socioeconomic status, and prior attainment" (Creemers and Kyriakides 2008, p. 12).

Taken literally, this definition includes ILSA, as these studies also intend to explain differences in student outcomes, taking into account a broad array of variables from all cells of the CIPO matrix. In fact, "educational effectiveness" has become an umbrella for quite a fuzzy set of studies, from surveys unveiling general characteristics of schools (e.g., leadership, trust (Bryk et al. 2010), and reliability (Teddlie and Stringfield 1993)) to experimental studies identifying effects of specific instructional interventions (e.g., training of self-regulation, peer learning, reading programs). In order to face current challenges (see the section on "Challenges to the EER paradigm" below), more sophisticated designs are needed (see the section on "Examples of enriched (longitudinal) designs integrating LSA and EER" below), including longitudinal data collection and experimental or quasiexperimental assignment to treatments, accompanied by more complex methods (which I will not focus on here) and more substantial theory.

Let me illustrate the need for more sophisticated theoretical and empirical work by just one cell in the CIPO matrix, namely classroom level processes, i.e., instruction—mainly because this cell will play a major role in subsequent examples.

In the early tradition of behaviorist psychology, the *time needed to achieve certain learning goals* was supposed to be a major criterion for instructional effectiveness. Following Carroll (1963), numerous studies have shown that learning time is a major predictor of student outcomes in many subjects. Accordingly, the notion of *opportunity to learn*, introduced by John Carroll in the early 1960s, was initially meant to indicate whether students had sufficient time and received adequate instruction to learn (Carroll 1963; cf. Abedi et al. 2006). *Quality of instruction* was operationalized as the reduction of learning time reached in a specific instructional setting, compared to a standard setting.

The notion of opportunity to learn (OTL) has since become an important concept in international student assessments (Husén 1967, 1974; Schmidt and McKnight 1995; Schmidt et al. 2001), and it was shown to be strongly associated with student performance, especially in cross-country comparisons (Schmidt and Maier 2009, pp. 552–556). At the same time, the construct received a much broader meaning. Stevens (1993, pp. 233–234) already identified four kinds of OTL variables most prevalent in research:

- Content coverage variables: These measure whether instruction covers the curriculum for a particular grade level or subject matter.
- Content exposure variables: These take into consideration the time allowed for and devoted to instruction (time on task) and the depth of the teaching provided.
- Content emphasis variables: These describe which topics within the curriculum are selected for emphasis and which students are selected to receive instruction

emphasizing lower order skills (i.e., rote memorization) or higher order skills (i.e., critical problem solving).
- Quality of instructional delivery variables: These reveal how classroom teaching practices (i.e., structuring of lessons) affect students' academic performance.

Thus, for certain authors, OTL has become more or less a synonym for the quality of instruction experienced by the student. Schmidt and Maier (2009), however, in their review argue that OTL is a rather uncomplicated concept: "What students learn in school is related to what is taught" (p. 541), and they intentionally focus on OTL "in the narrowest sense: Student's content exposure" (p. 542).

Schmidt and Maier acknowledge that although OTL may be a straightforward construct, it is difficult to measure. In order to explain differences in the achieved curriculum, teachers and/or students have traditionally been asked whether and how certain curricular content has been realized in instruction (the implemented curriculum), sometimes using logs (Rowan et al. 2004). In addition, curriculum experts have been asked whether and how content elements have been covered within curricular documents like syllabuses, textbooks, and standards (the intended curriculum). From these raw data, various indicators have been extracted. In many cases, the content taught has been judged twofold, in terms of topic and level of demand, while at the system level, indices for coherence, rigor, and focus have been derived (Schmidt and Maier 2009).

In addition to OTL as described above, a number of other processes at the classroom level have been found to be relevant for educational effectiveness (Creemers and Kyriakides 2008; Harris and Chrispeels 2006; Hopkins 2005; Scheerens and Bosker 1997). Well-structured lessons with close monitoring, adequate pacing and classroom management, clarity of presentation, and informative and encouraging feedback (i.e., the key aspects of "direct instruction") are positively linked to student performance. These components help create an orderly classroom environment and maximize effective learning time. Yet student motivation and noncognitive outcomes benefit from additional characteristics of instructional quality, such as a classroom climate and teacher–student relations that support student autonomy, competency and social relatedness (Deci and Ryan 1985). Furthermore, in order to foster conceptual understanding, instruction has to use challenging content (Brown 1994). Also, different student subpopulations may benefit from different instructional practices. Thus, teachers have to orchestrate learning activities in a way that serves the needs of their specific class. Klieme et al. (2009) condensed this knowledge into a framework of three "basic dimensions of instructional quality": (a) clear, well-structured classroom management, (b) supportive, student-oriented classroom climate, and (c) cognitive activation with challenging content. Several independent studies of secondary school mathematics education have since confirmed this triarchic structure of instructional quality and given some support for the cognitive and motivational impact that was hypothesized (*TIMSS-Video*: Klieme et al. 2001; *COACTIV*: Baumert et al. 2009; *Pythagoras*: Lipowsky et al. 2009). Klieme and Rakoczy (2003) as well as Kunter et al. (2008) identified similar structures within national extensions to PISA. The triarchic model is also revealed in observational data on elementary and primary education in the United States (Pianta and Hamre 2009) as well as in the Ohio teacher efficacy scales (OSTES) developed by Tschannen-Moran and Woolfolk Hoy (2001).

Challenges to the EER Paradigm

The paradigm of EER faces a number of severe theoretical and empirical challenges when conceptualizing and operationalizing the general model in more detail. The main challenges seem to be:

(a) The adaptive nature of educational processes: Practices may neither be equally effective for all students within a school nor for all education systems, local contexts, and schools. Moreover, depending on the kind of outcomes emphasized, different conclusions may be drawn (Kyriakides and Tsangaridou 2004). Hence, modern research into educational effectiveness also takes interactions with input into account and examines differential effectiveness and adaptive practices. A considerable amount of research has been carried out in this field (e.g., Creemers and Kyriakides 2008; Scheerens 2000; Teddlie and Reynolds 2000).

(b) The dynamic nature of educational processes: When turned into a dynamic model of school effectiveness (see Creemers and Kyriakides 2008), outcomes become inputs for further development. Mathematics anxiety, for example, can be an outcome of schooling as well as an input—impacting, for instance, students' homework activities. Moreover, inputs may have reciprocal mutual effects. For example, a school's socioeconomic composition in many education systems is correlated with funding, parental involvement, or even teacher quality. This, in turn, allows for other (better) teaching-learning environments to be offered, which attract students (or, rather, parents) from higher socioeconomic backgrounds, so that, in the end, social stratification, resources, and process quality are mixed and are difficult to disentangle (see "Examples of enriched (longitudinal) designs integrating LSA and EER" below for empirical results on that topic).

(c) The complexity of mediating processes: It is reasonable to assume that not all effects on student outcomes are direct. Comparatively weaker effects on student outcomes are often found for policies at the school and system level, as compared to student background variables and classroom processes (e.g., Wang et al. 1993). This may, in part, be because the former variables do not exert a direct effect on students, but are rather related to school or classroom processes, which in turn have an effect on student performance. Moreover, school level variables such as school climate, shared values and norms, or procedures to deal with behavioral problems, may have a direct effect on noncognitive outcomes (e.g., learning motivation, academic aspirations) and student behavior (e.g., truancy, violence), while school effects on student performance and other subject-related outcomes (e.g., interest and self-efficacy beliefs) probably will be mediated by teaching and learning within classrooms.

(d) The importance of moderating variables: Based on a constructivist understanding of student learning, current educational theory assumes that student learning is largely dependent on self-regulated processes, which are moderated by school, classroom, and teacher factors. Modeling such differences requires the examination of interaction/moderation effects. Contemporary research findings indicate that the relevance of school characteristics does not remain consistent across subjects and classes, and varies according to the constellation of a student population (Ditton and Krecker 1995; Luyten and de Jong 1998; Sammons et al. 1997; Scheerens and Bosker 1997). In line with the theory of differential effectiveness (e.g., Kyriakides and Tsangaridou 2004), it is important to acknowledge that relationships between variables may not be similar in different subgroups. For example, there is some evidence that students from diverse social backgrounds may benefit from different instructional techniques (e.g., Brophy 1992; Walberg 1986).

(e) The weakness of distal effects, especially school effects: Within the multilevel CIPO model, "effects" are usually supposed to cascade from the upper to the lower levels. However, meta-analyses of school and instructional effectiveness that are grounded in this model (Hattie 2009; Seidel and Shavelson 2007; Scheerens and Bosker 1997; Wang et al. 1993) force us to acknowledge that prerequisites of learning and individual activities bear more significance to the students' learning results than the characteristics and processes of instruction, whereas instruction and teacher competencies, in turn, bear more significance to student outcomes than school level factors. School effectiveness research thus concludes that learning conditions, norms, and practices at the school level do provide a framework for learning and teaching processes, but they are more distant to the students' learning achievement and thus bear less predictive power than the teaching and learning activities in the classroom (Creemers 1994; Ditton 2000, 2007; Fend 1998; Sammons 1999; Slavin 1996; Stringfield 1994). This view is supported by cognitive models of learning and teaching, which do not define instruction as an "immediately effective" measure, but rather as social interactions and learning opportunities that the students use for acquiring competencies, pursuant to their individual abilities and preexisting knowledge. Hence, individual learning activities are considered more meaningful for acquiring competencies than classroom instructional characteristics, and even more so compared to school process characteristics (Seidel and Shavelson 2007).

(f) The fundamental difference between status (at a given moment) and individual growth or organizational change (over time): Individual growth and organizational change (i.e., longitudinal outcomes of education) have to be studied distinctively, because explaining and predicting change is quite different from explaining and predicting levels of outcomes in cross-sectional comparison.

(g) While a vast body of evidence exists from English-speaking countries and the Netherlands regarding characteristics of effective schools, which have been retrospectively gained from analyzing high achieving schools (see Sammons et al. 1997) and school effectiveness studies (Scheerens and Bosker 1997), sound assessments of school developments are lacking from a longitudinal perspective. International surveys on school improvement research have been published in recent years (Lee and Williams 2006; Hopkins 2005; Harris and Chrispeels 2006) but they can merely report on case study effects or repeat the well-known meta-analyses of school effectiveness research; a longitudinal assessment involving schools as units of observation, objective criteria measures, and reliable sample sizes scarcely has been realized so far.

American school research in the 1970s and early 1980s brought processes of school development forward to large questionnaire-based studies, the Rand Change Agent Study and the DESSI study (Dissemination Efforts Supporting School Improvement) and thus highlighted these processes without being able to evaluate their effectiveness. It thus became clear that it is impossible to plan and predict school development in a harmonized way, but that it is locally adjusted, with "ownership" of the staff (which is an important condition for sustainable change) resulting from experiencing practical success (Teddlie and Stringfield 2006, p. 26 f.). From the late 1980s onwards, the principle of treating individual schools as units of action ("site-based management") also brought changes to research: for instance, Teddlie and Stringfield (1993) observed 16 schools over a period of 10 years, developing the concept of reliable schools. At present, longitudinal analyses are conducted on effects of "comprehensive school reform" (see the overview in Borman et al. 2003). These analyses are mainly based on school statistical data and standardized achievement tests. It is thus possible to determine whether schools participating in specific reform programs differ from other schools regarding the development of achievement. In some cases, recognizable effect sizes are reported. However, this line of research reveals hardly anything about processes and conditioning factors of school development.

(h) The incoherence and instability of effect sizes: According to Scheerens and Bosker (1997, p. 81), stability and consistency of school effects are "one of the most fundamental issues in school effectiveness research," but one that has been widely neglected. Current accountability policies are based on strong but questionable assumptions: that student achievement can legitimately be attributed to school (as opposed to teacher or department, for example) effects; that we can measure progress on the school level in a reliable manner; and that *change* in school-level effects is an indicator for successful school improvement, not an artifact due to unreliability and instability (see Goldschmidt et al. 2004 for statistical models that allow testing of these assumptions). Most recently, Bryk et al. (2010) took the analysis of school development a huge step forward, presenting complex data records from the evaluation of the Chicago school reform. But in this latter case, the indicators were rather descriptive.

(i) Early work by Willms and Raudenbush (1989) indicated that the overall achievement level of a school is remarkably consistent, has been challenged by British researchers. For example, Thomas et al. 1997, p. 194, state that "only a minority of schools performed both consistently (across subjects) and with consistency (over time) and ... these schools are at the extremes of the effectiveness range (i.e., strongly positive or strongly negative)." But those cases of well-performing or failing schools, these authors argued, can be understood considering our school effectiveness knowledge base. They hypothesized that high achievement expectations, a shared vision, strong and flexible leadership, high quality instruction, and strong parental involvement are among the factors that support positive school development in a longitude (Sammons et al. 1995, p. 93). These hypotheses were confirmed in part by a followup study using interviews with school headmasters.

Problems (f) and (g) will be illustrated in the following section with an example from a German school survey.

Comparing Value-Added Status, Growth, and Change Indicators for Schools: An Empirical Study

Klieme et al. (2010b) evaluated extracurricular activities in some 230 lower secondary schools all over Germany, using a multicohort longitudinal design. As a global measure of language competency, standard vocabulary tests were administered three times, in 2005, 2007, and 2009. Each time, students from grades 5, 7, and 9 participated, allowing for identification of individual growth over a two- or even four-year period for most of the students. All data were standardized within age groups. Also, student background information (gender, socioeconomic status, and migration status) is available. Thus, on the school level, different indicators for school quality can be derived:

(a) Based on data from the most recent wave of measurement, 2009, achievement scores can be calculated and adjusted for student background variables. The adjusted test score, aggregated for the school, can be used as a proximal indicator for the school's added value. This indicator represents the kind of data that would be available in a purely cross-sectional survey such as traditional ILSAs. This indicator turns out to possess stability—calculated as the correlation coefficient for $n=232$ schools—of about 70, which indicates the school results are relatively stable in Germany.

(b) For those students who were observed twice, a difference score can be calculated, describing the relative gain (or loss) in achievement between 2007 and 2009 relative to the respective age groups. Aggregated on the school level, this indicator measures "achievement gain" over two years.
A similar indicator can be derived for the period between 2005 and 2007. Both indicators correlate significantly, but only at $r=0.305$, indicating limited stability of this effect.

(c) An even more complex indicator can be calculated as the difference between the mean growth rate 2005–2007 and the mean growth rate 2007–2009. We consider this as an indicator for change in value-added of individual schools, i.e., as a statistical aspect that may reflect effects of organizational change.

As can be seen from the plots in Fig. 7.2, (a) and (b) correlate moderately ($r=0.39$, $p<0.001$), while the change indicator (c) is uncorrelated to both (a) and (b).

Fig. 7.2 Relationships between three indicators of school effects in $n = 232$ German secondary schools

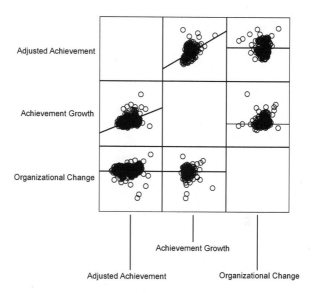

This finding illustrates that studies on school effects that can only use cross-sectional data will trigger misinterpretations—even if student background characteristics are controlled for. Cross-sectional estimates of "value-added" are weakly correlated or even uncorrelated to indicators that actually cover growth and change. Findings from cross-sectional studies should not be interpreted as explanations of school development.

How Can Educational Effectiveness Research Inform ILSAs? The PISA Design as an Example

One of the consequences of the issues raised here is that rather than being a sound foundation for educational effectiveness research, cross-sectional ILSAs depend on input from EER studies and theories. Factors that have been demonstrated to be relevant for educational effectiveness or efficiency in the research literature are premier candidates for continuous monitoring within ILSAs and for incorporation into the broader system of educational indicators.

For example, a recent version of the CIPO model, as shown in Table 7.2, covers practically all constructs that have been suggested for inclusion in the design of background questionnaires in the PISA 2012 study (Klieme et al. 2010a). The first column displays four levels: students, classrooms, schools, and countries. The three production phases are then given in the remaining columns, i.e., inputs, processes and outcomes, respectively. As the major achievement domain in PISA 2012 will be mathematics, the table focuses on student outcomes in this domain.

The choice of constructs in ILSAs is based on a combination of policy priorities and research evidence. Policymakers on the PISA Governing Board decide upon

Table 7.2 Overview of constructs covered by PISA 2012 (from Klieme et al. 2010a)

	Input	Processes	Outcomes
Students	Gender, grade level, socioeconomic status	Attendance/truancy	Mathematical literacy
	Educational career, grades	Outside-class activities—e.g., participation in after school programs	Mathematics-related attitudes, beliefs and motivation
	Immigration background	Motivation, engagement	General school-related attitudes and behavior, e.g., commitment, truancy
	Family environment and support		
	ICT experience, attitudes, skills	Learning and thinking strategies, test taking strategies	Learning motivation, educational aspirations
	Openness, problem solving styles	Learning time (including homework and private tuition)	
Classrooms	Class size, socio-economic background and ethnic composition	Quality of instruction: structure, support, challenge	Aggregated student variables
	Teacher education/training, expertise	Opportunity to learn: implemented curriculum, assigned tasks, mathematics-related activities	
		Instructional time, grouping, assessment and feedback	
Schools	Socioeconomic background and ethnic composition	Achievement orientation, shared norms, leadership, teacher morale and cooperation, professional development	Aggregated student variables
	Affluence of the community		
	School funding, public vs. private	Admission and recruitment policies, tracking, course offerings/school curriculum, evaluation	Promotion/retention and graduation rates
	School size		
	Parental involvement	Teacher-student relations, supportive environment	Attendance
Countries (Systems)	Economic wealth	School funding, tracking and allocation, policies for professional teacher development, support for special needs and language minority students, hiring and certification policies	Aggregated student variables
	Social (in)equality		
	Diversity policies	Accountability and evaluation policies, locus of decision-making	Average graduation level

the goals and research questions, while experts, building on extensive knowledge in EER, choose the appropriate constructs, instruments, and variables. For example, the definition of "mathematical literacy" as the most important outcome variable, and the decision to include mathematics-related attitudes and relations as outcome variables, are both based on policy decisions, reflecting general curriculum goals, and goals of the educational system shared by most participating countries. The constructs we use, however, and how these are operationalized, mainly reflect insights gained from research literature. Also, input and process variables are included if there is strong research evidence that they have an impact on the outcomes.

Some input factors are fairly stable and difficult to change, while others can be shaped by school development activities or policy decisions. Processes are usually more malleable, at least indirectly (e.g., by teacher education and professional development), and outcomes reflect the effects of the inputs and processes. Note, however, that the discrimination between the three strands of variables is by no means clear cut: Outcomes from one educational setting become an input for the next, while some process aspects (e.g., learning strategies) may well be treated as either input or outcome, depending on a given theoretical perspective, research design, or practical considerations.

As PISA is a trend study, assessing the same set of achievement domains every three years, it is crucial to define a core of variables that will be kept constant. Only if trend variables are kept unchanged—or moderately edited, leaving at least some anchor items unchanged—can policymakers and researchers be informed about change on the system level. Once again, the selection of constructs and variables is based on a combination of policy arguments and input from research studies. The PISA 2012 Questionnaire Framework (Klieme et al. 2010a) suggests the following design structure:

1. General (i.e., domain-independent) trend variables

General input variables:

- Student level inputs (grade; gender; socioeconomic background: parental education and occupation/family wealth/educational resources/cultural possessions; migration data: immigration status/heritage language/age on arrival in country; family support)
- School level contexts and inputs (community size, resources, qualifications of teaching staff)

General process variables:

- School level processes (decision-making, admission policies, assessment and evaluation policies, professional development, student-teacher-relations, parental involvement)
- Instructional processes (learning time, disciplinary climate, teacher support)

General outcome variables:

- General noncognitive outcomes—Commitment to learning (behavioral: truancy; personal goal: educational aspirations; motivational: learning engagement, affective: sense of belonging)

2. Domain-specific trend variables

- Domain-specific cognitive outcomes (math, science, reading literacy)
- Domain-specific noncognitive outcome variables (strategies and metacognition, domain-related beliefs, self-related beliefs, motivation)
- Domain-specific process variables (opportunity to learn, instructional quality, system and school level support)

3. Thematic extension variables (extensions within individual cycles)

- International options (e.g., in PISA 2012, educational career/second language learners; information and computer technology (ICT) literacy)
- Context variables for additional domains (e.g., ICT-related experiences relevant for computer-based problem solving)
- Descriptive and explanatory variables for specific reports (e.g., in PISA 2012: mathematics-related motivations and intentions)
- Malleable variables at the school level (e.g., in PISA 2012: truancy policies) that are specifically selected for descriptive purposes or for causal inference

4. System level data, gained from the OECD's international system of indicators, or from a system-level questionnaire

- Output of educational institutions (e.g., certificates)
- Financial and human resources invested into education
- Access to and participation in education
- Learning environment and organization of schools

How ILSAs May Contribute to Our Knowledge of Educational Effectiveness and School Development

Much of the value of ILSAs is based on a constant interplay between assessments such as PISA as a monitoring survey and more rigorous kinds of effectiveness research done elsewhere. As shown before, factors that have been demonstrated to be relevant for educational effectiveness or efficiency in the research literature are prime candidates for continuous monitoring and for incorporation into the OECD system of educational indicators. In the following, the inverse kind of link will be discussed. Even while causal inferences are not warranted, ILSA data can be put to substantial use for gaining insights in educational effectiveness: (1) Correlational and other exploratory results from ILSAs may lead to hypotheses that can subsequently be tested in more robust designs, namely longitudinal, experimental, or intervention studies. As an example, the next section discusses the German TIMSS video study, which led to the formulation of the triarchic theory of instructional quality; (2) Hypotheses from EER can be tested in ILSAs, making use of broad, representative samples, high participation rates, and good measurement quality. In presenting results of such tests, our theory of instructional quality is again referred to. (3) Last but not least, ILSAs allow for checking the cross-cultural and cross-national validity of EER findings.

ILSAs as a Means of Exploration and Hypothesis Generation: Findings from TIMSS and PISA

The TIMSS 1995 video study, an add-on to the international ILSA in grade 8, had a huge impact on instructional research in the United States (Stigler and Hiebert 1999) and in Germany (Baumert et al. 1997, Kunter et al. 2006), the two countries that participated along with Japan. Compared to Japan, with its strong focus on high level thinking, especially in the areas of geometry, open-ended problem solving, and a choreography that included extended seat work and group work as well as teacher lecturing, instruction in both Germany and the United States looked rather narrow. The instructional "script" found in Japanese classrooms was understood by many to be the cause for the high level of mathematics achievement that TIMSS as well as previous IEA studies and—later—the OECD PISA studies found in that country. However, as there was no overlap between the TIMSS video samples and the TIMSS assessment samples in Japan and the United States, this hypothesis could not be tested within the video study itself. Later, the 1998 TIMSS video study, which included another five high-achieving countries (Korea, the Czech Republic, the Netherlands, Switzerland, and Australia), would show that high achieving countries had quite different profiles in teaching practices, devaluating any attempt at directly linking student achievement to teaching practices on a national level (Hiebert et al. 2003; Pauli and Reusser 2006).

Within country, between-classrooms differences could be studied in depth for Germany, where TIMSS achievement tests had been implemented in the 1995 video sample, and a broad range of student and teacher questionnaire scales had been added, including a longitudinal followup one year later. Also, a number of high-inference video ratings were performed (Clausen 2002). Three basic (second-order) dimensions of instructional quality were identified in these ratings and shown to have specific effects on the classroom level, as seen in Table 7.3: (1) student-oriented, supportive climate and practices were related to positive development of student motivation; (2) so-called cognitive activation (e.g., Socratic deep-level questioning, use of complex problems) was related to achievement growth; (3) efficient classroom management with low level of disruptive student behavior seemed to underlie both (Klieme et al. 2001). Effects were quite small, but in subsequent ILSAs, namely PISA 2000 (Klieme and Rakoczy 2003) and PISA 2003 (Kunter et al. 2006), the basic pattern could be reproduced. Thus, ILSA studies served as the foundation for theory development, which was of course later augmented with arguments from educational and psychological research (see Klieme et al. 2009).

Hypotheses generated from ILSA data may later be tested in (quasi)experimental and/or longitudinal designs, as has been the case in the "Pythagoras" study on instructional quality (Klieme et al. 2010). This study, conducted in 2003/2004 in

Table 7.3 Second order factors of classroom practice based on high-inference video-ratings (TIMSS-Video 1994 Germany: national sample, 100 lessons; see Klieme et al. 2001)

Classroom management	Supportive climate	Cognitive activation
Effective treatment of interruptions: "teacher intervenes immediately, before disturbance may evolve"	Social orientation: "teacher takes care of her/his students' problems"	Teacher's ability to motivate students: "can present even abstract content in an interesting manner"
Clarity of rules • Interruptions (–) • Waste of time (–) • Monitoring • Time on task • Teacher unreliability (–)	Teachers' diagnostic competency with regard to social behavior	
Clarity and structuredness of the Instruction	*Individual reference norm in evaluation* • Rate of interaction (–) • Pressure on students (–)	*Errors as opportunities* *Demanding tasks* • Practicing by repetition (–)

Switzerland and Germany, adapted many design elements, techniques, and procedures from the TIMSS video studies. However, the content of the lessons to be videotaped was controlled for: all participating classes were filmed during their first three lessons of introduction to the Pythagorean Theorem. Instructional approaches were controlled to some extent, too: teachers were asked to do a proof (of any kind) during the lessons. The content focus set by design could be used to develop and implement tailored assessments and questionnaires that directly addressed teaching and learning within the lessons that had been taped.

The sample consisted of 20 Swiss and 20 German classes from two secondary school types. Because participation was voluntary, the sample is not representative. The analyses draw on data from a maximum of 1,015 students in the ninth grade (Germany) or the eighth grade (German-speaking part of Switzerland).

In addition to video ratings, student ratings of instructional quality were implemented to test the triarchic theory. In fact, all three dimensions of instructional quality could be assessed by student questionnaires and were shown to be highly predictive of general achievement growth over the school year. Student ratings for (a) structure, (b) teacher support, and (c) process-oriented approach to homework, as an indicator of cognitive activation, all correlate highly (0.47–0.52) with changes in achievement on the class level.

ILSAs as a Means of Testing Hypotheses from EER: Findings from PISA

Our theory of instructional quality predicts that classroom management has a strong positive correlation with student achievement, while supportive climate would be related to student motivation. These hypotheses were tested with the international

PISA 2000 data set. A three-level hierarchical regression model was specified, involving individual, school, and country level predictors. The International Socio-Economic Index of Occupational Status (ISEI)—more precisely, the maximum of mothers ISEI and fathers ISEI called HISEI—was used as a control variable, and two scales from the PISA student questionnaire were used as predictors at the individual level, while their aggregated analogues were used as predictors on the school and the system level. The model was run twice: once with reading literacy, a cognitive variable, as the dependent, and once with interest, an affective variable, as the dependent variable (Fig. 7.3).

ILSAs as a Means of Understanding the Systemic and Cultural Context of Education and How It Moderates EER Results: Findings from TALIS and PISA

A behavior-oriented version of the triarchic model of instructional quality was implemented in the OECD TALIS study by asking teachers how often they implemented each of 13 given practices in their teaching:

- Structuring practices (5 items): e.g., "I explicitly state learning goals." Other items include summary of former lessons, homework review, checking the exercise book, and checking student understanding during classroom talk by questioning students.
- Student-oriented practices (4 items): e.g., "Students work in small groups to come up with a joint solution to a problem or task." Other items include ability grouping, student self-evaluation, and student participation in classroom planning.
- Enhanced activities (4 items): e.g., "Students work on projects that require at least one week to complete." Other items include making a product, writing an essay, and debating arguments.

Based on TALIS main study data from 23 countries, it has been shown that (a) the three dimensions can be differentiated across countries (i.e., the triarchic model has some cross-cultural validity), (b) structuring practices, as hypothesized, are associated with higher levels of classroom discipline (as perceived by teachers), and (c) participation in professional development as well as teaching high-ability classes is correlated with a higher frequency of using these practices. Mathematics and science teachers report less student orientation and less frequent use of enhanced activities than teachers of other subjects (Klieme and Vieluf 2009).

Quite often, questionnaire scales show strange behavior when individual, school, and country level relations are compared. Especially for self-reported Likert-type questions, a number of negative correlations with student achievement have been found on the country level, although on the individual level, the correlation is positive. This kind of reversion of a correlation, when considering the aggregated level of states rather than the familiar individual level, can often be found in ILSA data records. Explanations so far mostly refer to culture-specific

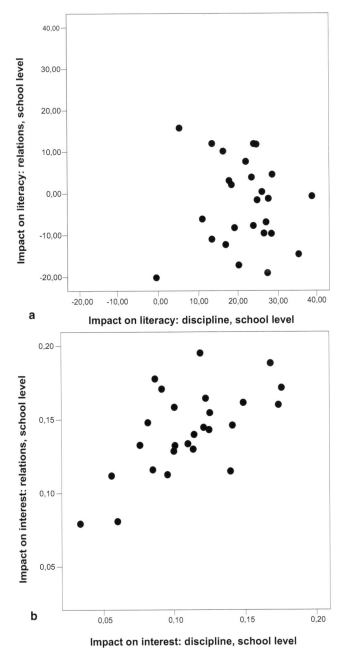

Fig. 7.3 a Effects of perceived classroom discipline and perceived quality of teacher-students-relation on reading literacy. *Each dot* represents one participating country. For each country, the graph shows the country-specific school level parameters. Apparently, effect sizes are larger for disciplinary climate than teacher-student-relations, as predicted. **b** Effects of perceived classroom discipline and perceived quality of teacher-students-relation on reading interest. *Each dot* represents one participating country. For each country, the graph shows the country-specific school level parameters. Apparently, effect sizes are larger for teacher-student-relations than for disciplinary climate

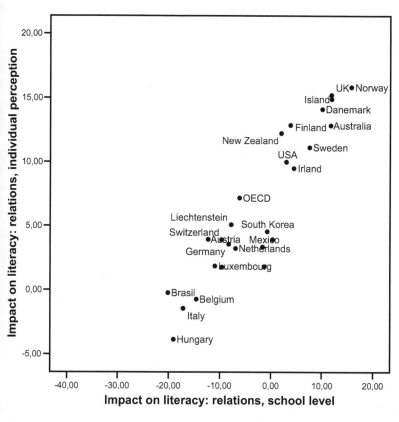

Fig. 7.4 School level effect (*horizontal*) and individual level effect (*vertical*) of perceived teacher-student-relations on reading literacy for various countries; data from a three-level hierarchical regression analysis

response styles. Figure 7.4 shows that in some countries this phenomenon occurs on the school level as well.

The countries depicted in Fig. 7.4 clearly fall into two distinctive categories: In systems with strong and early tracking, such as the German-speaking countries as well as Hungary, Italy, and some non-European countries, the effect is negative on the between-school level, and close to zero on the individual, within-school level. Both effects can be interpreted referring to selection and framing processes that typically operate within those tracked systems: Students are allocated to secondary school types according to their overall achievement level. In low track schools, teachers tend to be more supportive and less demanding. This is clearly reflected in student perceptions, causing the negative correlation on the school level. Within schools, however, variation in student perceptions is quite small because of the selection process; therefore, correlation is about zero.

In systems with less tracking, however, as in Nordic and Anglo-Saxon countries, both between-school and within-school parameters are clearly positive. In those

Table 7.4 Design enhancements to PISA (national options) in Germany

Level of analysis	Cross-section	Longitude
Students	Individual competency level	*Individual learning progress (PISA Germany 2003/2004)*
Classroom	*Competency levels of school classes*	*Instructional effectiveness (PISA Germany 2003/2004)*
Schools	Mean competency level of schools	*School development (PISA Germany school panel 2000/2009)*
School systems (states)	"Output" of educational systems	State trends

systems, schools are more equal, so that each school has a relatively wide range of achievement levels as well as a wide range of student perceptions, allowing for higher correlations.

The example shows how effects measured between and within schools are shaped by system characteristics.

Examples of Enriched (Longitudinal) Designs Integrating ILSAs and EER

Furthermore, the ILSA design may be enhanced by oversampling as well as adding additional instruments, allowing for quasiexperimental add-ons and for longitudinal studies on the school and/or the individual level. For example, several such enhancements have been implemented as national options for the PISA studies in Germany (See Table 7.4).

Two examples of such enhancements will be presented: (1) a national large-scale assessment (NLSA) study on language competencies in Germany (DESI) reassessed students one year after the first NLSA allowed studying the impact of school level factors on classroom instruction and student growth. (2) PISA/Germany 2009 reassessed schools nine years after their first participation in that NLSA, allowing the study of school development over nearly a decade.

Longitudinal Design on the Individual Level: The German National Study on Language Learning, DESI

This section reports on a representative study of language development in ninth grade, $n=209$ schools, 1,579 teachers, 9,980 students. Hierarchical linear modeling (HLM) specifies the impact of school level (achievement orientation, strength of competency goals, cooperation among German language teachers) and classroom level factors (structure, teacher support, cognitive challenge, frequency of opportunities for language learning). Drawing on a school achievement study that is representative for Germany regarding the subjects of German and English (DESI; see Klieme et al. 2008), we assess how far differences in the development of achievement in terms of language awareness and learning motivation in the subject of German in ninth-year students can be explained by differences in the school norms and teaching practices and by differences in the norms and practices in German instruction. We also assess what pattern of relations can be identified between the school and classroom instructional characteristics. In each school, two classes from grade 9 were assessed. Data were analyzed with a series of three-level models, allowing for an analytical dissection of school, class, and individual levels.[1]

For teaching German to ninth-year students, we intend to assess how far differences in the development of achievement in the area of "language awareness" and motivation to learn can be explained by school norms and practices among the teaching staff and by characteristics of German instruction quality. The DESI subtest on language awareness is used here because it bears the best measurement characteristics of all tests applied to German lessons, and because the pertinent demands on German lessons can be measured comparatively well by surveying student perceptions.

At the level of (German) lessons, we once again identified three basic dimensions of instructional quality:

1. clear, well-structured teaching, (structuredness)
2. a supportive learning climate that is oriented towards the students (teacher support), and
3. challenging, cognitively activating demands (cognitive challenges)

However, only student self report of perceptions during lessons were available. In contrast to expert coded videotaped lessons, student self reports are limited particularly in assessing the third quality dimension. We administered a questionnaire scale regarding the perceived importance of correct language use, which should be able to model high demands on the achievement criterion of "language awareness." We also took into account a fourth scale for questions regarding the frequency of language-related learning opportunities in the classroom.

Following the learning and teaching theory assumptions outlined above, we expect supportive teacher behavior to be crucial to the development of motivation, while cognitively challenging lesson design is important for achievement development. Both of these criteria are likely to be positively influenced by well-structured instruction. Contrary to the three basic dimensions, the fourth scale pertinent to the frequency of learning opportunities in the field of language awareness constitutes a "surface characteristic" of methodological-didactic design, and we do not expect this scale to bear an effect on learning development.

The following predictors are applied at the school level: achievement expectations of the German teachers, norms that are shared among the German teaching staff (here: the relevance of language competency goals) as well as cooperation among the German teaching staff. These aspects of professional action among

---

[1] These analyses have first been published in German by Klieme et al. 2010c.

colleagues are generally assumed to influence the quality of instruction and also cognitive and motivational learning processes. We can specifically anticipate high expectations of achievement and respective competency goals of teachers to lead to more challenging lessons, thus mediating the improved development in achievement.

First, we are looking for effects of school level processes on instructional quality, as perceived by students (Table 7.5). Considering the model with control variables (model II), the following picture emerges: Explanation of perceived instruction is least successful for the surface characteristic of "learning opportunities." For the three deep level dimensions of instructional quality—i.e., structuredness, support and challenge—we can, however, state that the school type has significant impact, because all three dimensions of quality were assessed more positively in the educational track of Hauptschule (general secondary school) than at schools from the Gymnasium (grammar school) or Realschule (intermediate secondary school) tracks. Moreover, the aspects of professional work we assessed among the teaching staff (cooperation, competency goals, and expectations of achievement) do not reveal any significant effects, thus they do not contribute to the students' perceptions of instructional quality beyond the control variables we considered.

In a final analytical step, the effects of the school and instruction level on the increase in learning and motivation are assessed (see Table 7.6). Regarding our main research question, we can establish that none of the three characteristics of professional work at the school level impacts upon achievement and motivation. This applies when simultaneously taking control variables into account (in each case, models II), but also when only looking at the school characteristics as such (models I).

However, the findings outlined in Table 7.6 support our model of instructional quality. The indicator of cognitively challenging lessons used here, "demand on correct language use," bears a significant and also sizable effect on the increase in achievement, at both the individual and the classroom levels. This implies that a high cognitive challenge, as commonly perceived by the students, influences achievement development in a positive way; moreover, within a class, those students who perceive this aspect of instructional quality in a more positive light than their peers are distinguished by an even higher increase in achievement. Pursuant to our assumptions, teacher support is particularly important for the development of motivation.

Thus, the theoretical assumption that school quality, and more precisely the professional norms and cooperation among teaching staff, mediated by instructional quality, influences the development of students, receives no support from the DESI data on German lessons. Contradicting the assumptions of school research, and even more contrary to the expectations of school development researchers, our study does show indications of an effect of school characteristics on the development of learning and motivation in German lessons.

At the level of classroom instruction, however, an effect can be ascertained for cognitively demanding lesson designs (promoting achievement development) as

Table 7.5 Three-level model for explaining instructional characteristics

Predictors	Structuredness		Support		Demand language use		Learning opportunity	
	I	II	I	II	I	II	I	II
Student level								
Social status		-0.034*		-0.053*		-0.047*		-0.013
Basic cognitive abilities		-0.030*		0.027		0.065*		-0.051*
Gender female		0.072*		0.206*		0.365*		0.023
German as first language		-0.033		0.082*		0.029		0.051
Classroom level								
Social composition		0.062		0.234		0.298*		-0.046
Cognitive composition		0.027		-0.003		0.152**		-0.002
Proportion of girls		-0.339*		-0.140		0.186		-0.151
Proportion of first language German		-0.347*		-0.370*		-0.413*		-0.266
School level								
Expected achievement	-0.016	0.020	0.006	0.019	0.045	0.014	<0.001	0.048
Cooperation	0.054*	0.015	-0.017	-0.037	-0.036	0.019	0.054*	0.026
Competency goals	-0.046*	-0.002	-0.032	-0.010	0.020	-0.011	-0.082*	-0.033
School with Hauptschul-educational track		0.343*		0.325*		0.176*		0.168*
Grammar school		0.079		-0.028		-0.049		-0.138

$*p<0.05$; $**p<0.07$

Table 7.6 Three-level model for explaining achievement gains and motivational development

Predictors	Achievement gains			Increase in motivation		
	I	II	III	I	II	III
Student level						
Social status		0.001	0.001		0.009	0.009
Basic cognitive abilities		0.123*	0.122*		−0.075*	−0.076*
Gender female		0.077	0.077		0.190*	0.191*
German as first language		0.006	0.006		0.025	0.027
Demand language use		0.085*	0.085*		0.055	0.055
Structuredness of lessons		0.039	0.039		0.064*	0.064*
Learning opportunities		−0.017	−0.017		0.010	0.010
Teacher support		0.029	0.029		0.205*	0.204*
Classroom level						
Social composition		−0.151	−0.001		−0.040	0.018
Cognitive composition		0.204	0.274*		0.132	0.180
Proportion of girls		0.056	0.063		−0.207	−0.200
Proportion German first language		−0.221	−0.322		−0.547*	−0.559*
Demand language use		0.332*	0.335*		0.126	0.120
Structuredness of lessons		−0.141	−0.139		0.087	0.074
Learning opportunities		−0.147	−0.166		0.110	0.099
Teacher support		0.147	0.135		0.232*	0.216*
School level						
Expected achievement	−0.030	−0.034	−0.037	−0.049	−0.020	−0.017
Cooperation	−0.008	0.040	0.034	0.050	0.049	0.035
Competency goals	−0.008	−0.033	−0.024	−0.006	0.007	0.025
School with Hauptschule educational track			0.106			0.150
Grammar school			−0.205			−0.043

*$p<0.05$; **$p<0.07$

well as supportive teacher behavior (promoting motivation). DESI thus supports the teaching quality model that assumes three basic dimensions, with cognitive challenges presenting the most important predictor of achievement, whereas teacher support determines motivation development. Both are described as "deep level characteristics" in instructional research. Corresponding to theoretical assumptions, the frequency of learning opportunities in terms of a "surface characteristic" does not correlate with learning and motivation development.

We can summarize this pattern of findings as follows: Basic dimensions of instructional quality prove to be effective in the subject of German, while it is impossible to match the professional instructional activities with the professional actions at school level (i.e., cooperation, expected achievement, and competency goals among staff). The school level factors influence instructions particularly regarding characteristics of the diversity of learning opportunities, which other than supportive measures and cognitive challenges, do not render any significant contribution to instructional effectiveness.

Enhanced ILSA Designs Allow for Testing Organizational Change: Longitudinal Studies on the School Level—The German PISA School Panel

The mainstream of school improvement research is still largely grounded in case studies (cf. Hopkins 2005; Lee and Williams 2006). Large-scale international student assessments like TIMSS and PISA can provide new insights into the mechanisms of school change, because they offer high quality achievement data and a broad array of context and process data (including school policies, curricular and extracurricular opportunities, school climate, and many more). However, from a school effectiveness point of view, these studies have limited explanatory power because they are all cross-sectional. Effects caused by school policies and school-level processes cannot be separated from selection bias.

"The often-heard plea for more longitudinal research in school effectiveness can only be repeated here. Not only effects should be measured at more than one point in time, but also input and process variables" (Scheerens and Bosker 1997, p. 315).

A national enhancement to the PISA studies luckily provides longitudinal information for hundreds of schools. The results presented here are built on national enhancements to the OECD PISA studies that were administered in 2000, 2003, and 2006.[2] In each of those years, the "international" PISA sample in Germany, which consisted of about 200 schools, has been enhanced by a national sampling scheme, which applies PISA tests and background questionnaires to 1,500 schools all over Germany, allowing for a comparison between federal states.

Within those very large data sets, 506 schools could be found that had been assessed at least twice in 2000 and in 2003. Most of those schools are located in small federal states, so the sample is by no means representative for Germany. However, it can help to study stability in school variables.

We applied hierarchical linear modeling, with students both from 2000 and 2003 included in a virtual sample, and membership in one of the two cohorts as a level 1-indicator (see Fig. 7.5 and Table 7.7 for the associated parameter estimates).

With a 0.93 correlation between mean school achievement in 2000 and in 2003, this variable shows high stability. However, the extremely high parameter also results from the stability of school *type* (track) differences. When looking at the lowest track (Hauptschule) only, the stability of achievement over three years decreases to 0.84; while for grammar schools only, it is down to 0.57. Thus within the German school system, there is some instability of school results. Schools move up or down, and we might try to explain those changes by changes in school input and school processes.

As we had assumed, there is a complex interplay between school composition (i.e., mean student SES) and student achievement (Fig. 7.6). Schools with a com-

---

[2] This research has been initiated by Klieme and Steinert 2008; the findings cited here have first been presented by Hochweber et al. (2010).

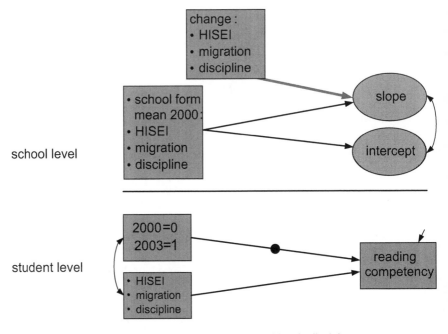

Fig. 7.5 Multilevel model for the analysis of organizational longitudinal data

Table 7.7 Parameter estimation and significance test for the model in Fig. 7.5

	I	II
Dependent: 2000 reading level		
School form: HS educational track	−32.4	−32.2
School form: GY	36.2	36.6
Proportion of migrant students	−12.3	−12.0
Mean HISEI	31.8	31.5
Discipline, school climate	−11.5	−12.8
Dependent: change in reading 2000–2003		
School form: HS educational track	−0.5	1.7
School form: GY	0.9	−4.5
Proportion of migrant students	*−3.4*	−1.7
Mean HISEI	−3.2	0.1
Discipline, school climate	*4.2*	*3.7*
Difference migration		*−4.0*
Difference HISEI		*3.4*
Difference school climate		*3.9*

*$p < 0.05$

paratively high achievement can maintain or improve their social composition. This finding leads to a better understanding of the relation between student composition and school outcome. Traditionally, only the impact of individual SES and student composition on student learning and outcomes has been considered.

Fig. 7.6 Cross-lagged panel analysis (school level only) of the interrelation between reading and SES background

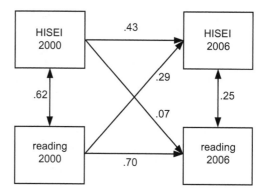

What about school level input and processes? Results indicate that classroom discipline, mean SES, and proportion of migrant students explain the (aggregated) achievement status on school level. The better the disciplinary climate, and the lower the proportion of migrant students, the better reading competency develops over three years. And, finally, schools that succeed in increasing disciplinary climate, attracting students from higher SES backgrounds, and a reduced proportion of migrant students will show higher gains in reading achievement.

Summary and Conclusion

The main purpose of international large-scale assessment is to provide indicators for continuous monitoring of educational systems. Compared with the complexity and theoretical challenges of Educational Effectiveness Research, however, ILSAs show severe limitations—the most important being the absence of longitudinal data, especially baseline information on prior achievement. Without longitudinal designs, it is practically impossible to build adequate, complex explanatory models or to draw causal inferences.

However, there are ways to enhance the design of national as well as international large-scale assessments to allow for stronger explanatory power. This chapter reported on two such enhancements implemented in Germany: adding a short-term longitudinal assessment on the student and classroom level covering one school year (implemented within the language assessment study DESI), and resampling schools to study school development as an organizational process (implemented within national extensions to PISA). We recommend that ILSA studies move in those directions to increase validity as well as policy relevance.

Nevertheless, useful links already exist between ILSAs and EER. First, ILSAs need constructs and instruments and theoretical insight from Educational Research, including EER, to design and analyze the studies. Thus, designing advanced ILSA studies is a challenge to Effectiveness Research, which may even initiate new developments in theory and empirical work, as has been the case with the notion of "opportunity to learn." Second, ILSAs can help foster EER by allowing explorative analyses and generating hypotheses, by testing research hypotheses, and by studying the intercultural biases and culture-specific context factors that shape the functioning of educational systems.

Hopefully the future will see further advancements in the interaction between Educational Effectiveness Research and international large-scale assessments. To reach this goal, the research community has to gain support of policymakers.

Acknowledgment The present author gratefully acknowledges contributions from Johannes Hartig, Jan Hochweber, Nina Jude, Ulf Kröhne, Katrin Rakoczy, Brigitte Steinert, Svenja Vieluf, all from DIPF, Center for Research on Educational Quality and Evaluation. Martina Kenk and Gwen Schulte have been especially helpful in editing this chapter.

References

Abedi, J., M. Courtney, S. Leon, J. Kao, and T. Azzam. 2006. *English language learners and math achievement: A study of opportunity to learn and language accommodation (CSE Report 702, 2006)*. Los Angeles: University of California, Center for the Study of Evaluation/National Center for Research on Evaluation, Standards, and Student Testing.

Baker, D. P. 2009. The invisible hand of world education culture. In *Handbook of education policy research*, eds. G. Sykes, B. Schneider and D. N. Plank, 958–968. New York: Routledge.

Baumert, J., R. Lehmann, M. Lehrke, B. Schmitz, M. Clausen, and I. Hosenfeld, et al. 1997. *TIMSS—Mathematisch-naturwissenschaftlicher Unterricht im internationalen Vergleich. Deskriptive Befunde*. Opladen: Leske + Budrich.

Baumert, J., M. Kunter, W. Blum, M. Brunner, T. Voss, and A. Jordan, et al. 2009. Teachers' mathematical knowledge, cognitive activation in the classroom, and student progress. *American Educational Research Journal* 47:133–180.

Borman, G. D., G. M. Hewes, L. T. Overman, and S. Brown. 2003. Comprehensive school reform and achievement: A meta-analysis. *Review of Educational Research* 73:125–230.

Brophy, J., ed. 1992. *Planning and managing learning tasks and activities: Advances in research on teaching (Vol. 3)*. Greenwich: JAI Press.

Brown, A. L. 1994. The advancement of learning. *Educational Researcher* 23(8):4–12.

Bryk, A. S., P. B. Sebring, E. Allensworth, S. Luppescu, and J. Q. Easton. 2010. *Organizing schools for improvement. Lessons from Chicago*. Chicago: University of Chicago Press.

Carroll, J.B. 1963. A model of school learning. *Teachers College Record* 64:723–733.

Clausen, M. 2002. *Unterrichtsqualität: Eine Frage der Perspektive?* Münster: Waxmann.

Creemers, B. P. M. 1994. *The effective classroom*. London: Cassell.

Creemers, B. P. M., and L. Kyriakides. 2008. *The dynamics of educational effectiveness: A contribution to policy, practice, and theory in contemporary schools*. London: Routledge.

Deci, E. L., and R. M. Ryan. 1985. *Intrinsic motivation and self-determination in human behavior*. New York: Plenum Press.

Ditton, H. 2000. Qualitätskontrolle und Qualitätssicherung in Schule und Unterricht. *Zeitschrift für Pädagogik* 41(Beiheft):73–92.

Ditton, H. 2007. Schulqualität – Modelle zwischen Konstruktion, empirischen Befunden und Implementierung. In *Qualität von Schule*, eds. J. van Buer and C. Wagner, 83–92. Frankfurt a. M.: Lang.

Ditton, H., and L. Krecker. 1995. Qualität von Schule und Unterricht. Empirische Befunde zu Fragestellungen und Aufgaben der Forschung. *Zeitschrift für Pädagogik* 41(4):507–531.

Fend, H. 1998. *Qualität im Bildungswesen. Schulforschung zu Systembedingungen, Schulprofilen und Lehrerleistung*. Weinheim: Juventa Verlag.

Goldschmidt, P., K. Choi, and F. Martinez. 2004. *Using hierarchical growth models to monitor school performance over time: Comparing NCE to scale score results. CES Report 618.* Los Angeles: Center for the study of evaluation, University of California.

Gustafsson, J.-E. 2007. Understanding causal influences on educational achievement through analysis of differences over time within countries. In *Lessons learned: What international assessments tell us about math achievement,* ed. T. Loveless, 37–63. Washington, D.C.: The Brookings Institution.

Hanushek, E. A., and L. Woessmann. 2009. Do better schools lead to more growth? Cognitive skills, economic outcomes, and causation. NBER Working Paper No. 14633, National Bureau of Economic Research, Cambridge. http://www.nber.org/papers/w14633.pdf. Accessed 3 Nov 2011.

Hanushek, E. A., and L. Wossmann. 2010. The economics of international differences in educational achievement. NBER Working Papers 15949, National Bureau of Economic Research, Cambridge. http://www.nber.org/papers/w15949.pdf. Accessed 3 Nov 2011.

Harris, A., and J. H. Chrispeels., eds. 2006. *Improving schools and educational systems: International perspectives.* London: Routledge.

Hattie, J. 2009. *Visible learning. A synthesis of over 800 meta-analyses relating to achievement.* London: Routledge.

Hiebert, J. R., H. Gallimore, K. B. Garnier, H. Givven, J. Hollingsworth, and A. M.-Y. Jacobs, et al. 2003. Teaching mathematics in seven countries: Results from the TIMSS 1999 video study. US Department of Education, National Center for Education Statistics, Washington, D.C.

Hochweber, J., B. Steinert, J. Gomolka, and E. Klieme. 2010. Schulentwicklung 2000–2003–2006: Befunde auf Basis der PISA-Studien. Paper presented at the 2010 Congress of the German Society for Educational Science (DGFE), Mainz, Germany.

Hopkins, D., ed. 2005. *The practice and theory of school improvement: International handbook of educational change.* Springer: Dordrecht.

Husén, T. 1967. *International study of achievement in mathematics (Vol. 2).* New York: Wiley.

Husén, T. 1974. Introduction to the reviews of three studies of the International Association for the Evaluation of Educational Achievement (IEA). *American Educational Research Journal* 11(4):407–408.

Klieme, E., and K. Rakoczy. 2003. Unterrichtsqualität aus Schülerperspektive. In *PISA 2000. Ein differenzierter Blick auf die Länder der Bundesrepublik Deutschland,* eds. J. Baumert, C. Artelt, E. Klieme, M. Neubrand, M. Prenzel, U. Schiefele et al., 333–359. Opladen: Leske + Budrich.

Klieme, E., and B. Steinert. 2008. Schulentwicklung im Längsschnitt. Ein Forschungsprogramm und erste explorative Analysen. *Zeitschrift für Erziehungswissenschaft* 10(Sonderheft):221–238.

Klieme, E., and S. Vieluf. 2009. Teaching practices, teachers' beliefs and attitudes. In *Creating effective teaching and learning environments. First results from talis,* ed. OECD. Paris: Organisation for Economic Co-operation and Development. http://www.oecd.org/dataoecd/17/51/43023606.pdf.

Klieme, E., G. Schümer, and S. Knoll. 2001. Mathematikunterricht in der Sekundarstufe I: Aufgabenkultur und Unterrichtsgestaltung. In *Bundesministerium für Bildung und Forschung (BMBF)* ed. TIMSS—Impulse für Schule und Unterricht. Forschungsbefunde, Reforminitiativen, Praxisberichte und Video-Dokumente, 43–57. München: Medienhaus Biering.

Klieme, E., A. Helmke, R. Lehmann, G. Nold, H.-G. Rolff, K. Schröder, et al. eds. 2008. *Unterricht und Kompetenzerwerb in Deutsch und Englisch. Ergebnisse der DESI-Studie.* Weinheim: Beltz.

Klieme, E., C. Pauli, and K. Reusser. 2009. The Pythagoras study: Investigating effects of teaching and learning in Swiss and German classrooms. In *The Power of Video Studies in Investigating Teaching and Learning in the Classroom,* eds. T. Janik and T. Seidel, 137–160. Münster: Waxmann Verlag.

Klieme, E., E. Backhoff, W. Blum, J. Buckley, Y. Hong, D. Kaplan, H. Levin, J. Scheerens, W. Schmidt, F. van de Vijver, and S. Vieluf. 2010a. *Designing PISA as a sustainable database for educational policy and research: The PISA 2012 Context Questionnaire Framework.* Paris: OECD.

Klieme, E., N. Fischer, H. G. Holtappels, T. Rauschenbach, and L. Stecher. 2010b. *Ganztagsschule – Entwicklung und Wirkungen*. Frankfurt a. M.: DIPF.

Klieme, E., B. Steinert, and J. Hochweber. 2010c. Zur Bedeutung der Schulqualität für Unterricht und Lernergebnisse. In *Schulische Lerngelegenheiten und Kompetenzentwicklung. Festschrift für Jürgen Baumert,* eds. W. Bos, E. Klieme and O. Köller, 231–255. Münster: Waxmann.

Kröhne, U. 2010. Comparison of quasi-experimental methods for large-scale assessments: Estimating the effect of bilingual instruction based on a subsample of the DESI study. Invited presentation at the 2010 Symposium on Causality, Jena University, Germany.

Kunter, M., T. Dubberke, J. Baumert, W. Blum, M. Brunner, A. Jordan, et al. 2006. Mathematikunterricht in den PISA-Klassen 2004: Rahmenbedingungen, Formen und Lehr-Lernprozesse. In *PISA 2003: Untersuchungen zur Kompetenzentwicklung im Verlauf eines Schuljahres,* eds. M. Prenzel, J. Baumert, W. Blum, R. Lehmann, D. Leutner, M. Neubrand et al., 161–194. Münster: Waxmann.

Kunter, M., Y.-M. Tsai, U. Klusmann, M. Brunner, S. Krauss, and J. Baumert. 2008. Students' and mathematics teachers' perception of teacher enthusiasm and instruction. *Learning and Instruction* 18:468–482.

Kyriakides, L., and N. Tsangaridou. 2004. School effectiveness and teacher effectiveness in physical education. Paper presented at the 85 Annual AERA Meeting, American Educational Research Association, Chicago, USA.

Lee, J. C., and M. Williams. 2006. *School improvement: International perspectives.* New York: Nova Science Publishers.

Lipowsky, F., K. Rakoczy, C. Pauli, B. Drollinger-Vetter, E. Klieme and K. Reusser. 2009. Quality of Geometry instruction and its short-term impact on students' understanding of the Pythagorean theorem. *Learning and Instruction* 19:527–537.

Luyten, H., and R. de Jong. 1998. Parallel classes: Differences and similarities. Teacher effects and school effects in secondary schools. *School Effectiveness and School Improvement* 9(4):437–473.

Organisation for Economic Co-operation and Development. ed. 2007a. *Education at a glance.* Paris: Organisation for Economic Co-operation and Development.

Organisation for Economic Co-operation and Development. ed. 2007b. *PISA 2006. Science competencies for tomorrow's world.* Paris: Organisation for Economic Co-operation and Development.

Organisation for Economic Co-operation and Development. ed. 2008. *Education at a glance.* Paris: Organisation for Economic Co-operation and Development.

Organisation for Economic Co-operation and Development. ed. 2009a. *Education at a glance.* Paris: Organisation for Economic Co-operation and Development.

Organisation for Economic Co-operation and Development. ed. 2009b. *PISA 2009 Assessment framework key competencies in reading, mathematics and science.* Paris: OECD.

Pianta, R. C., and B. K. Hamre. 2009. Conceptualization, measurement, and improvement of classroom processes: Standardized observation can leverage capacity. *Educational Researcher* 38(2):109–119.

Purves, A. C. 1987. The evolution of the IEA: A memoir. *Comparative Education Review* 31(1):10–28.

Rowan, B., E. Camburn, and R. Correnti. 2004. Using teacher logs to measure the enacted curriculum in large-scale surveys: Insights from the study of instructional improvement. *Elementary School Journal* 105:75–102.

Sammons, P. 1999. *School effectiveness: Coming of age in the 21st century.* Lisse: Swets & Zeitlinger.

Sammons, P., D. Nuttall, P. Cuttance, and S. Thomas. 1995. Continuity of school effects: A longitudinal analysis of primary and secondary school effects on GCSE performance. *School Effectiveness and School Improvement* 6(4):285–307.

Sammons, P., S. Thomas, and P. Mortimore. 1997. *Forging links: Effective schools and effective departments.* London: Paul Chapman Publishing Ltd.

Scheerens, J. 2000. *Improving school effectiveness. Fundamentals of educational planning series, IIEP, Vol. 68.* Paris: United Nations Educational, Scientific, and Cultural Organization (UNESCO).

Scheerens, J., and R. J. Bosker. 1997. *The foundations of educational effectiveness.* Oxford: Pergamon Press.

Schmidt, W. H., and A. Maier. 2009. Opportunity to learn. In *Handbook of Education Policy Research,* eds. G. Sykes, B. Schneider and D. N. Plank, 541–559. New York: Routledge.

Schmidt, W. H., and C. McKnight. 1995. Surveying educational opportunity in mathematics and science: An international perspective. *Educational Evaluation and Policy Analysis* 17(3):337–353.

Schwerdt, G., and A. C. Wuppermann. 2011. Is traditional teaching really all that bad? A within-student between-subject approach. *Economics of Education Review* 30:365–379.

Seidel, T., and R. J. Shavelson. 2007. Teaching effectiveness research in the last decade: The role of theory and research design in disentangling meta-analysis results. *Review of Educational Research* 77:454–499.

Slavin, R. E. 1996. *Education for all.* Lisse: Swets & Zeitlinger.

Stanat, P., and G. Christensen. 2006. *Where immigrant students succeed—a comparative review of performance and engagement in PISA 2003.* Paris: Organisation for Economic Co-operation and Development.

Stevens, F. 1993. Applying an opportunity-to-learn conceptual framework to the investigation of the effects of teaching practices via secondary analyses of multiple-case-study summary data. *Journal of Negro Education* 62(3):232–248.

Stigler, J. W., and J. Hiebert. 1999. *The teaching gap: Best ideas from the world's teachers for improving education in the classroom.* New York: Free Press.

Stringfield, S. 1994. A model of elementary school effects. In *Advances in school effectiveness research and practice,* eds. D. Reynolds, B. P. M. Creemers, P. S. Nesselrodt, C. Teddlie, E. C. Shaffer and S. Stringfield, 153–187. Oxford: Pergamon.

Teddlie, C., and D. Reynolds. eds. 2000. *The international handbook of school effectiveness research.* New York: Routledge.

Teddlie, C., and S. Stringfield. 1993. *Schools make a difference. Lessons learned from a 10-year study of school effects.* New York: Teachers College Press.

Teddlie, C., and S. Stringfield. 2006. A brief history of school improvement research in the USA. In *Improving schools and educational systems: international perspectives,* eds. A. Harris and J. Chrispeels, 131–166. London: Routledge.

Thomas, S., P. Sammons, P. Mortimore, and R. Smees. 1997. Stability and consistency in secondary schools' effects on students' GCSE outcomes over three years. *School effectiveness and school improvement* 8(2):169–197.

Tschannen-Moran, M., and A. Woolfolk Hoy. 2001. Teacher efficacy: Capturing an elusive construct. *Teaching and Teacher Education* 17(7):783–805.

Walberg, H. J. 1986. Syntheses of research on teaching. In *Handbook of research on teaching (3rd edn.),* ed. M. C. Wittrock, 214–229. New York: Macmillan.

Walker, D. A. 1976. *The IEA six-subject survey: An empirical study of education in twenty-one countries. International studies in evaluation.* New York: Wiley.

Wang, M. C., G. D. Haertel, and H. D. Walberg. 1993. Toward a knowledge base for school learning. *Review of Educational Research* 63(3):249–294.

Willms, J. D., and S. W. Raudenbush. 1989. A longitudinal hierarchical linear model for estimating school effects and their stability. *Journal of educational measurement* 26(3):209–232.

Chapter 8
Prospects for the Future: A Framework and Discussion of Directions for the Next Generation of International Large-Scale Assessments

Henry Braun

Introduction

There is an old adage, "Be careful what you wish for." In the case of education policy, the old lament that the results of international large-scale assessments (IL-SAs) were not a "front burner" issue has been replaced by the lament that they are now too politicized. Whether or not this is the case, it is certainly true that education policy debates stemming from international comparisons have attained unprecedented prominence, partly because of the ascendancy of the human capital model of competitive advantage among nations. In fact, in some countries, the reports of ILSAs have been key drivers of reform. The continuing expansion of the number of participating jurisdictions testifies to their global importance. Indeed, ILSAs are seen as providing unique, credible information that can—and should—inform broad policy decisions. In this landscape, holding a conference in March 2011 in Princeton, NJ, on the role of ILSAs in education policy was both timely and much needed. As this volume reveals, a broad range of topics was covered and different suggestions for future innovations put forward. The principal aim of this chapter is to offer a preliminary framework for considering ILSA-related issues, and to situate the chapters of this book—based on presentations given at the conference at Educational Testing Service in Princeton—within this framework. It concludes with some thoughts on future directions.

The largest and most influential global ILSAs are Trends in International Mathematics and Science Study (TIMSS) and Progress in International Reading Literacy Study (PIRLS), both sponsored by the International Association for the Evaluation of Educational Achievement (IEA), and the Programme for International Student Assessment (PISA) and the International Adult Literacy Survey (IALS), both spon-

H. Braun (✉)
Center for the Study of Testing, Evaluation and Education Policy, Lynch School of Education
Boston College, 140 Commonwealth Ave, 02467 Chestnut Hill, MA, USA
e-mail: braunh@bc.edu

M.von Davier et al. (eds.), *The Role of International Large-Scale Assessments:*
Perspectives from Technology, Economy, and Educational Research,
DOI 10.1007/978-94-007-4629-9_8, © Springer Science+Business Media Dordrecht 2013

sored by the Organisation for Economic Co-operation and Development (OECD). At the conference there was also discussion of the International Civics and Citizenship Survey (ICCS) and the forthcoming Programme for the International Assessment of Adult Competencies (PIAAC). It was noted that an important role is played by regional large-scale assessments confined to nations in western, southern, and eastern Africa, and Latin America and the Caribbean. Although there are certainly policy issues specific to each, this chapter aims to address issues that apply to most, if not all, global ILSAs.

To begin at the beginning, the primary purpose of education is to adequately prepare all children to lead productive, satisfying lives that contribute to the common good. The role of education policy is to design, manage and monitor the education system so it accomplishes its purpose. Braun and Kanjee (2006) posited that this purpose subsumes four component goals, namely: access, quality, effectiveness, and efficiency. ILSAs typically have been used to address the goals of quality and effectiveness of educational systems. In particular, they help to answer three key questions:

1. What are the essential skills, dispositions and habits of mind required for success in the 21st century?
2. In view of the response to No. 1, how does each nation fare in comparison to other participating nations or jurisdictions?
3. What can be expected with respect to growth over time and attainment of these essential precursors to success?

With respect to quality, the rigorous and intensive process that precedes agreement on the blueprint for an ILSA represents an international consensus on valued outcomes for the focal cohort of students. Individual countries can examine their curricula to gauge alignment with these outcomes. Turning to effectiveness, comparisons with other countries with respect to both current level and trend provide at least a rough indication of the relative effectiveness of a country's education system. (Of course, more nuanced interpretations require due consideration of contextual differences.) As far as growth over time, the spectrum of results offers nations a choice of targets, both short term and long term.

Thus, the answers to the three questions can inform policymakers' deliberations. To this point, Ritzen (this volume) provides empirical evidence on the differential impact of PISA 2006 results on policy formation across participating countries. Not surprisingly, evidence, however credible and relevant, is not sufficient to drive macro-level educational policy.

More recently, ILSAs have also been used to address one aspect of the efficiency goal. In particular, various authors have sought to identify some characteristics common to the education systems of the jurisdictions that are at or near the top of the league tables, or have achieved substantial and sustained improvement in their standings over time (see, for example, Paine and Schleicher 2011). The implication is that other jurisdictions would do well to emulate these exemplars. I will return to this point below.

ILSAs: Theory of Action

It is evident that the primary contribution of ILSAs is to facilitate direct international comparisons of achievement; that is, in the absence of a common assessment, each nation's system remains "hermetically sealed," and it is well nigh impossible to make meaningful comparisons among them. Differences in high school completion rates, for example, are potentially confounded by differences in requirements, economic conditions, and so on. Thus, policy leaders are free to make assertions regarding their nation's relative standing in regard to educational achievement without fear of contradiction.

With this in mind, Ritzen (this volume) argues for the importance of the transparency provided by ILSAs and suggests different mechanisms by which they can serve as agents for change. Of course, transparency can be a double-edged sword (as if WikiLeaks didn't demonstrate that sufficiently). In the present instance, the most common presentation of ILSA results is in the form of a ranking of jurisdictions based on score means, the so-called league tables. These rankings can be over-interpreted or misinterpreted, with possibly negative consequences. What is called for is a more nuanced examination of the results at various levels of aggregation—but this is rarely done by reporters, pundits, or legislators. Although the sponsors not only publish massive tomes after each administration to provide supplemental analyses and greater insight, but also supply data files for secondary analyses, these rarely get the attention of the league tables and the accompanying commentary. A key issue, then, is how ILSAs can evolve both to mitigate negative outcomes and to better contribute to constructive change.

But how can transparency lead to improvements in education? Theoretically, the process should work like this: The surveys generate and disseminate widely accepted evidence on the relative performance of different jurisdictions on relevant constructs such as student knowledge and skills in reading, mathematics, or science. This "transparency" spurs reflection and review on the part of government officials, policymakers and other stakeholders in education. A consensus is reached on appropriate modifications to policy and practice that are informed, at least in part, by the policies and practices of the most successful jurisdictions. Moreover, the publicity resulting from the release of the results on a fixed cycle supports the political will to allocate sufficient resources over a long period of time to achieve sustainable improvement.

What are the essential conditions for such a theory to approximate reality? There are at least five. They are as follows:

1. The reported outcomes are considered credible, relevant, and sufficiently accurate.
2. There is acknowledgment of the correspondence between these outcomes and the national goals.
3. The interpretations of the outcomes, both absolutely and comparatively, are approximately correct.

4. Stakeholders are inspired (or spurred) by the results, as well as the accompanying public reaction, to propose new policies and allocate (or reallocate) resources.
5. Policymakers maintain a sustained but flexible focus on these policies.

Let us consider each one in turn, with references to chapters in this volume as appropriate.

Credibility and Relevance

Before each administration, there is a lengthy process, which typically involves all participating jurisdictions, to achieve consensus on the operational definitions of the target constructs and carry out a test development process that results in an instrument appropriate to a heterogeneous set of student populations comprising many different educational, cultural, and linguistic traditions. Both the rigor of the process and its products contribute to the credibility of the outcomes. In addition, because comparability is the touchstone for utility, such factors as sample selection and degree of participation, accuracy, and appropriateness of the translations/ adaptations, candidate motivation, and fidelity to administrative protocols are addressed and monitored. Although these factors were not central to any of the presentations at the conference, the impact of any major changes in the design of an ILSA on these factors would have to be evaluated. Relevance is supported by the rationale proposed for each target construct, which includes an argument linking proficiency to success in further academic studies and/or in the workplace and civic life (Kirsch et al. 2007). Clearly, doubts about credibility undermine the argument for relevance.

Conference presenters did address different facets of both credibility and relevance. With respect to the latter, Hanushek and Woessman (this volume) argue that the core cognitive skills measured by ILSAs are key components of human capital and assert the importance of the direct measurement of skills in contrast to statistics on proxies for achievement, such as educational attainment and the like. There are at least two main difficulties with distal indicators such as educational attainment. First, they are not comparable across jurisdictions and, second, there is wide variation in the distribution of proficiency at each level of attainment. See, for example, results from the National Adult Literacy Survey (1993). Further, the authors cite empirical findings that relate country-level variation in human capital to differences in economic growth and development. They do acknowledge, however, that returns to skills vary by country due to differences in such factors as level of development, political structure, cultural issues, and the like.

With respect to credibility, critics of standardized testing typically focus on the twin criteria of depth and breadth. The former is usually framed in terms of construct representation. That is, the tests fail to address the more complex facets of the target constructs, leading to an incomplete, and too optimistic, portrait of achievement. With regard to breadth, the argument is that the target constructs are too narrowly construed, with the consequence that important skills do not receive the necessary attention and resources.

Presenters addressed the issue of breadth and credibility, making the case for particular ensembles of constructs: Torney-Purta and Amadeo (this volume) speak to the importance of civic engagement and citizenship, while Levin (this volume) speaks to noncognitive skills. Although the authors certainly acknowledge the enduring importance of foundational skills, they argue that other constructs deserve considerably more attention if we are to capture the full spectrum of human capital relevant to success in the 21st century.

The chapter by Torney-Purta and Amadeo argues for looking beyond purely economic considerations to measuring dispositions related to civil society and participatory democracy. They provide a useful review of past assessments, making the case that they attained a high level of psychometric quality and, moreover, that secondary analyses of the results has yielded important insights with respect to both crossnational and subnational comparisons. In particular, it has been possible to identify multidimensional profiles of individuals with distinctly different beliefs and attitudes. Such findings complement the empirical findings that higher levels of cognitive skills are associated with greater participation in the economic, social, and civic life of the state.

The chapter by Levin urges that so-called noncognitive skills be assessed along with cognitive skills because there are strong theoretical and empirical rationales for the important roles that these skills play in individual success both in school and work. Thus, these skills should be considered integral components of human capital and deserving of attention. He also cites evidence that schooling influences the development of these skills, strengthening the argument that they should be included as target constructs in the design of school-based surveys. Further, Levin makes the important point that neglect of these constructs can skew policy choices.

As is the case with the assessment of civic dispositions, there is ample precedent for including noncognitive skills in ILSAs. For example, an instrument labeled an "Inventory of Student Approaches to Learning" was administered as part of PISA 2000 (OECD 2003). The instrument assessed such constructs as motivation, self-related beliefs, and approaches to learning. Psychometric and other analyses indicate that the instrument met the stringent criteria required for an international study. Since then, there has been considerable activity in this arena, as documented in a recent review (Author 2008).

In contrast to accountability-related assessments, the low stakes associated with ILSAs (at least for students) make them a suitable vehicle for assessing noncognitive skills. As ILSAs transition to computer-based delivery, the potential for high-quality measurement of a broad array of such skills and dispositions is greatly enhanced. It should also be acknowledged that the distinction between "cognitive" and "noncognitive" is increasingly viewed as anachronistic: Many noncognitive skills have a strong cognitive component, and cognitive skills are applied most effectively when noncognitive skills are engaged. Thus, ILSAs should consider adopting a more expansive and holistic view of their focal constructs.

Role of Technology

Bill Gates is said to have remarked that "we overpredict the impact of technology in the short run and underpredict its impact in the long run." That rings true in the case of educational assessment in the United States, despite some undeniable advances in introducing computer delivery in a few states, as well as introducing it to such sectors as graduate admissions testing and professional licensure. With the continuing development of cheaper and more powerful mobile computing/communication devices and the completion of the next generation of the Internet and communication networks, one can reasonably hope that we are leaving the short run and entering the long run.

In the context of a particular ILSA, the strategic use of technology depends on a holistic view of the goals of the program and a realistic view of the constraints under which it operates: Would the introduction of computer delivery lead to improvements in construct representation and data utility that are sufficiently compelling to justify a major initial investment and, perhaps, larger operating costs? Could it lead to unintended biases? How would it affect participation of jurisdictions and of certain subpopulations in different jurisdictions?

Notwithstanding these and other related questions, there is a general sense that the introduction of technology in the administration of ILSAs is both inexorable and to be welcomed. Beller (this volume) shares that view. She offers a useful, comprehensive review of technology initiatives at the national and international levels. In particular, she briefly describes a number of interesting technology-based supplemental assessments undertaken or planned by both IEA and OECD.

There are a number of goals that can be envisioned for technology-based assessments. These include improving alignment and accuracy for measures of current target constructs, and facilitating the measurement of new constructs, such as problem-solving and computer/information literacy. These two, as well as other constructs that lend themselves more to technology-based assessments, could contribute to increased credibility and relevance of technology-based ILSAs, not least by strengthening links to the world outside schools. However, the assessment of new constructs will certainly raise challenging methodological issues. The introduction of more complex stimuli, as well as the desire to evaluate both processes and outcomes, will call for more sophisticated psychometric models and data-analytic strategies.

The conjunction of more ambitious targets of assessment and new means of delivery will also require different ways of organizing the work. The dynamics of the interactions among the various specialists are bound to become more complex as well. Technology will help here. As Beller points out, technology can increase efficiency and cost effectiveness by supporting new methodologies for collaborative assessment design and development, machine scoring of open-ended responses, and dissemination of results. Further advances are on the horizon. However, she does acknowledge the formidable challenges in conducting a computer-based administration internationally.

On this point, PIAAC, which is in the field in 2012, is a bellwether as it has been designed from the outset to be fully computer delivered.[1] Many lessons (some painful) have already been learned about conducting an ILSA on a new technology platform. If PIAAC can be carried out with reasonable success, it will surely provide an impetus for a broader move to computer-based ILSAs. Presumably, the infrastructure built for PIAAC can be leveraged for other OECD initiatives. The example of PIAAC demonstrates that, despite the challenges, many countries are eager to participate in a next-generation assessment.

Informing Policy

It is certainly true that volumes can be written concerning both the proper use of ILSA results and decrying the misuse of those same results. As mentioned earlier, ILSA results are most commonly viewed through the lens of league tables. Such tables are clear and irresistible, and appear to tell a very simple story. Too often, however, commentators focus on ranks (or changes in ranks) without due regard to the corresponding score differences. In many cases, substantially different ranks may mask small score differences (Bracey 2004). Although crossnational comparisons are of obvious interest, subnational comparisons may have greater immediate use. Unfortunately, these are too rarely given equal attention. An interesting hybrid is the simultaneous crossnational comparison of both levels of achievement and within jurisdiction variation (Sum et al. 2002) that directly addresses issues of equity.

ILSAs offer a well-designed framework to instantiate important constructs, and the outcomes do offer compelling examples of the high level of accomplishment that large proportions of students can reach in some jurisdictions. The contrasts among jurisdictions can be a powerful call to action, with a natural tendency to look to leading nations for policy prescriptions. Indeed, there is now burgeoning mini-industry based on culling "lessons learned" from the study of high-performance education systems. Delegations from lagging jurisdictions have been routinely dispatched to such destinations as Finland, Singapore, and Ontario to ferret out the secrets of their success. Commissioned reports drawing on the policies and practices of several leading nations purport to have distilled the keys to improved achievement, See for example, the reports by McKinsey (2007, 2010) and by Paine and Schleicher (2011).

Despite the enthusiasm of the authors and the certainty they communicate, caution is in order. Policy prescriptions implicitly rely on some form of causal attribution. As Hanushek and Woessman (this volume) acknowledge, there are serious impediments to making unassailable causal inferences from ILSAs. Although par-

---

[1] There is provision to administer a paper-and-pencil form when computer administration is infeasible or inadvisable.

ticipating jurisdictions form a natural experiment, high rankings or rapid progress are likely due to a confluence of factors, both educational and extraeducational. Focusing on certain common features of education policy offers only a partial and perhaps misleading picture. Hargreaves (2011) makes this point by noting that the Canadian provinces of Alberta, Ontario, and Quebec all do well in ILSAs but have rather different policies. He speculates that their advantage over the United States may be as much a function of economic, social and community conditions as the specifics of their educational systems.

From a methodological perspective, a necessary (but not sufficient) step would be to analyze the policies of a comparable group of "laggard" jurisdictions and determine that they indeed differ systematically from those of the leaders. Further, one would have to amass evidence to discredit alternative explanations for the differences in outcomes (Campbell 1957; Braun 2008). Another issue is whether differences in PISA outcomes truly reflect differences in performance of different jurisdictions or whether they are also due, in part, to the fact that the meaning of the background variables characterizing individuals and groups may vary across jurisdictions. Unfortunately, analyses that examine whether background characteristics of students in countries can be directly compared are rarely done. The patterns highlighted in the various reports, then, may be suggestive and even "common-sensical," but they are not scientifically impregnable. Caveat emptor is the watchword.

In a useful counternarrative, Klieme (this volume) offers a thoughtful analysis of the difficulties inherent in making inferences from ILSAs that are directly relevant to policymakers. He notes that the cross-sectional nature of ILSAs limit the strength of any causal claims and, in particular, points out the futility of carrying out credible value-added analyses. In a more positive vein, he suggests there is the possibility of a productive dynamic between ILSAs and what he terms "education effectiveness research." This is illustrated by an example of how Germany enhanced the value of an ILSA through the addition of a carefully designed and executed longitudinal component. More generally, there can be real value in secondary analyses of ILSA results, especially through focused subnational comparisons.

Because of the comprehensiveness of the data collected, going well beyond the cognitive results, ILSAs and related surveys offer a rich treasure trove for secondary analysts and have yielded important insights not available from single-country data. Hanushek and Woessman (this volume) cite an example from macroeconomic policy, but there are many others. As usual, special care is required in drawing conclusions from these data.

Policymakers and other stakeholders should not underestimate the obstacles to profiting from participation in an ILSA. Given the inertia inherent in education systems and the time lag in effecting meaningful reforms, successful change requires a sustained focus that, in turn, requires a broad political consensus on a long-term plan. Strategies should incorporate intermediate milestones whose attainment can maintain interest and support. Periodic assessments can be helpful in this regard, particularly if the results accurately reflect a trend of incremental improvement.

Policy Action

Ritzen (this volume) presents a general model of the different channels through which ILSA results provide information to various groups of stakeholders and, in the case of PISA 2006, categorizes different jurisdictions in terms of its impact on their education policies. He speculates on the various factors that determine whether ILSAs have a substantial impact in a particular jurisdiction. Where there is sufficient interest and concern, however, ILSAs can provide both impetus and direction, as illustrated by some of the examples cited by Ritzen. Klieme (this volume) makes the case that leveraging an ILSA through complementary studies can substantially enhance the utility of the findings and, thereby, play a greater role in policymakers' decisions.

Of course, a country's decision making in the educational arena depends on the interaction of multiple factors including the political context, national ambition, and competing priorities. However, the increasing prominence of ILSA results makes it more difficult for political leaders to dismiss them as irrelevant and disengage from the collaboration. At the same time, good intentions must be matched by sustained commitment and sufficient capacity. Poorer nations and those beset by political instability can experience difficulties in providing the former and building the latter. ILSA sponsors should rethink how they can provide the necessary support and encouragement to a broader array of within-country champions, recognizing that there are political considerations involved in engaging stakeholders through non-governmental channels.

Looking Ahead

On balance, in my view, ILSAs have had a positive impact on global educational systems. The critical question is whether and how that positive impact can be increased. There are at least three different paths:

- Provide more useful information.
- Enhance the value of that information.
- Extend the reach of the ILSAs.

Presumably, forward-looking strategies should encompass all three paths. With respect to the first two, conference presenters argued for extending the range and depth of the target constructs. Meaningful progress in this direction will likely involve some combination of computer-based delivery and special studies. As mentioned earlier, this will surely require the development and implementation of more powerful methodologies to assure sponsors of the accuracy and comparability of the results.

Although technical issues were raised only peripherally at the conference, they merit serious attention in any strategic planning exercise. Setting more ambitious assessment goals may call for the introduction of adaptive testing algorithms, new psychometric models, or expert systems for evaluating complex student responses. Given the long lead times typically incorporated into ILSA schedules, there should be ample opportunity for sponsors and contractors to review the current status of these technologies, to project near-term developments, and to conduct pilot studies to obtain empirical results that can inform design choices. In any real-world setting, there will be conditions or demands that constrain what may be feasible from a technical point of view, necessitating various tradeoffs. Again, the experience with PIAAC can provide useful guidelines for future innovations.

An ILSA can also serve as the anchor for various time-linked complementary surveys conducted by individual countries or groups of countries sharing a common interest. One example, already cited, was provided by provided by Klieme (this volume). Earlier exemplars include the TIMSS teacher video study (Stigler et al. 1999), the OECD school leadership study (Pont et al. 2008), and the OECD teacher study (2009). Another direction is to link an ILSA to a national assessment, as has been done with TIMSS and NAEP (Phillips 2009; NCES 2011).

Such extensions greatly enhance the value of the core ILSA results. Further enhancements would accrue if ILSAs provided more interpretable descriptions of different levels of performance. This could be accomplished through a modified behavioral anchoring of selected points along the score scale or through segmenting the score scale and providing descriptions of the modal student in each segment. The former approach was pioneered with the National Assessment of Educational Progress (Beaton and Allen 1992) and is currently employed by TIMSS and PIRLS. The latter was developed for the NALS (Kirsch et al. 1993).

A viable alternative is suggested by the work of Torney-Purta and Amadeo (this volume), in which clusters of individuals with similar profiles are identified and described. The estimated population distributions across clusters in different jurisdictions provide useful comparative information.

With respect to the path of extending the reach, the most obvious strategy is to continue to add more jurisdictions to the roster of participants. However, this strategy has some potentially negative consequences. As the number of participating jurisdictions grows, it places an increasing burden on program staff, particularly if the additions involve new languages or nations with poor infrastructure. The question is whether staff could continue to achieve a broad consensus, preserve quality, and meet tight timelines. Failure to plan for the operational implications could lead ILSAs to become victims of their own success. To mitigate one aspect of the problem, the OECD specifies that only member countries participate in the design and item calibration. Other countries then pay for the opportunity to administer the assessment under supervised conditions, with the results reported on the common scale.

Fortunately, alternative strategies are available. Aspiring nations could ramp up to full participation by first using small, selected samples of students to sit for the assessment in order to gauge the appropriateness of the level for the full cohort. In some cases, it might be informative to have teachers take the assessment, although there likely would be political considerations involved in such a step. Intermediate levels of participation could also be organized through partnerships with regional consortia. This could also create a channel for ILSA staff to share resources and expertise with the staff of the consortia. Indeed, building the requisite capacity in the developing world is a powerful, if indirect, way to extend the reach of the high-profile global ILSAs. The OECD is pursuing another direction, through the proposed development of a PISA-like instrument that could be administered by schools with the results reported on the PISA scales.

ILSAs also appear to be developing more sophisticated media strategies. With each passing year, "results-release events" are accorded more prominent coverage, and follow-on events build continuing interest in the outcomes and their implications. The problem is how to support the organization of such occasions in most participating jurisdictions, recognizing, as Ritzen (this volume) points out, that there will be political constraints in some settings. Equally important, there should be an ongoing effort to educate both policymakers and members of the media on the proper use and interpretation of ILSA results. This is not a trivial effort as many of the relevant issues involve technical issues that are not easily communicated to lay audiences.

Concluding Remarks

In this chapter I have suggested a framework for considering key issues that confront ILSA sponsors and contractors as they look to the future, and indicated how the topics presented relate to the framework. I have also taken the liberty of briefly addressing other topics. It should be borne in mind, however, that in addition to the speakers and discussants, this conference brought together nearly 100 individuals with interest, experience, and expertise in ILSAs. The comments following the presentations, as well as the conversations in the ample time between sessions, added immeasurably to the richness of the event.

My sense is that there was a general consensus that these global partnerships are a valuable resource for the international community and should continue to thrive. On the other hand, there is a contrarian perspective, not represented at the conference, which decries both the economic focus of human capital development and the growing influence of international assessments on national education policy (Spring 2011). Although these are minority views, they do remind us that equity should be given attention equal to that of efficiency as we consider different paths.

Not surprisingly, each speaker had a different focus and somewhat different recommendations on future directions. Over the next few years, these and other options will compete in the crucible of political, economic and technical realities. What will emerge? No one today can say. However, we should all bear in mind that ILSAs represent perhaps the only major international educational commitment for many countries, and sometimes their only source of nationwide information about the educational system. It is imperative that the sponsors and governing bodies strive to adapt the surveys to the evolving needs of an increasingly diverse set of countries while maintaining sufficiently strong links to the past to preserve trends.

Negotiating these sometimes conflicting desiderata will call on the best skills of both the measurement community and associated technical specialties—not to mention extraordinary political talents. Despite inevitable frustrations and setbacks, we should all keep our eyes on the prize of contributing to information-rich education policy decision making.

References

Author. 2008. *Psychosocial assessment of college readiness: A prospectus*. Princeton: New Constructs Center, Educational Testing Service.

Beaton, A.E., and N.L. Allen. 1992. Interpreting scales through scale anchoring. *Journal of Educational Statistics* 17:191–204.

Bracey, G.W. 2004. *Setting the record straight*. 2nd ed. Portsmouth: Heinemann.

Braun, H. 2008. McKinsey report: How the world's best performing school systems come out on top. *Journal of Educational Change* 9(3):317–320.

Braun, H., and A. Kanjee. 2006. Using assessment to improve education in developing nations. In *Educating All Children: A Global Agenda*. eds. J. E. Cohen, D. E. Bloom, and M. B. Malin. Cambridge, MA: American Academy of Arts and Sciences.

Campbell, D. T. 1957. Factors relevant to the validity of experiments in social settings. *Psychological Bulletin* 54:297–312.

Hargreaves, A. 2011, January 26. *Canada's Culture of Excellence in Education*. Toronto Star.

Kirsch, I., A. Jungeblut, L. Jenkins, and A. Kolstad. 1993. *Adult literacy in America: A first look at results of the National Adult Literacy Survey*. Washington, DC: National Center for Education Statistics, U.S. Department of Education.

Kirsch, I., H.I. Braun, K. Yamamoto, and A. Sum. 2007. *America's perfect storm: Three forces changing our nation's future*. Princeton: Policy Information Center, Educational Testing Service.

McKinsey & Co. 2007. *How the world's best school systems come out on top*. New York: McKinsey & Co.

McKinsey & Co. 2010. *How the world's most improved school systems keep getting better*. New York: McKinsey & Co.

National Center for Education Statistics. 2011. http://nces.ed.gov/pubsearch/pubsinfo.asp?pubid=2011472

OECD. 2003. *Learners for life: Student approaches to learning, results from PISA 2000*. Paris: Organisation for Economic Co-operation and Development.

OECD. 2009. *Creating effective teaching and learning environments: First results from TALIS*. Paris: Organisation for Economic Co-operation and Development.

Paine, S.L., and A. Schleicher. 2011. *What the U.S. can learn from the world's most successful education reform efforts*. New York: McGraw-Hill Research Foundation.

Phillips, G.W. 2009. *The second derivative: International benchmarks in mathematics for U.S. states and school districts*. Washington, DC: American Institutes for Research.

Pont, B., D. Nusche, and H. Moorman. 2008. *Improving school practice. vol.1: Policy and Practice*. Paris: Organisation for Economic Co-operation and Development.

Spring, J. 2011. *The politics of American education*. New York: Routledge.

Stigler, J. W., P. Gonzales, T. Kawanaka, S. Knoll, and A. Serrano. 1999. *The TIMSS videotape classroom study: Methods and findings from an exploratory research project on eighth grade mathematics instruction in Germany, Japan, and the United States*. Washington, DC: National Center for Education Statistics.

Sum, A., I. Kirsch, and R. Taggart. 2002. *The twin challenges of mediocrity and inequality: Literacy in the U.S. from an international perspective*. Princeton: Policy Information Center, Educational Testing Service.

.

Printed by Publishers' Graphics LLC